OXFORD MONOGRAPHS IN INTERNATIONAL LAW

General Editors

PROFESSOR VAUGHAN LOWE QC

*Chichele Professor of Public International Law at the University of Oxford
and Fellow of All Souls College, Oxford*

PROFESSOR DAN SAROOSHI

*Professor of Public International Law
at the University of Oxford and Fellow of
The Queen's College, Oxford*

PROFESSOR STEFAN TALMON

*Director of the Institute of Public International Law
at the University of Bonn and Supernumerary Fellow
of St Anne's College, Oxford*

The Margin of Appreciation in International Human Rights Law

OXFORD MONOGRAPHS IN INTERNATIONAL LAW

The aim of this series is to publish important and original pieces of research on all aspects of international law. Topics that are given particular prominence are those which, while of interest to the academic lawyer, also have important bearing on issues which touch the actual conduct of international relations. Nonetheless, the series is wide in scope and includes monographs on the history and philosophical foundations of international law.

The Margin of Appreciation in International Human Rights Law

Deference and Proportionality

ANDREW LEGG

OXFORD

UNIVERSITY PRESS

OXFORD
UNIVERSITY PRESS

Great Clarendon Street, Oxford, OX2 6DP,
United Kingdom

Oxford University Press is a department of the University of Oxford.
It furthers the University's objective of excellence in research, scholarship,
and education by publishing worldwide. Oxford is a registered trade mark of
Oxford University Press in the UK and in certain other countries

British Library Cataloguing in Publication Data
Data available

Library of Congress Cataloging in Publication Data
Data available

ISBN 978-0-19-965045-3

Printed in Great Britain by
CPI Group (UK) Ltd, Croydon, CR0 4YY

For Hannah

Preface

The margin of appreciation doctrine is controversial and somewhat difficult to grasp. Notwithstanding this, it lies at the heart of many of the most important international human rights cases. Its use sometimes leads to calls for greater judicial restraint by international human rights courts, or, in other words, a broader margin of appreciation to the state. This call for judicial restraint was demonstrated, for example, by the outcry[1] in the UK as the deadline approached for the authorities to amend the blanket ban on prisoner voting, in accordance with the European Court of Human Rights' decision in *Hirst v UK (No. 2)* No. 74025/01 (2005) (ECtHR (GC)). Calls for judicial restraint have been articulated at the intergovernmental level, most notably in the Brighton Declaration, which concludes that a reference to the margin of appreciation should be expressly included in the Preamble to the Convention and invites the Committee of Ministers to adopt the necessary amending instrument by the end of 2013.[2] Academic criticism has tended in the other direction, arguing for greater judicial activism by international human rights courts, and at its most severe a banishing of the concept of the margin of appreciation from their reasoning altogether.

This book seeks both to provide an explanation of what the margin of appreciation is, and to respond to criticisms of it. Uniquely, the book addresses the concept of the margin of appreciation in three international human rights tribunals: the European Court of Human Rights; the Inter-American Court of Human Rights; and the United Nations Human Rights Committee.

Part One of the book provides a conceptual explanation of what the margin of appreciation is, arguing that it is a doctrine of judicial deference, and supporting this contention by reference to the philosophy of practical reasoning. Part One also provides the foundation for a justification of the margin of appreciation on the basis of three main factors: (i) democratic legitimacy; (ii) the current practice of states (the 'consensus' factor); and (iii) expertise. Part Two explores these factors in greater depth, explaining how each factor provides normative support for the margin of appreciation, and expounding relevant case law of the three tribunals, thereby providing a doctrinal account of how the margin of appreciation operates in practice. Part Three of the book looks at how the factors for a margin of appreciation interact with other factors in a case, such as 'the nature of the right', as part of the proportionality assessment. These chapters consequently explore the structure of reasoning in international human rights adjudication. Each part of the book is

---

[1] F Gibbs, 'Human Rights: Is it Time to Sever Ties with the European Court?' (2011) *The Times* 23 February, 55.
[2] Brighton Declaration, 19 April 2012, paragraph 12(b). The Declaration is a political document agreed by delegates of the High Level Conference on the Future of the European Court of Human Rights that met in Brighton on 19–20 April 2012.

likely to be of interest to academics and students of international human rights law, as well as those working with international human rights law. Practitioners are likely to find the categorization of case law in Chapters 4–6 of most use.

The book began as a doctoral thesis at the University of Oxford entitled *Deference in International Human Rights Law*. I am grateful to my supervisors, Professors John Finnis and Dan Sarooshi, for their support during this project, and to my examiners Professors Timothy Endicott and Dominic McGoldrick. Professors Chris McCrudden and John Merrills, who examined my MPhil thesis, also helped to shape the project's direction. Professors Vaughan Lowe and Guy Goodwin-Gill coordinated and chaired international law research seminars at All Souls College, Oxford, where I had the privilege of presenting aspects of my research on a variety of occasions. I profited from their, and my peers', astute and helpful questions.

I am thankful for the valuable research assistance provided by Gonzalo Candia, who helped me to update the case law from the Inter-American Court of Human Rights as the book neared completion. I am grateful to the Arts and Humanities Research Council for funding my doctoral research, and for the support of the Harvey Fellowship.

Above all, I would like to thank my wife Hannah, whose companionship, advice, patience, kindness, and joy have inspired me from the project's inception to its conclusion. The book is dedicated to her.

Andrew Legg

Lincoln's Inn Fields, London
April 2012

General Editors' Preface

Whether it is a sign of the maturity of the international legal system, or simply a reflection of the preoccupations of our times, the increasing focus on public law conceptions such as proportionality and legitimate expectations as tools for the judicial control and adjustment of exercises of power is a salient characteristic of contemporary law. The idea of a 'margin of appreciation' is of particular utility in regulating relations between different centres of power. Its operation in relation to related concepts such as justiciability gives it enormous potential in the development of the law, but also gives rise to important questions of principle concerning the relationship between judicial, executive, and legislative power.

In this important book Andrew Legg explores these issues in the context of human rights law with admirable clarity. His trenchant analysis will, however, be of great interest and value across a much wider field. It provides a principled account, firmly rooted in legal practice, of one of the most potent and interesting legal concepts to have emerged in international law in recent decades. Academics and practitioners alike will value it for its careful articulation of the basis and the contours of this fascinating doctrine.

AVL

Oxford
March 2012

Contents

Table of Cases

ENGLAND AND WALES

EUROPEAN COURT OF HUMAN RIGHTS

EUROPEAN COURT OF JUSTICE

INTER-AMERICAN COURT OF HUMAN RIGHTS

INTERNATIONAL COURT OF JUSTICE

IRELAND

SOUTH AFRICA

UN HUMAN RIGHTS COMMITTEE

UNITED STATES SUPREME COURT

Table of Treaties and Legislation

INTERNATIONAL TREATIES

DOMESTIC LEGISLATION

List of Abbreviations

ACHR	American Convention on Human Rights
AJIL	American Journal of International Law
BIICL	British Institute of International and Comparative Law
CAT	Committee against Torture (United Nations)
CEDAW	Committee on the Elimination of Discrimination against Women (United Nations)
CERD	Committee on the Elimination of Racial Discrimination (United Nations)
CLJ	Cambridge Law Journal
Cornell Intl LJ	Cornell International Law Journal
CUP	Cambridge University Press
EC Regulation	European Community Regulation
ECHR	European Convention on Human Rights
ECJ	European Court of Justice
ECtHR	European Court of Human Rights
ECtHR (GC)	European Court of Human Rights (Grand Chamber)
EHRLR	European Human Rights Law Review
ELJ	European Law Journal
EJIL	European Journal of International Law
Emory Intl LRev	Emory International Law Review
ESA	European Space Agency
EU	European Union
Harv LRev	Harvard Law Review
Harv UP	Harvard University Press
HRC	*See* UN HRC
HRLJ	Human Rights Law Journal
HRQ	Human Rights Quarterly
IACtHR	Inter-American Court of Human Rights
ICAO	International Civil Aviation Organization
ICCPR	International Covenant on Civil and Political Rights
ICJ	International Court of Justice
ICLQ	International and Comparative Law Quarterly
ICTY	International Criminal Tribunal for the former Yugoslavia
IJRL	International Journal of Refugee Law
IRA	Irish Republican Army
IVF	in vitro fertilization
KFOR	Kosovo Force (NATO)
LQR	Law Quarterly Review
Manchester UP	Manchester University Press
MIT Press	Massachusetts Institute of Technology Press
MLR	Modern Law Review
NATO	North Atlantic Treaty Organization
Northwestern ULRev	Northwestern University Law Review

Notre Dame Lrev	Notre Dame Law Review
OJLS	Oxford Journal of Legal Studies
OUP	Oxford University Press
PAS	parental alienation syndrome
PTSD	post-traumatic stress disorder
SAJHR	South African Journal of Human Rights
SCalLRev	Southern California Law Review
The Treaties	ACHR, ECHR, and ICCPR
The Tribunals	ECtHR, IACtHR, and UN HRC
UDHR	Universal Declaration of Human Rights
UNHCR	United Nations High Commissioner for Refugees, or UN Refugee Agency
UN HRC	United Nations Human Rights Committee
UNSC	United Nations Security Council
UNSC Resolutions	Resolutions of the United Nations Security Council
VCLT	Vienna Convention on the Law of Treaties
WTO	World Trade Organization
Yale LJ	Yale Law Journal
YILC	Yearbook of the International Law Commission

1

Introduction

When human rights cases are tried before international courts, judges must consider in each case that comes before them whether to follow a particular state's interpretation of international human rights law or to adopt their own approach. Whichever way they decide, judges thereby set the limits of state sovereignty in the sphere of human rights. Doctrines of judicial deference, such as the margin of appreciation in the European Court of Human Rights (ECtHR), significantly influence a tribunal's approach to this adjudication.[1]

The concept of the margin of appreciation in international human rights law is frequently viewed as problematic. While some commentators simply view it as unsatisfactorily confused,[2] others oppose what they regard as its pernicious connotations for human rights law: that the doctrine betrays the universality of human rights,[3] or that it undermines the protection of human rights[4] according to common standards. Those who accept that the margin of appreciation is a useful adjudicative technique tend to limit their discussion to a description of its role and how it seems to operate.[5] This book employs a different approach by seeking to establish a conceptual justification for the doctrine of the margin of appreciation that both reflects and explains the approach taken by international human rights tribunals.

The conceptual justification for the margin of appreciation focuses on it being a doctrine of judicial deference whereby judges are influenced by factors outside of the immediate pros and cons of a particular decision related to their own institutional competence. These factors are referred to as 'external factors' throughout this

---

[1] For example, RSJ Macdonald, 'The Margin of Appreciation' in RSJ Macdonald, F Matscher, and H Petzold (eds) *The European System for the Protection of Human Rights* (Martinus Nijhoff, Dordrecht; London 1993) 123 and JG Merrills, *The Development of International Law by the European Court of Human Rights* (2nd edn, Manchester UP, Manchester 1993) 174–5.

[2] Lester describes the margin of appreciation doctrine as 'slippery and elusive as an eel': A Lester, 'Universality versus Subsidiarity: A Reply' (1998) 1 EHRLR 73, 75. See also Macdonald (n1) 85.

[3] E Benvenisti, 'Margin of Appreciation, Consensus, and Universal Standards' (1999) 31 International Law and Politics 843, 844.

[4] Commentators speak of the 'abdication of judicial responsibility' in this context. This phrase is from TRS Allan, 'Human Rights and Judicial Review: A Critique of "Due Deference"'(2006) 65 (3) CLJ 671, 675, writing about deference in human rights adjudication in the UK. The argument is made at the international level, for example by Benvenisti (n3) 844, 852, and 854, claiming that international courts undermine their role by using the doctrine. See also C Feingold, 'The Doctrine of Margin of Appreciation and the European Convention on Human Rights' (1977–78) 53 Notre Dame LRev 90, 95.

[5] See Chapters 2.1 and 3.4.c.

book, although they might also be regarded as 'institutional factors'. This approach, which considers the impact of external factors on the reasoning of courts, draws on theories of second-order reasoning from the philosophy of practical reasoning. Second-order reasons are reasons that affect how decisions are made, which are not part of the immediate pros and cons. Although the label 'second-order reasons' is a technical philosophical term, it is a label describing a common phenomenon. We all recognize, for example, that tiredness affects our decision-making. We also know that how well we know or value somebody affects those decisions we make that impact them. Likewise, this type of second-order (or external) reasoning exists in the field of judicial decision-making. They are often referred to as 'doctrines of deference'. The approach adopted in this book argues that the margin of appreciation is a version of this familiar aspect of judicial decision-making, albeit with unique characteristics in international human rights law.

International human rights law itself is not a unified concept.[6] There are numerous human rights treaties that deal with matters ranging from declarations on the whole of international human rights law,[7] to conventions on only single issues such as torture[8] or specific spheres such as children's rights.[9] In addition, there are numerous different types of dispute resolution mechanism that implement and interpret human rights conventions.

The international human rights tribunals studied in this book are the European Court of Human Rights (ECtHR), the Inter-American Court of Human Rights (IACtHR), and the United Nations Human Rights Committee[10] (UN HRC) acting under the First Optional Protocol to the International Covenant on Civil and Political Rights (ICCPR), which gives it competence to examine individual complaints of alleged violations of the Covenant by state parties. Hereafter these three tribunals are referred to collectively as 'the Tribunals', and the treaties they interpret are referred to as 'the Treaties'.[11] Whilst other international human rights bodies might have been included,[12] the Tribunals have been selected for two main

---

[6] I Brownlie, *The Rule of Law in International Affairs: International Law at the Fiftieth Anniversary of the United Nations* (Martinus Nijhoff, The Hague; London 1998) 65–6.

[7] UN Declaration of Human Rights 1948.

[8] UN Convention against Torture 1984.

[9] UN Convention on the Rights of the Child 1989.

[10] While the HRC submits 'views' in response to 'communications' submitted by individuals and can be regarded as only 'quasi-judicial', it is sufficiently judicial to warrant inclusion in this study since its views are regarded as providing authoritative interpretations of the Covenant. Views of the HRC are the only decisions of an international body interpreting a comprehensive human rights document. Thus, while the HRC is not strictly a tribunal, it is deemed as 'of a judicial nature', and 'similar' to an international court in certain respects by various members of the HRC, in particular when it examines communications under the Optional Protocol: see D McGoldrick, *The Human Rights Committee: Its Role in the Development of the International Covenant on Civil and Political Rights* (Clarendon Press, Oxford 1991) 54–5.

[11] The European Convention on Human Rights (ECHR), the American Convention on Human Rights (ACHR), and the International Covenant on Civil and Political Rights (ICCPR) respectively.

[12] For example, UN bodies such as the Committee on the Elimination of Discrimination against Women (CEDAW), the Committee against Torture (CAT), and the Committee on the Elimination of Racial Discrimination (CERD), or possibly another regional body such as the African Commission on Human and People's Rights.

reasons, other than practical limitations. First, there are evident similarities between the Tribunals' approaches to the margin of appreciation that strengthen the conceptual and doctrinal arguments of the book. Whilst each of the Tribunals has a unique approach to interpreting and applying the Treaties, and on the whole comparisons between the systems cannot be easily made,[13] the approach to the margin of appreciation taken in this book is quite clearly reflected in the practice of each of these Tribunals. Secondly, the Treaties are more or less comprehensive. This is important because it is often said that the nature of the right or the type of case is one of the factors for a margin of appreciation. The book argues instead that the margin of appreciation operates, structurally at least, in the same way irrespective of the type of right or the nature of the case. Although these factors may affect how much impact the margin of appreciation can have in different cases, it is analytically useful not to regard them as factors for a margin of appreciation: see particularly Chapter 8.

1. The margin of appreciation in the ECtHR, IACtHR, and the UN HRC

The ECtHR was the first of the Tribunals to deploy the concept of the margin of appreciation. Indeed, the margin of appreciation is a judicial creation that was developed by the Strasbourg Court.[14] There is no textual peg on which to hang the doctrine in the European Convention. Its origins have been traced to analogous concepts of judicial deference in the administrative law of a number of European countries.[15]

In English law, deference as a separate concept is a relatively recent idea, but has some relation to the older, familiar concept of *Wednesbury*[16] unreasonableness, which is likewise similar to the *Chevron*[17] doctrine in US constitutional law. These concepts reflect a traditional judicial unwillingness to interfere with determinations made by other branches of government except where clearly warranted by the

---

[13] See 'Legal orders and comparisons', Chapter 3.2.d.

[14] For a helpful discussion of the origins of the doctrine, dating back to the inter-state case of *Greece v UK* No. 175/56 (1958) (European Commission of Human Rights), see D Spielmann, 'Allowing the Right Margin: The European Court of Human Rights and the National Margin of Appreciation Doctrine—Waiver or Subsidiarity of European Review?' (Centre for European Legal Studies Working Paper Series, Cambridge 2012) 4–5.

[15] For example, the *marge d'appréciation* in French administrative law, and similar concepts in German constitutional law: Y Arai-Takahashi, *The Margin of Appreciation Doctrine and the Principle of Proportionality in the Jurisprudence of the ECHR* (Intersentia, Antwerpen; Oxford 2002) 2–3 and HC Yourow, *The Margin of Appreciation Doctrine in the Dynamics of European Human Rights Jurisprudence* (DPhil, University of Michigan 1995; Kluwer Law International, The Hague 1996) 14–15. For an overview of similar concepts in France, Germany, Spain, and the UK, see B Goold, L Lazarus, and G Swiney, *Public Protection, Proportionality and the Search for Balance* (Ministry of Justice Research Series 10/07, HMSO, London 2007).

[16] *Associated Provincial Picture Houses v Wednesbury Corporation* [1948] 1 KB 223 (CA).

[17] *Chevron USA Inc v Natural Resources Defense Council Inc* 467 US 837 (1984) (SC).

circumstances. In various parts of the world today, there appears to be a growing consensus amongst scholars of an emerging 'culture of justification'[18] in public law, particularly in relation to fundamental or human rights. More exacting standards of judicial review of government action domestically have required increasingly refined understandings of deference than in the past. But such debates in some domestic systems have lagged behind the development in Europe of the margin of appreciation. Although deference in European human rights law may originate in domestic public law, its rapid development, along with that of the principle of proportionality, is likely to contribute back to discussions about deference domestically. In English law, in the field of human rights, standards of review have become increasingly exacting, triggered in no small measure by incorporation of the European Convention on Human Rights (ECHR) by the Westminster Parliament in the Human Rights Act 1998 and a concomitant increasing reliance on Strasbourg jurisprudence.

Given that the doctrine of the margin of appreciation is a judicial creation, it is unsurprising that a theory of deference has not been set out comprehensively in the decisions themselves, which are confined to their specific facts. Since the doctrine's early use,[19] it has featured in hundreds of decisions, and it continues to be of huge importance today. Many commentators have written about the doctrine; some supportively, which has largely involved explaining its ramifications and impact in European human rights law; and others critically, preferring that it be banished as a concept in international human rights law.[20] However, startlingly little has been written examining how the margin of appreciation operates conceptually in international human rights law or offering a justification for it. One of the aims of this book is to address this gap in the existing literature.

The IACtHR has not considered as many cases involving interpretation of human rights standards as its European counterpart, and has instead dealt largely with cases in which there were findings of fact relating to gross and systematic violations of human rights. Many cases have alleged forced disappearances or brutal murders that, if proven on the facts, would clearly constitute violations of Articles 4 (right to life), 5 (personal integrity, prohibition of torture), and 7 (liberty and security) of the American Convention on Human Rights (ACHR).

Given that most cases to have reached the IACtHR have largely involved findings of fact, it is unsurprising that there are far fewer examples of cases employing concepts of deference compared with the ECtHR's resort to the margin of appreciation. As Tom Farer, former President of the Commission, states:

As long as governments were simply torturing and maiming, interpretation was hardly necessary. But with governments striving with varying degrees of effort to establish the rule

---

[18] This phrase was coined by South African scholar Etienne Mureinik, and popularized by former South African and now Canadian scholar David Dyzenhaus. See further D Dyzenhaus, 'Law as Justification: Etienne Mureinik's Conception of Legal Culture' (1998) SAJHR 11.

[19] For example, *Handyside v UK* No. 5493/72 (1976) (ECtHR).

[20] See Chapters 2 and 3.

of law, the Commission naturally began to receive more cases from the gray borderland where the state's authority to promote the general interest collides with individual rights.[21]

It is only as interpretation of these more 'grey' cases has emerged that the Court has been able to consider issues relevant to the margin of appreciation. Whilst many cases have not yet raised questions of cultural difference or dynamic interpretation in the same distinct ways as the ECtHR, David Harris predicted that there would be an increasing role for the margin of appreciation in the Inter-American system as follows:

[I]t may be anticipated that, as the American system evolves, with the number and percentage of ordinary, as opposed to gross, human rights violations increasing, these kinds of issues will arise for the Inter-American Commission and Court. Certainly there are varying conceptions of morality and honour and kinds of legal systems in different parts of South and North America.[22]

This prediction has been verified, as can be seen in relevant discussion of the IACtHR case law throughout this book.[23] As yet, there is very little academic commentary of the role of the margin of appreciation in the IACtHR.

As with the IACtHR, there is very little written about the margin of appreciation in the UN HRC. Another aim of this book is to offer a conceptual account of the margin of appreciation that reflects the practice of the HRC and IACtHR as well as the ECtHR, and to collate and discuss the relevant decisions of these tribunals.

The lack of commentary on the margin of appreciation in the HRC is likely to be explained by two main factors. First, many cases before the HRC have (like those before the IACtHR) simply required factual determination. For instance, prior to the 1980s a high proportion of the HRC's cases considered allegations of torture, disappearance, and extended arbitrary detention by the Uruguayan military government; since the 1980s a high proportion of cases scrutinized Caribbean death penalty trials and detention. Secondly, and more speculatively, the regular change in members of the Committee every two years is likely to affect the consistent development of judicial doctrine.[24] Other reasons why little has been written about the margin of appreciation in the HRC might be that: the Committee meets only three times per year; it has a burdensome workload that includes assessing Country Reports; and it has a growing backlog of individual communications.

Although commentators have not written extensively about the margin of appreciation in the cases before the HRC, there are nevertheless a number of different perspectives about whether or not it exists at all in practice. Sarah Joseph

---

[21] T Farer, 'The Rise of the Inter-American Human Rights Regime: No Longer a Unicorn, Not Yet an Ox' in DJ Harris and S Livingstone (eds) *The Inter-American System of Human Rights* (Clarendon Press, Oxford 1998) 32.

[22] D Harris, 'Regional Protection of Human Rights: the Inter-American Achievement' in ibid, 12.

[23] See in particular Chapter 2.4.b . See also JM Pasqualucci, *The Practice and Procedure of the Inter-American Court of Human Rights* (CUP, Cambridge 2003) 51.

[24] S Joseph, J Schultz, and M Castan, *The International Covenant on Civil and Political Rights: Cases, Materials, and Commentary* (2nd edn, OUP, Oxford 2004) 30.

claims that 'the HRC has been more radical than the European bodies in its apparent rejection of the cautious doctrine of the margin of appreciation'.[25] She does not explain in detail what the margin of appreciation is, but focuses instead on two decisions of the HRC that reject the terminology of the margin of appreciation. This is not the end of the matter. Relying on the Committee's 'apparent rejection' of the margin of appreciation in these few cases places too much reliance on what terminology is used instead of assessing the substance of what the HRC decides.

A better view has been put forward by James Crawford as follows: the Committee has been 'speaking silently the language of the margin'.[26] By this, Crawford seems to be saying that whilst the Committee has not been committed to the terminology of a margin of appreciation, the ideas that this terminology entails have nevertheless been expressed in its communications. Numerous cases are discussed in this book that bear out Crawford's approach.[27] There is certainly scope for further development of the concept of the margin of appreciation in the HRC,[28] but there is ample evidence supporting the proposition that it forms part of the HRC's practice. It seems as if a more nuanced approach to the margin of appreciation in the work of the HRC might even be acceptable to Joseph when she says elsewhere:

Indeed, the uncertainty entailed in ICCPR limitations introduces flexibility to human rights interpretation, and generates ideological and cultural debate over the content of human rights guarantees. It is possible that the HRC might apply these limitations differently in the context of different cultural or economic circumstances.[29]

2. Book structure

This book addresses the question 'Is the way in which the margin of appreciation in international human rights law affects the reasoning of the Tribunals justified?' in three parts. Part One (Chapters 2 and 3) identifies the conceptual basis for the margin of appreciation and responds to arguments critical of the margin of appreciation, thereby offering a sustained justification of the doctrine. Part Two

---

[25] Ibid. For a similar view, see D Feldman, 'Freedom of Expression' in D Harris and S Joseph (eds) *The International Covenant on Civil and Political Rights and United Kingdom Law* (Clarendon Press, Oxford 1995) 408–9.

[26] Quotation from James Crawford's Preface to Arai-Takahashi (n15) ix. A similar view is taken in D Harris, 'The International Covenant on Civil and Political Rights: An Introduction' in D Harris and S Joseph (eds) *The International Covenant on Civil and Political Rights and United Kingdom Law* (Clarendon Press, Oxford, 1995) 14.

[27] Also see M Schmidt, 'The Complementarity of the Covenant and the European Convention on Human Rights: Recent Developments' in ibid, 657–8.

[28] What Dominic McGoldrick wrote in the 1990s remains the case today, although to a somewhat lesser extent—'It is as yet too early to know how widely the doctrine of the margin of appreciation will be interpreted in the HRC's jurisprudence': McGoldrick (n10) 160.

[29] S Joseph, J Schultz, and M Castan, *The International Covenant on Civil and Political Rights: Cases, Materials and Commentary* (OUP, Oxford 2000) 25. This same quotation appears again in the second edition of this work (n24) 43, but the last sentence quoted here is omitted, which may indicate that Joseph disputes even the existence of this more implicit operation of deference.

(Chapters 4–6) explores the three factors that justify the margin of appreciation in practice and catalogues the case law in relation to these factors. Part Three (Chapters 7–8) explores how the factors for a margin of appreciation interact with other relevant factors in a case (such as the 'nature of the right') as part of the proportionality assessment. Accordingly, Part Three assesses the structure of decision-making in human rights law. The content of each of the chapters is summarized further as follows.

Chapter 2 argues that the margin of appreciation is the judicial practice of assigning weight to a respondent state's reasoning in a case on the basis of three factors: (i) democratic legitimacy; (ii) the common practice of states; and (iii) expertise. Where there are fewer grounds for a margin of appreciation to the respondent state's reasoning as a result of these external factors, then there is heightened scrutiny of the state's reasoning by the Tribunals. This account of how the margin of appreciation affects the reasoning of the Tribunals is grounded in theories of deference that form part of the philosophy of practical reasoning. Chapter 2 also argues that this conception of the margin of appreciation is reflected in the practice of the Tribunals.

Having articulated how the margin of appreciation, as a doctrine of deference, affects the reasoning of the Tribunals, Chapter 3 argues that this practice is justified. A variety of issues are discussed in this chapter that can be split into two groups: first, about the nature of human rights and their legal protection; and secondly, about what is the proper role of the Tribunals in interpreting inter-national human rights standards. The first group of issues raises the following questions: does the margin of appreciation doctrine, which allows a certain latitude for differential human rights protection across states, result in relativism about human rights and a betrayal of the universality of human rights? What does 'universality' mean? Does it entail legal uniformity? For human rights defenders everywhere, if the charge of relativism is sustained, it could be a knockout blow for the margin of appreciation. For this reason, the concern is addressed at the outset. It is argued that a proper account of universality entails the legitimate differentiation of value. There is consequently scope for different instantiations of human rights from place to place and time to time. If reasons for a margin of appreciation on occasion result in different human rights rules for different places, this does not necessarily mean that the standards are different, or that there is relativism about human rights, but rather that there can be different ways of protecting the same human right. Even if this argument were accepted, it would not necessarily follow that states within the same legal system should take different approaches to the protection of human rights. For example, it might be said that France and Poland can legitimately protect freedom of religion in ways that reflect their own cultures and traditions, but that the same legal standards ought nevertheless to apply to both states as a result of the nature of the European Convention system that binds them both. This sort of argument raises the second group of issues.

The second group of issues discussed in Chapter 3 is debated using two main approaches to the role of the Tribunals in interpreting international human rights standards. The first approach prefers the Tribunals to set common human rights standards and is consequently suspicious of a margin of appreciation, seeing it as an abdication of the Tribunals' role and responsibility. As long as the Tribunals get the standards right, this approach favours an activist tribunal. Three accounts by different commentators are set out in Chapter 3 that can be categorized under this first approach. The extreme opposite approach to this, of conservative tribunals that implement only standards that are clearly discernible from the text of the treaties or the intention of the treaty signatories at the time of entry into force,[30] has been rejected by the Tribunals and commentators alike, and thus is not discussed in depth in this book.[31] Instead, the second approach discussed, and the approach adopted by this book, is more nuanced. It is not suspicious of, but is instead supportive of, judicial deference to states. This approach accepts that the Tribunals have the authority to set standards when interpreting the Treaties, but nevertheless argues that the margin of appreciation is important because it reflects the subsidiary role of the Tribunals in the protection of human rights.

Having argued generally that the margin of appreciation is justifiable, Chapters 4, 5, and 6 discuss when the external factors for a margin of appreciation provide good reasons to assign weight to arguments of the state and whether the practice of the Tribunals is reflective of these normative arguments. Chapter 4 argues that there is an appropriate factor for a margin of appreciation to the state where there are clear democratic grounds for the approach taken by the state. The question central to this argument is: what is the role of democracy in the formation of human rights norms? The debates in constitutional theory surrounding judicial review of legislation provide a helpful analogy explaining why there are reasons for deference to states in international human rights law when interpretations of human rights standards are democratically grounded. The chapter sets out (from the case law of the Tribunals') decisions that show that the margin of appreciation is affected by considerations of democratic legitimacy. This shows that the Tribunals view their own role as respecting the democratic formation of human rights norms, but nevertheless scrutinize states' reasoning. The case law exposition assesses the extent to which a margin of appreciation is granted on the basis of democratic legitimacy. The reasons why the Tribunals give a margin of appreciation or heighten scrutiny of states' reasoning on the basis of democratic legitimacy contribute to the development and shaping of a norm of democratic governance in international law.

Chapter 5 argues that there is a reason for granting a margin of appreciation to the state where there is a lack of consensus amongst the practice of contracting states about the correct interpretation of the relevant human rights standard. This is a controversial matter and raises questions about the proper interpretation of international treaties, and whether there is anything distinctive about international human rights treaties. The chapter argues that given that the international order is based on the sovereign equality of states, and that international law norms are based on state agreement even where there is scope for tribunals to set standards, cognizance of and margins of appreciation on the basis of current state practice is

---

[30] For example, as seen in *travaux préparatoires*.
[31] But see Chapter 5.3.a.

appropriate, even in the field of human rights. This approach is reflected in the Vienna Convention on the Law of Treaties (VCLT). Decisions of the Tribunals are set out in this chapter that show how current state practice operates as a second-order (external) reason for a margin of appreciation or heightened scrutiny of the state's reasoning. This chapter also touches on the related matter of margins of appreciation to other international bodies and norm-making institutions, such as the European Union (EU) or the United Nations Security Council (UNSC). This is an emerging issue with a relatively small body of decisions at present, but nevertheless affects the margin of appreciation given to states by the Tribunals when reasons for deference to other international actors are at play.

Chapter 6 argues that the expertise or greater competence of the state is a reason for a margin of appreciation. This is a common ground for deference in domestic legal contexts and is less controversial than the other external factors for a margin of appreciation. The chapter addresses the question of whether deference on the basis of superior state expertise is compatible with a full determination of the relevant factors—that is, whether it entails non-justiciability. Decisions of the Tribunals showing a margin of appreciation on this basis are assessed, and decisions showing what sorts of expertise provide reasons for deference are expounded. Cases are also studied that show where the Tribunals regard themselves as having greater expertise and hence provide grounds for employing heightened scrutiny of the state's reasoning.

Having looked at the different reasons for a margin of appreciation in practice, Chapter 7 examines in greater detail the question of how the margin of appreciation impacts the reasoning of the Tribunals, arguing that a proper account of proportionality answers this question. Too often, the proportionality assessment is analysed as being about how to determine what the content of a right is, looking only at the immediate reasons and omitting discussion of external factors for a margin of appreciation. This has given rise to accounts of proportionality dominated by theories of rights. The chapter takes a closer look at proportionality. First, the origins of proportionality are assessed, showing that the contemporary role of proportionality has moved beyond its more limited instantiation in ethics discourse to involve an assessment of the legitimacy of states' standards of human rights protection. Secondly, different accounts of proportionality grounded in competing theories of rights are examined critically. The main aim of this section is to determine whether and how these different accounts incorporate an assessment of external factors for a margin of appreciation along with the immediate or first-order reasons. The chapter argues that these accounts do not adequately incorporate the assessment of external factors/second-order reasons for a margin of appreciation as required, and consequently sets out a new account of proportionality. Some commentators recognize that proportionality limits grounds for a margin of appreciation and keeps the doctrine within its proper bounds, but they do not explain how. The new account of proportionality set out in Chapter 7 attempts to do exactly this, as well as to show how this approach is consistent with the jurisprudence of the Tribunals.

It is often said that the nature of the right or the type of case is a factor that affects the margin of appreciation, but very little explanation is proffered as to why this might be so. Chapter 8 addresses the question of whether the nature of the right or the type of case is a factor for a margin of appreciation. The chapter argues that the nature of the right relates to the first-order reasons in a case, and consequently affects how strong reasons for a margin of appreciation need to be in order to impact the decision-making of the tribunal. This affects the outcome of the proportionality assessment, and not the reasons for a margin of appreciation themselves. Thus the nature of the right is not a factor for a margin of appreciation per se, but it affects the impact of factors for a margin of appreciation. The chapter goes on to argue that the type of case is also not a reason for deference, but rather that certain types of case produce similar considerations and thus such categorizations of cases provide guidance to the Tribunals about how earlier judges assessed a similar case. This is not binding precedent, but it can be informative. Accounts of decisions that discuss margins of appreciation or deference categorized by the type of case or right can be beneficial to lawyers and decision-makers because they can provide guidance about the sorts of factors that will impact future cases. But there is room here for caution: each case will likely turn on its own facts, and whilst previous decisions can guide the decisions of future tribunals, they are not formally binding.

3. Approach

Making sense of the margin of appreciation in international human rights law requires engagement with and development of a variety of different theoretical ideas present within relevant literature and prompted by the practice of the Tribunals. It also requires a substantial engagement with and analysis of the decisions of the Tribunals. There are consequently two guiding methodological approaches that interact throughout the book: the first is theoretical; and the second is the exposition of case law.

The theoretical discussions undertaken in this book would not need to reflect the practice of the Tribunals since they could involve theorizing in the abstract or suggesting significant reform of the current practice of the Tribunals. However, in order for theory to relate to these systems, a sufficient degree of overlap between the theory and practice is required. For example, whilst some constitutional theory can involve the philosophy of constitutional arrangements generally, other constitutional theory engages with particular constitutional arrangements, for example the sovereignty of the Westminster Parliament or the supremacy of the United States Supreme Court's interpretation of the US Constitution. The theorizing in this book is of the latter type, engaging with the Tribunals as they exist, and taking account of the decisions they have made and how they have acted.

As already discussed, there are a number of different theoretical questions raised by this book, some of which are descriptive and some of which are evaluative. The descriptive theoretical inquiries include such questions as 'how does the margin of appreciation operate?', drawn from the philosophy of practical reasoning, or 'what does universality mean?', from moral theory, and whether different instantiations of human rights standards lead to relativism, from human rights theory. An important part of the book involves a (descriptive) assessment of how rights are determined, drawn from the theory of legal rights. Of particular importance here is how second-order reasoning operates in a theory of adjudication, with the related descriptive question: 'Does judicial deference involve some sort of non-justiciability doctrine?' Some of the evaluative questions are, for example: 'Is a margin of appreciation justifiable in international human rights law?', 'Does the role of the Tribunals envisage such deference to the state?' or 'Are there grounds for a margin of appreciation to the state on the basis of democratic legitimacy?', or 'What is the role of the current practice of states in interpreting international human rights treaties?' These evaluative questions involve normative international institutional theory, a sort of constitutional theory for the international human rights sphere.

It is not suggested here that there is any hard-and-fast distinction between evaluation and description for the purposes of legal theory. Indeed, very often they overlap.[32] It is unsurprising to note, then, that the descriptive accounts of this book support the evaluative positions taken in other parts of the book. However, it is intended that the evaluative and the descriptive accounts could be separated. Consequently, if a reader were to disagree with the arguments in favour of a margin of appreciation, he or she could hold a different view as to the role that the margin of appreciation should have in international human rights tribunals, yet nevertheless concur with the conceptual account of the margin of appreciation as the practice of assigning weight to the reasons for a decision on the basis of external factors, drawn from the theory of second-order reasoning.

The second methodological approach in this book is the exposition of legal decisions. Traditionally, this involves a more 'black letter' approach to scholarship that records the internal coherence of a body of law. Aspects of this book do record the decisions of the Tribunals on the margin of appreciation, showing how the Tribunals give deference on the basis of certain factors. This record involves what Chris McCrudden has called 'constructing explanatory "models" from the legal material'.[33] In this book, the explanatory modelling is undertaken in a context of some controversy. It is certainly the case that the assessment of legal decisions in this book 'takes place within a normative context' and consequently 'includes normative elements'.[34]

Does the normative context within which the more traditional case law exposition is undertaken cause methodological difficulties? It might be said that the interaction between case law exposition of decisions involving a margin of appreciation in the Tribunals and the theorizing undertaken in the book is problematic because it would not be possible to give a faithful account of the conduct of the Tribunals whilst simultaneously advancing normative arguments about the role of

---

[32] See J Finnis, *Natural Law and Natural Rights* (Clarendon Press, Oxford 1980) ch 1.
[33] C McCrudden, 'Legal Research and the Social Sciences' (2006) 122 LQR 632, 634.
[34] Ibid.

deference in the Tribunals. But such a concern overlooks the symbiosis between much of the theoretical discussion in the book and the exposition of the case law.[35] This symbiosis can be evidenced in three ways. First, there are a number of normative assumptions in the practice of the Tribunals when exercising deference. These assumptions have been subject to criticisms. This book sets out arguments in favour of, for example, a margin of appreciation on the basis of democratic legitimacy. Such theoretical positions are merely assumed by the Tribunals and adopted in their practice. Thus the normative discussion that defends such deference on the basis of democratic legitimacy supports the exposition of decisions that undeniably give a margin of appreciation on that basis. Secondly, the decisions of the Tribunals involving a margin of appreciation themselves affect the role of the Tribunals, and thus normative debates about the role of the Tribunals ought to consider these decisions. Thirdly, and most importantly, this book argues that the account of the margin of appreciation advanced in Chapter 2 is the best way of explaining the practice of the Tribunals as they show deference to states.[36]

   To avoid the danger of cherry-picking decisions that simply support the theoretical positions adopted in this book, the case law study undertaken in preparing the book was systematic. All decisions (as of January 2012) of the Grand Chamber of the ECtHR were read and studied with a view to identifying aspects of decisions that would contribute to a discussion about the margin of appreciation. In addition,

---

[35] The overlapping of different methodologies is noted in McCrudden (n33). The connection between legal analysis and theory mirrors the overlap of discipline in social sciences noted by Finnis (n32). In the preface to that book, Finnis states that the chapters in the second part of his book 'sketch what the textbook taxonomists would label an "ethics", a "political philosophy", and a "philosophy of law" or "jurisprudence". *We may accept the labels, as a scholarly convenience, but not the implications that the "disciplines" they identify are really distinct and can safely be pursued apart*' [emphasis added]. In addition, a fascinating approach to international law, inspired by the Yale Law School teachings of Myers McDougal amongst others, found in R Higgins, *Problems and Process: International Law and How We Use It* (Clarendon Press, Oxford 1994) 2–12, shows how international law is formed and impacted by numerous other factors (such as policy) that require transparent exploration.

[36] Dr Jeroen Shrokkenberg significantly influenced the chapter in P van Dijk and GJH van Hoof, *Theory and Practice of the European Convention on Human Rights* (3rd edn, Kluwer Law International, The Hague; London 1998) in which the following appears (at 82), which affirms the arguments of this paragraph:

> When reviewing cases under the Convention, the Commission and the Court proceed on the basis of a certain understanding of their role and responsibilities within the framework of the Convention system in relation to those of the Contracting States. The text of the Convention offers some guidance for such an understanding, but they are no more than a starting point. According to Article 1, it is for the Contracting Parties to 'secure to everyone within their jurisdiction the rights and freedoms defined in Section I of this Convention.' The Commission and the Court have been set up 'to ensure the observance of the engagements undertaken by the High Contracting Parties' (Article 19). The respective roles, within the Convention system, of the States on the one hand and the Strasbourg organs on the other can thus be summarized as follows: the Contracting States are to observe the obligations they have undertaken, while the Commission and the Court are charged with supervising compliance with the obligations on the part of the Contracting States. Obviously, this does not yet answer the question of how exactly, given these respective roles, the Commission and the Court should exercise their supervisory powers. In order to understand the way in which these organs perceive their role in the Convention system, one must turn to their case law.

a significant number of Chamber decisions were studied that have contributed to the development of the margin of appreciation. All decisions of the IACtHR and the UN HRC (as of January 2012) were similarly read and studied. Decisions that do not fit with the descriptive or evaluative theoretical approaches taken in this book are explicitly included and discussed so that exposition of the case law remains accurate.

The decisions selected for inclusion in this study do not attempt to categorize the case law involving deference comprehensively. As Steven Greer notes, the case law of the ECtHR does not form 'an integrated system of judicially constructed "legal rules"',[37] and such decisions are formally non-precedential. Greer explains that judgments tend to 'illustrate how a relevant principle applies to certain facts'.[38] The same can certainly be said of the IACtHR and HRC decisions. Also, numerous judgments cite verbatim the principles set out in previous cases. For these reasons, the case law selection in the book is not comprehensive; it would be unnecessary and tedious to attempt such. Instead, relevant case law has been selected to illustrate the approach of each tribunal on the matter under discussion. Although not attempting to be comprehensive, the selection of cases does attempt to capture the approach of each tribunal accurately.

Thus far, the term 'doctrinal' exposition has been avoided, although methodologically it is more common to refer to 'doctrinal' legal analysis than an exposition of 'decisions'. This is because, in the context of a margin of appreciation, there is some controversy about whether or not there ought to be a label 'doctrine' attached to its use at all. In the ECHR system, it is common to refer to the 'doctrine' of the margin of appreciation, but there is no such recognized doctrine in the Inter-American or UN HRC context. The controversy surrounding whether or not the concept of deference can give rise to the label 'doctrine' has been robustly debated by English public law commentators in recent years. The critic that makes the most coherent argument against attributing the label 'doctrine' to judicial deference is Tom Hickman. Hickman presents what he calls a 'non-doctrinal account' of deference.[39] He argues that if deference were to be a doctrine, this would lead to predetermination about what factors are relevant and how much weight to assign to them.[40] Hickman is right that this sort of predetermination would be entirely inappropriate and undesirable for the practice of deference, but is wrong to say that this is what is required by the concept of a doctrine—it implies that all legal doctrine prescribes a court's approach to a case, which is obviously not so. The concept of legal doctrine is under-studied.[41] The term 'doctrine' sometimes refers to a set of rules, which can be more or less prescriptive and detailed. At other times, the term 'doctrine' refers to a set of standards that operate as 'amorphous guides to resolving disputes, often listing a set of factors to be considered and balanced'.[42] An

---

[37] S Greer, *The European Convention on Human Rights: Achievements, Problems and Prospects* (CUP, Cambridge 2006) xvii.
[38] Ibid.
[39] T Hickman, *Public Law after the Human Rights Act* (Hart, Oxford 2010), especially ch 5.
[40] Ibid, 137–9.
[41] E Tiller and F Cross, 'What is Legal Doctrine?' (2006) 100 Northwestern ULRev 517, 517.
[42] Ibid.

example of this latter type of 'doctrine' from English law is the concept of 'fair, just and reasonable'[43] as an element of the legal doctrine that determines whether or not there is a duty of care in the tort of negligence. The 'fair, just and reasonable' test clearly involves a set of amorphous standards. Nevertheless, the courts consider and imbue these vague concepts with meaning as more decisions are based on them. Hickman's concern that the label 'doctrine' would predetermine a court's approach to deference is unwarranted.

Consequently, if this broader conception of 'doctrine' were to be employed, the margin of appreciation could rightly be called a 'doctrine'. In the ECtHR, it makes greater sense to speak of the margin of appreciation as a doctrine because it is so widely recognized, utilized, and incorporated in decisions and arguments before the Court. In the IACtHR and the UN HRC, the same cannot be said. Instead, whilst decisions of these bodies show a margin of appreciation in substance, they do not self-consciously resort to the concepts or labels of the margin of appreciation in the same way as do decisions of the ECtHR. It would consequently be premature to refer to the 'doctrine' of the margin of appreciation in the IACtHR or the HRC.

There is no exact science surrounding when something becomes prevalent or discussed sufficiently to warrant the label 'doctrine'. Even in its most discussed context in the ECHR system, the margin of appreciation is still regarded as uncertain and its parameters and principles unclear. It might therefore be questioned, even using the broader idea of 'doctrine' presented above, whether the European margin of appreciation is still too indeterminate to be called a doctrine. But this would be mistaken: the European concept of a margin of appreciation is so widely used and capable of explanation, and its principles so capable of articulation, that it is appropriate to refer to it as a doctrine. Indeed, as well as providing a theoretical account of the margin of appreciation, this book expounds the contours of the doctrine of the margin of appreciation in the ECHR system. Whilst it is premature to refer to a doctrine of the margin of appreciation in the Inter-American and UN HRC systems, this book gathers together decisions that show the beginnings of a judicial practice that may in time become detailed and clear enough (even if it remains abstract) for the term 'doctrine' also to be considered appropriate in these jurisdictions. The remainder of the book will use the term 'doctrine of the margin of appreciation' or 'doctrine of deference' loosely in the context of the IACtHR and HRC to refer to decisions that involve deference to states.

---

[43] *Caparo Industries Plc v Dickman* [1990] 2 AC 605 (HL), 618 (*per* Lord Bridge).

PART I

THEORY: CONCEPTUALIZING AND JUSTIFYING THE MARGIN OF APPRECIATION

The margin of appreciation is a judicially created doctrine. It has been developed and become increasingly refined over time through case law. The doctrine has not been the subject of sustained conceptual or theoretical explanation by its founders. It has been the subject of much commentary, some of which is strongly critical of the doctrine and concerned, for example, that it may lead to relativism about human rights.

Part One of the book seeks to address the underconceptualized nature of the margin of appreciation and to explain its theoretical foundation as a doctrine of judicial deference, exploring the concept of deference in the literature of 'practical philosophy', or the philosophy of practical reasoning, in Chapter 2. Chapter 3 addresses the main criticisms of the margin of appreciation doctrine, and sets out the foundation for a justification of the doctrine that is consistent with the universality of human rights. This foundation for justifying the margin of appreciation is developed in Part Two of the book, where the three factors for a margin of appreciation that contribute to a comprehensive defence of the margin of appreciation are explored in greater detail.

Part One, with its focus on the conceptual and normative basis for the margin of appreciation, is likely to appeal primarily to academics and students of international human rights law. Readers interested in arguments in favour of the margin of appreciation are also likely to find relevant material in the early sections of Chapters 4–6, which provide a justification for the three factors in favour of a margin of appreciation.

2

Deference: Reasoning Differently on the Basis of External Factors

1. Introduction

Those who regard the concept of the margin of appreciation as a useful technique of adjudication in international human rights law tend to limit their discussion to a brief description of its role and how it seems to operate. Such accounts describe, for example, deference or the margin of appreciation as an interpretational tool that determines which matters properly require a uniform international human rights standard and which allow legitimate variations from state to state.[1] Or, for example, such accounts refer to the margin of appreciation as a doctrine that establishes whether it is a matter of national sovereignty or for the Tribunals to demarcate the contours of a particular human rights standard.[2] These sorts of descriptions contain accurate observations. However, a number of important questions remain, such as what sort of interpretational tool the margin of appreciation is, and *how* the doctrine determines whether it is a matter of national sovereignty or for the Tribunals to establish the content of a particular human rights standard.

This book employs a different approach by expounding the nature of deference as the practice of assigning weight to reasons for a decision on the basis of external factors. The book argues that the margin of appreciation in international human rights law is the judicial practice of assigning weight to the respondent state's reasoning in a case on the basis of one or more of three external factors: democratic legitimacy; the common practice of states; and expertise. This understanding of the margin of appreciation is an example of second-order reasoning and draws from the philosophy of practical reasoning. The book contends that this is a familiar aspect of judicial decision-making with unique characteristics in international human rights law.

This analysis of deference has two consequences for a proper account of the margin of appreciation in international human rights law: first, it provides a robust

---

[1] For example, P Mahoney, 'Universality versus Subsidiarity in the Strasbourg Case Law on Free Speech: Explaining Some Recent Judgments' (1997) 4 EHRLR 364, 370.

[2] JG Merrills, *The Development of International Law by the European Court of Human Rights* (2nd edn, Manchester UP, Manchester 1993) 174–5 and P van Dijk and GJH van Hoof, *Theory and Practice of the European Convention on Human Rights* (3rd edn, Kluwer Law International, The Hague; London 1998) 95.

theoretical explanation for the practice of the Tribunals;[3] and secondly, it explains how the external factors impact the reasoning of the Tribunals.

2. Assigning weight differently on the basis of external factors

Philosophers of practical reasoning, or 'practical philosophy' as it is sometimes called, have only relatively recently been discussing the practice of assigning weight to reasons for a decision differently on the basis of external factors. For ease of reference, this practice is in this chapter referred to as 'second-order reasoning', and the external factors are referred to as 'second-order reasons'. One of Joseph Raz's major contributions to scholarship was the clarification of reasoning by observing that people commonly consider second-order reasons when making decisions. Second-order reasons are reasons to act or to refrain from acting on one's own assessment of the first-order balance of reasons, or the balance of reasons in issue. This definition of second-order reasons is broad,[4] and encompasses a number of different types of second-order reason. Philosophers distinguish between 'exclusionary' and 'non-exclusionary' second-order reasons. The distinction is discussed in this section, and it is argued that deference involves the Tribunals considering non-exclusionary second-order reasons to uphold the states' interpretation of their international human rights obligations.

Exclusionary second-order reasons are the subclass of second-order reasons that Raz developed most clearly. Raz exemplified them using the example of Ann, who, because of her tiredness, decided not to assess whether or not to accept an investment proposal, thus losing the opportunity.[5] In this example, Ann's assessment of

---

[3] It is true, as Letsas states, that 'the best theory of the margin of appreciation may not be the one that ECtHR judges, one by one, share or have fully developed in their judgments': G Letsas, 'Two Concepts of the Margin of Appreciation' (2006) 26 (4) OJLS 705, 706. However, the contention of this book is that the theory developed here closely corresponds to the practice of the Tribunals, and enables a coherent exposition of doctrine. See here P Soper, *The Ethics of Deference: Learning from Law's Morals* (CUP, Cambridge 2002) 18, fn13, on the relationship between theory and practice. See also Chapter 1.3.

[4] Stephen Perry argues, in 'Judicial Obligation, Precedent and the Common Law' (1987) 7 OJLS 215, 223, that Raz's conception of second-order reasons is too narrow, but this overlooks the fact that 'reasons' to act or refrain from action are not, in the general definition of second-order reasons, held to be determinative, or exclusionary. Instead they can be of varying weight. It appears, then, that Raz's general definition of second-order reasons remains sound and is compatible with Perry's definition (ibid), which is as follows:

> A second-order reason is a reason for treating a first-order reason as having a greater or lesser weight than it would ordinarily receive, so that an exclusionary reason is simply the special case where one or more first-order reasons are treated as having zero weight. The two modes of practical reason which Raz distinguishes can thus be regarded, in effect, as the two extremes of a continuum; at one end action is to be assessed on the basis of a balance of reasons in which no reason has been assigned anything other than its ordinary weight, while at the other end action is to be assessed by a balance of reasons some of which have been assigned, on the basis of second-order reasons, a non-ordinary weight of zero. Between these two extremes lies an indefinitely large number of further possibilities, all of which are variations on the idea of a weighted balance of reasons.

[5] J Raz, *Practical Reason and Norms* (OUP, Oxford 1999) 37–8.

whether or not to invest involved considering the first-order reasons, for example whether or not there would be a good return, what risks were involved, for how long the funds would be tied up, etc. Ann's awareness of her own tiredness was not a first-order reason, but rather influenced Ann to decide not to make an investment decision. Her tiredness was a second-order reason—in other words, 'a reason not to act on the balance of reasons'.[6]

Raz deployed the concept of exclusionary second-order reasons in legal theory to explain how legal rules claim authority in one's reasoning process. Where there is a law requiring or prohibiting certain conduct, this excludes (albeit not entirely) the need to engage in one's own balance of reasoning whether or not to engage in that conduct. Law is not intended to operate as merely one factor to be weighed in one's reasoning. Legal rules are supposed to be determinative. Their status as law operates as a second-order exclusionary reason to act. Sometimes, exclusionary reasons can exclude one or some reasons amongst many: for example, of the many activities that could be undertaken on a stag weekend, we exclude the illegal options, and hence make a choice amongst the remaining legal options.

Exclusionary reasons do not in fact exclude their targeted factors entirely from consideration. Once such factors are known, the decision is still made cognizant of the factors that ought to be excluded. Since such factors cannot be erased from consideration entirely, it is difficult to decide what impact such reasons have in the deliberative process. It is possible, then, that the concept of exclusionary reasons collapses into the more general body of second-order reasons. Another possibility is that the label 'exclusionary' could be descriptive rather than proscriptive. Whilst exclusionary reasons are intended to exclude first-order reasoning, where they in fact often do so (or where they significantly reduce the weight of such first-order reasons in the deliberative process), this observation could lead to that second-order reason warranting the label 'exclusionary'; where the reasons do not in fact exclude other reasoning (for example, there are first-order reasons of such great importance that they override the second-order reasons to act in a contrary way), then the label 'exclusionary' cannot apply. This looser rendition of the term 'exclusionary' can apply in a number of legal contexts, for example finding that a court lacks jurisdiction because an agreement to arbitrate disputes applies, or finding that a case has been brought outside of a limitation period. It is clear that the concept of exclusionary reasons does not apply when states seek a margin of appreciation to their interpretation of their international human rights obligations. This would be tantamount to saying that states claim the authority to determine the content of these international obligations, which would make nonsense of the judicial process. Reasons for a margin of appreciation are instead non-exclusionary or general second-order reasons.

The more general second-order reasons, non-exclusionary second-order reasons,[7] are less well discussed by philosophers and legal theorists. Recently, Stephen Perry has

---

[6] Ibid, 36.
[7] From this point onwards, where mention is made of second-order reasons, it will be to non-exclusionary or general second-order reasons unless stated otherwise.

developed the concept of second-order reasons more substantially. Perry argues that second-order reasoning often requires 'at least some familiarity, and often a great deal, with the ultimate values and other justifying reasons which figure in first-order practical reasoning'.[8] This is particularly the case in legal contexts in which a court makes decisions that involve second-order reasons. One application of general second-order reasons is the presumption of innocence in criminal law,[9] which requires stronger grounds for guilt than the mere balance of first-order reasons when convicting (the standard is 'beyond reasonable doubt' in English law). In a civil suit, if the same set of facts were to require determination, this second-order reason would not apply and the balance of first-order reasons would normally suffice.

Another application of the more general form of second-order reasoning discussed by Perry is the system of precedent in common law reasoning.[10] Precedent operates as a second-order reason by cautioning against a *de novo* assessment of the case according to the balance of first-order reasoning, leaning instead towards consistency with previous decisions. The level of preference or weight given to prior decisions varies from case to case and according to the level of the court within the legal system's hierarchy. The weight of this second-order reason affects the extent to which the court will be able to extend the law to new situations, to distinguish precedent, or even to overrule cases. The latter power is normally the preserve of a system's highest court alone. Often, precedent will determine how a case before the court ought to be decided, and in this sense appears to act as an exclusionary reason. But this is inaccurate. When considering whether or not to apply an existing precedent, no reasons are excluded. The court assesses all of the reasons for and against the outcome required by precedent (for simplicity, let us call these options 'A' and 'B', respectively). The court then applies the second-order reasons to follow precedent resulting in strengthening the reasons for A. This may or may not lead to outcome A. Other factors may override the need for consistency, leading either to more nuanced legal doctrine by extending the law to include situation B, or it may mean that there are strong grounds for overruling precedent and establishing a new rule that leads to B rather than to A.

Other common legal situations that involve second-order reasoning include deference to the finding of facts of lower courts and deference in judicial review to non-judicial branches of government or technical agencies in domestic public law. However, they are rarely discussed as examples of second-order reasoning.[11] The concept of deference intrinsically involves second-order reasoning, as explained in the next section, and consequently deference in international human rights law is

---

[8] S Perry, 'Second-Order Reasons, Uncertainty and Legal Theory' (1988–89) 62 SCalLRev 913, 915.

[9] Ibid, 933.

[10] Ibid, 963–72, and see 969–70 in particular for contextual reweighting. Perry's broader aim, which is not of concern here, is to improve understanding of common law legal theory.

[11] For an account of judicial review in constitutional theory as involving second-order reasoning, see A Kavanagh, 'Deference or Defiance: The Limits of the Judicial Role in Constitutional Adjudication' in G Huscroft (ed) *Expounding the Constitution: Essays in Constitutional Theory* (CUP, Cambridge 2008).

best understood as involving the allocation of weight to second-order reasons to follow the respondent states' approach to the interpretation and application of international human rights standards. This assigning of additional weight to the views of the state requires justification, and does not prevent consideration of the first-order reasons. We turn now to an analysis of deference as second-order reasons or on the basis of external factors, before looking at how this is exemplified in the practice of the Tribunals.

3. Deference on the basis of external factors

Comparing the way in which requests and orders, which are both second-order reasons for action, affect the reasoning process helpfully elucidates the practice of giving deference,[12] because it provides an analogy of second-order reasoning that does not prevent the consideration of first-order reasons.

Requests can provide second-order reasons for action that are to be weighed along with the ordinary first-order reasons for action. For example, if one is asked for money by a stranger, or a friend, or a neighbour in need, the request will be weighed in the reasoning process along with the reasons related to how to use one's financial resources. Orders, by contrast, imply 'some special priority or weight'[13] such that they might 'pre-empt or outweigh all other reasons that bear on the decision'.[14]

The weight allotted to a request in the reasoning process depends upon a variety of factors, for example the nature of the relationship and the appropriateness of deferring to the requestor. The reason for the additional weight attached to orders flows from the nature of the relationship with the person issuing the command. If there is a relationship of authority with the commander, this determines the weight attached to the command as a reason for action, such that it may become pre-emptive. If one's 11-year-old child orders payment to himself or herself of a 10 per cent tax on one's income, this would not cause one to do so, and would provide no weight in deciding how to apportion one's income. An authoritative order by contrast, for example from the tax revenue authorities, is determinative of one's reasons for action, including if one personally feels that the action is unjustified.

Reasons for deference operate in the reasoning process in a similar way to a request, in that they do not pre-empt consideration of the first-order reasons. As a result of external factors, some of the reasons in favour of a decision are strengthened in the reasoning process, but they do not prevent the consideration of all of the relevant first-order reasons.

---

[12] Soper (n3) 20–7.

[13] Ibid, 20.

[14] Ibid, 21. Raz argues that an order is binding whereas a request is not, because an order is an exclusionary second-order reason, whereas a request is not: (n5) 101.

The operation of second-order reasoning can helpfully be illustrated by the use of a quasi-mathematical formula. In practice, it would not be desirable to quantify all of the variables in this way since some variables might be of negligible importance or their value might be intangible and a matter of discretion. Nevertheless, the formula illustrates the impact of the operation of external factors on the first-order reasoning. For example, if there are three (first-order) reasons (a, b, and c) related to a decision, two of which are in favour of one outcome (x) and the third is in favour of outcome (y), the extrinsic factor or second-order reason (s) can operate as follows.

(i) x (a + b) considered along with y(c)(s)

(ii) (a(s) + b) considered along with y(c)

(iii) x (a + b(s)) considered along with y(c)

(iv) x (a + b)(s) considered along with y(c)

In example (i), the second-order reason (s) affects reason (c) either to strengthen or to reduce reasons to produce outcome (y): (s) might be crucial in swinging the decision in favour of (y); it might either strengthen or reduce the weight of (c), but overall have no effect; or it might so reduce the weight of (c) so as to tilt the decision in favour of outcome (x). In examples (ii)–(iv), the external factor (s) affects the reasons in favour of outcome (x) in a variety of ways. Again, in these different ways, the decision might be unaffected by (s) or it might determine whether the decision favours outcome (x) or (y). An important point to note here is that the effect of the external factor can be determined only once all of the reasons have been considered. The structure of this reasoning process is exemplified below in section 5 of this chapter, and discussed further in Chapter 7.

Giving deference on the basis of external factors in the above example can strengthen both outcome (x) and (y) depending on the quantities and variables. If outcome (x) were the view of one person and outcome (y) were the view of another, then we could speak of giving deference to the views of one of them on the basis of (s). In the context of international human rights law, the same descriptive terminology is not easily transferable. This is because the parties are normally an individual applicant and a respondent state. Where there is no common trend amongst states about the scope and definition of a particular international human rights standard, it could be said that this is a ground for deference (a 'margin of appreciation') to the state. However, the opposite statement—that is, that if the approach of the applicant were strengthened and the approach of the state were weakened by a common trend amongst states, then this would be a ground for deference to the applicant—does not aptly describe the practice of the Tribunals. This is because the external factors all relate to the state—to its democratic legitimacy in reaching the standard, to the level of common practice amongst other states to back up its approach or to imply diverse approaches, and to the level of expertise held by the state. Rather than saying, then, that there is deference or a margin of appreciation to the view of the applicant, another expression is required. In domestic public law, this is commonly referred to as the 'variable intensity of review' or 'standards of review'. In the US, in cases in which there are fewer grounds for deference to the government, this is referred to by the courts as 'heightened review' or 'strict scrutiny', depending on the nature of the case.[15] It is helpful to see the impact of each second-order reason on a state's arguments as on a scale between greater deference and stricter scrutiny. The nature of the reasons involved in a case will depend on whether there is a margin of appreciation (or strengthened first-order reasons) in a case or whether there is greater scrutiny of the first-order reasons. However, it is useful to give the overall process of considering external factors a single label. The label adopted in this book is 'deference', and its legal application in international human rights law is referred to as the 'margin of appreciation', but another label could be chosen.[16]

It is not appropriate to speak of deference when one has been ordered to act, for the order implies some legitimate authority to determine the outcome. The power dynamic involved in giving deference implies that the decision-maker was free to reject arguments to assign weight to the views of another, but had logical reasons to attach this additional weight to such views. In the context of international human rights law, respondent states do not, when claiming a margin of appreciation, have authority over the Tribunals. Instead, the Tribunals are competent to consider all of the issues before them, but may consider that there are reasons to assign weight to or to heighten scrutiny of the views of the respondent state.[17] Deference in the prime sense used herein does not, then, result in servility.[18] Although 'being deferential' in common parlance sometimes refers to a characteristic of bowing to another's preferences, perhaps out of politeness or station, the same sense need not apply to the action of giving deference. In a judicial context, which requires a rational assessment of all of the reasons in a case, there is no room for servility in the practice of deference. Instead, reasons are required for judges to give deference. This leads us to the next stage of enquiry: what reasons are there for deference, in particular in international human rights law?

---

[15] See Chapter 8.

[16] See Chapter 9.

[17] Judge Spielmann, Section President of the ECHR, refers extrajudicially to the idea that relying on the margin of appreciation might be akin to a waiver of the European Court of Human Rights' power of review: D Spielmann, 'Allowing the Right Margin: The European Court of Human Rights and the National Margin of Appreciation Doctrine—Waiver or Subsidiarity of European Review?' (Centre for European Legal Studies Working Paper Series, Cambridge 2012) 3. One has to have authority to be able to waive it. Accordingly, reference to the concept of waiver accurately captures the notion that the margin of appreciation does not take certain issues outside of the Court's formal competence, jurisdiction, or authority. However, the problem with the concept of 'waiver' is that it implies that the Court chooses not to exercise its authority to consider the substance of a case. If this were true, it would be tantamount to an abdication of judicial responsibility. However, it does not accurately reflect the practice of the Tribunals, which consider grounds for a margin of appreciation to be part of a decision-making process that includes the consideration of all of the factors in a case. See further section 5 of this chapter.

[18] See Lord Hoffmann's concern that using the label 'deference' in a judicial context carries 'overtones of servility' in *R(ProLife Alliance) v BBC* [2004] AC 185 (HL), [75].

4. Types of reason for deference

This section discusses types of reason for deference generally, as well as introducing the external factors for a margin of appreciation in international human rights law. The first group of reasons for deference is based on the nature of the relationship and the role of the actor. The second group of reasons for deference is based on the expertise of the actor and the epistemic limitations of the decision-maker.

a. Relationships and comity

The discussion in the previous section about how reasons for deference operate like a request, but unlike an order, referred to examples from interpersonal relationships. In such examples, it is clear that the nature of the relationship affects whether or not there is a relationship of authority between the parties and, where there may not be strict authority, how much weight is to be attributed to one request over another. In personal relationships, when assessing requests and reasons for deference, we look at who is seeking deference and why. Sometimes, people seek deference from us simply so that we can please them by favouring their preferences. At other times, there may be reasons to defer on the basis of the importance and value of the relationship. So, if spouses disagree over the type of school to which they should send their children, both views must be taken into account. Both will have reasons to defer to the other, based on the nature and importance of their relationship and of their marriage. Their final decision will be based on a number of factors, such as the 'relative strength of each spouse's conviction'.[19] It is clear that deference in this instance is unrelated to the first-order reasons about the school, financial considerations, etc. These remain relevant, and may be determinative, but there are reasons for deference to the other spouse's view that are independent of these first-order considerations.

Other reasons for deference include respecting the role of the other actor. For example, grandparents of a 10-year-old decide to rent a movie chosen by the parents, which is certified as suitable for 12-year-olds. Were it up to them, they would not allow their grandchild to watch this movie until she reached the age of 12, because they think it is too scary. But, in deference to the parents who are happy for their child to watch the movie, the grandparents allow their grandchild to rent it. Here, the significant issue is that they respect the role of the parents in making such selections for their child.

When assessing deference in the legal context of adjudication, giving deference to the state because of the intrinsic value of the relationship with the Tribunal is clearly inappropriate. In interpersonal relationships, one might defer to another as an expression of friendship. But in the setting of international human rights law the concept of friendship is out of place, since the role of the Tribunals is to act as

---

[19] Soper (n3) 23.

impartial arbitrators, sitting in judgment on the actions of the state. For the Tribunals to show deference to a state simply to please the state is entirely inappropriate, whereas deference to one's spouse for this reason is entirely reasonable. In the context of adjudication, reasons for deference require logical justification, and cannot simply be relational.

Two external factors for inter-institutional deference based on respecting the role of the other actor are identifiable in the practice of the Tribunals: (i) the democratic legitimacy of the state's action; and (ii) the level of common practice amongst states. These reasons for a margin of appreciation are grounds for comity between different authorities.[20] 'Comity' is defined by Timothy Endicott as 'the duty of one authority to support the proper function of other authorities'.[21]

Deference on the basis of democratic legitimacy is not unique to the Tribunals. It is also recognizable in domestic public law and judicial review. Reasons for deference to the state on the basis of democratic legitimacy entail the state effectively saying: 'Give deference to us. After all, we have a democratic mandate to decide this matter of human rights.' The view that one takes of the role of the Tribunals, discussed in Chapter 3, will affect the way in which this operates as a reason for deference. Chapter 4 considers why democratic legitimacy is a reason for deference, and how it operates in the practice of the Tribunals.

Deference on the basis of the level of common practice amongst states is specific to the Tribunals. Reasons for deference to the state on the basis of common practice entail the state effectively saying something like: 'Give deference to us. After all, other states agree we are right about what this human right standard is.' There are differences of view both amongst theoreticians and in the case law about whether the level of common practice should be relevant to the determination of international human rights standards. Again, such views are influenced by the position one takes about the role of the Tribunals. The approach an international tribunal takes to this issue affects its approach to second-order reasoning and thus the strength of reasons for a margin of appreciation on this basis. Chapter 5 assesses these debates in greater depth, as well as the practice of the Tribunals.

b. Epistemic limitations and expertise

If a person has expertise in a particular area, then a decision-maker has reason to defer to that person's views to produce a better decision. Sometimes, expertise operates as an exclusionary reason, since decision-makers take the word of the experts at face value and no longer deliberate on the first-order reasons themselves. However, this need not be the case, and partly depends on the dynamic and the role of the individuals. For example, if one were to go to a garage to find out how to fix one's car, one could take the mechanic's word as the final answer; alternatively, one could take it into account and do one's own research to make up one's own mind.

---

[20] See Chapter 3.4.b.
[21] TAO Endicott, *Administrative Law* (OUP, Oxford 2009) ix.

Likewise, the level of deference accorded to a more experienced mechanic will differ as a result of the extent of one's own expertise.[22]

The significance of the expertise can vary depending on the decision-maker's level of knowledge and the strength of other second-order and the first-order reasons. It remains the role and responsibility of the decision-maker to make a decision, but in making that decision it is reasonable in principle for the decision-maker to lean on the assessment of facts that are given by those in a better position to know about them.

There are a number of different contexts in which reasons for deference on the basis of expertise arise. In some of them, it is more apt to use the label 'giving deference to superior expertise', and in other contexts it makes better sense to refer to 'superior competence' or the fact that the state is better placed to make the decision. The Tribunals' confidence in their own ability to make a decision accurately influences the extent to which they give a margin of appreciation to those with greater skills, experience, or knowledge.[23] Such epistemological limits are common in practical reasoning and, in the context of the margin of appreciation in international human rights law, are a key external factor affecting the reasoning of the Tribunals.

Reasons for deference to the state on the basis of expertise or competence entail the state effectively saying: 'With due respect, give deference to us because, after all, we know better than you do about these matters.' This external factor is less controversial than the other reasons for a margin of appreciation and is sometimes argued away as simply being part of the ordinary reasoning process. Perhaps this is because resort to such reasoning is common practice in legal reasoning. This reason for a margin of appreciation is discussed in Chapter 6.

5. Cases that demonstrate this approach in practice

Some commentators do not regard deference in legal tribunals as the practice of assigning weight on the basis of second-order reasoning; rather, they understand the operation of deference by tribunals as a sort of non-justiciability doctrine,[24] because, on their view, deference involves the courts failing to engage with reasons that require determination, and instead bowing to the state's approach to the issues.[25] But non-justiciability is a doctrine that operates as a substantive bar on adjudication, which means that the tribunal does not make a decision because it is

---

[22] Soper similarly refers to two doctors discussing a diagnosis, contrasted with a doctor speaking with a patient: (n3) 36, fn1.

[23] Perry refers to such reasons for deference as 'epistemic limitations': (n8) 933–45.

[24] See TRS Allan, 'Human Rights and Judicial Review: A Critique of "Due Deference"' (2006) 65 (3) CLJ 671, E Benvenisti, 'Margin of Appreciation, Consensus, and Universal Standards' (1999) 31 International Law and Politics 843, and C Feingold, 'The Doctrine of Margin of Appreciation and the European Convention on Human Rights' (1977–78) 53 Notre Dame LRev 90. See also T Jones, 'The Devaluation of Human Rights under the European Convention' (1995) Public Law 430, 732.

[25] TRS Allan (n24) 689 opines: 'Due deference turns out, on close inspection, to be non-justiciability dressed in pastel colours.'

domestic margin of appreciation thus goes hand in hand with a European supervision. Such supervision concerns both the aim of the measure challenged and its 'necessity'; it covers not only the basic legislation but also the decision applying it, even one given by an independent court.

The Court in this case decided that there was no breach of Article 10 largely because it deferred to the national authorities' view of the effect on morals within their locality, which furthermore was held to be proportionate, notwithstanding the acknowledged importance of the right to freedom of expression, because a slightly revised edition of *The Schoolbook* was permitted to circulate in England. The purpose here is not to assess whether or not the decision was correct, but simply to highlight that the decision involved the operation and interrelation of first-order and second-order reasons. Much of the rest of the book will discuss the nature of the second-order reasons, and how and why they operate to affect deference.

Another early ECtHR case that exemplifies the role of second-order reasoning is *Sunday Times v UK*.[33] In that case, by contrast with *Handyside*, the ECtHR found that Article 10 had been violated. An injunction was served against the *Sunday Times* newspaper preventing it from printing details about the book *Spycatcher* written by Peter Wright, a former intelligence official of the UK government. The book had already been published in the US, and was consequently already in the public domain, but the Attorney General argued that the newspaper's publications would radically increase exposure to this breach of confidence within the UK, which, it was claimed, could have hazardous consequences for national security, a matter that is usually accorded a wide margin of appreciation by the Court.[34] In making its decision, the Court acknowledged that contracting states have a margin of appreciation and reiterated that this would be subject to their supervision. The Court went on to explain how this supervision operated. In the following extract, the idea that all of the first-order reasons are relevant and are to be weighed alongside the second-order reasons can be seen:

The Court's task, in exercising its supervisory jurisdiction, is not to take the place of the competent national authorities but rather to review under Article 10 the decisions they delivered pursuant to their power of appreciation. This does not mean that the supervision is limited to ascertaining whether the respondent State exercised its discretion reasonably, carefully and in good faith; what the Court has to do is to look at the interference complained of in the light of the case as a whole and determine whether it was 'proportionate to the legitimate aim pursued' and whether the reasons adduced by the national authorities to justify it are 'relevant and sufficient'.[35]

Some of the 'reasons adduced by the national authorities', such as the fact that state parties are better placed to assess the standard of protection necessary for national security, are second-order reasons. In this case, the Court found that there was a legal basis for the interference in Article 10, that it pursued a legitimate aim, but

---

[33] *Sunday Times v UK (No. 2)* No. 13166/87 (1991) (ECtHR).
[34] Ibid, 234–5. See further Chapter 6.4.a.
[35] Ibid, 242.

decided that the injunctions were not 'necessary', basing its decision on the fact that the material had already entered the public domain and that the injunctions were serving merely as a containment measure.[36] This case provides a clear example of second-order reasons being considered, but not being regarded as sufficiently weighty to strengthen the first-order reasons in favour of the state to override the first-order reasons of the applicant.

In *Hatton v UK*,[37] in which the applicants complained about sleep loss as a result of living close to Heathrow airport, allegedly in contravention of Articles 8 and 13, the Grand Chamber of the ECtHR emphasized that the impact of reasons for deference vary according to the strength of the first-order reasons as follows: 'The scope of this margin of appreciation is not identical in each case but will vary according to the context.'[38] In this case, the Court found that the state had struck a fair balance between the economic interests involved and the right of residents to undisturbed sleep, taking into account its margin of appreciation.

A case that exemplifies how second-order reasons for deference affect the balance of first-order reasons is *Stoll v Switzerland*.[39] During the course of the judgment, the relevant second-order and first-order reasons are discussed and set out; an explanation as to the weight allocated to these reasons is given at the end of the judgment.[40] Of course, the judges do not categorize the relevant considerations into first-order and second-order reasons, and they refer back and forth between these two types of reason in the judgment. In this case, Swiss journalists were fined for printing information leaked to them. The information revealed snippets of sensitive correspondence between the Swiss ambassador to the US and Swiss government officials relating to claims by Jewish Holocaust survivors for compensation from Swiss banks that were enriched as a result of deposits made by victims of the Holocaust. The Court noted[41] the importance of freedom of the press and the protection of political comment in the decision, which are first-order reasons, along with such matters as the diversity of approaches that European states take in responding to the leaking of confidential information, which is a second-order reason. The Court goes on to discuss in depth the content of the news items, weighing such first-order reasons as well as the impact of second-order reasons, and concluding that the state had not imposed a disproportionate fine on the applicants, given the context of that case.

---

[36] Ibid, 243.
[37] *Hatton v UK* No. 36022/97 (2003) (ECtHR (GC)).
[38] Ibid, [101], citing *Buckley v UK* No. 20348/92 (1996) (ECtHR), [74].
[39] *Stoll v Switzerland* No. 69698/01 (2007) (ECtHR (GC)).
[40] An interesting aspect of the case is that the dissenting judges criticize the format of the reasoning given by the majority. The minority argues that '[u]ntil they reach paragraph 147 of the judgment readers could easily believe that the Court is heading towards finding a violation of Article 10 of the Convention': ibid, second sentence of the dissenting opinion of Judge Zagrebelksy, joined by Judges Lorenzen, Fura-Sandstrom, Jaeger, and Popović. This complaint is misplaced. The fact that the majority explain the relevant factors to be considered is a useful exercise, even if the weightings can arguably be accorded differently.
[41] Ibid, e.g. [105]–[107], [115]–[116], [129].

The foregoing examples show how the ECtHR's margin of appreciation doctrine involves second-order reasoning. At this stage, the modest aim has been to show that the distinction between first-order and second-order reasoning taken from the philosophy of practical reasoning applies to the doctrine of the margin of appreciation. The reasons for deference are discussed in greater depth in subsequent chapters.

b. Inter-American Court of Human Rights (IACtHR)

Whilst the ECtHR has a well-established doctrine of deference, the same cannot be said of the IACtHR. Indeed, a number of cases seem to imply that there will be no deference to states. One example of this is *Herrera-Ulloa v Costa Rica*,[42] in which a journalist claimed a breach of Article 13 of the American Convention on Human Rights (ACHR) (freedom of thought and expression) because of legal action taken against him. This legal action was taken because he published articles on the immunity enjoyed by honorary Costa Rican diplomats. Because of the reporting, these posts began to be abandoned, but one of the diplomats took successful legal action against the applicant for damage to honour. One of the elements of the cause of action was 'malice'. The IACtHR stated that any infringement of free speech:

must be proportionate to the legitimate interest that justifies it and must be limited to what is strictly necessary to achieve that objective. It should interfere as little as possible with effective exercise of the right to freedom of expression.[43]

This phrase seems to imply that any interference by a state with free speech will be rigidly assessed only on the balance of first-order reasons. Reference is made in the judgment to ECHR jurisprudence about the level of appropriate interference with free speech,[44] but there is no reference to any margin of appreciation.

Does this mean that the IACtHR does not take into account second-order reasoning? On the contrary, second-order reasons for deference have as much relevance in the context of the Inter-American system of human rights protection as anywhere else, even if they have thus far been employed less frequently. They are used less often largely on the basis of the cases that are brought before it. Indeed, reasons for deference feature prominently only in cases in which there is not an obvious violation of the relevant convention.[45] In *Herrera-Ulloa*, the fines imposed were exorbitant and the reporting accurate. It was simply not necessary to discuss the fine limitations of state interference with free speech since the case clearly exceeded it. In other cases before the IACtHR, there is evidence of the second-order reasoning involved in deference.

---

[42] *Herrera-Ulloa v Costa Rica* Series C No. 107 (2 July 2004) (IACtHR).
[43] Ibid, [123].
[44] Ibid, e.g. [125]–[126].
[45] See Chapter 1.1 and S Greer, *The Margin of Appreciation: Interpretation and Discretion under the European Convention on Human Rights* (Council of Europe, Brussels 2000) 14.

The clearest resort to second-order reasoning by the IACtHR is from an Advisory Opinion. The Court opined, in *Proposed Amendments of the Naturaliza-tion Provisions of the Constitution of Costa Rica*,[46] on whether the relevant amend-ments were in accordance with the ACHR. The issues dealt with in the case included the increased time for which non-nationals were required to live in Costa Rica before they could apply for naturalization, including for spouses of nationals, and the requirements to read, write, and speak Spanish, and to pass a test on the history of the nation. The Court decided that the amendments did not obviously violate the Convention, citing the margin of appreciation reserved to states on such matters.[47] The major second-order reason is identified as follows:

[A]s far as the granting of naturalization is concerned, it is for the granting state to determine whether and to what extent applicants for naturalization have complied with the conditions deemed to ensure an effective link between them and the value system and interests of the society to which they wish to belong. To this extent there exists no doubt that it is within the sovereign power of Costa Rica to decide what standards should determine the granting or denial of nationality to aliens who seek it, and to establish certain reasonable differentiations based on factual differences which, viewed objectively, recognize that some applicants have a closer affinity than others to Costa Rica's value system and interests.[48]

It is possible to misinterpret this statement to mean that the naturalization provi-sions are non-justiciable, because they are 'within the sovereign power' of the state to determine. But note that it is only 'certain *reasonable* differentiations' that are within the sovereign power (emphasis added). It is thus for the Court to determine the limits of the sovereign power, and to do this it needs to weigh up all of the various first-order reasons, taking into account the second-order reason that it is primarily 'for the granting state' to assess the requirements for people to belong to it. Otherwise, the Court ought to have decided the case summarily as being outside its jurisdiction. Instead, the Court reasoned the case through, assessing all of the reasons, both first-and second-order, to test the compliance of the proposed amendment.

Whilst other IACtHR cases do not so explicitly employ second-order reasoning or a margin of appreciation, there are cases that show how such reasoning features in the judicial process. In *Ricardo Canese v Paraguay*,[49] an industrial engineer wrote reports about the hydroelectric power plant on the Paraná River, critiquing the chair of the board, a supporter of the then President of Paraguay. Later, that chairman and the applicant were competing candidates in the presidential cam-paign, and the applicant lost. The applicant was then charged with libel for bringing to light the former corruption of his contender, and his links to the former President. Without being able to give evidence, the applicant was convicted,

---

[46] *Proposed Amendments of the Naturalization Provisions of the Constitution of Costa Rica* Advisory Opinion OC-4/84 of 19 January 1984, Series A No. 4 (IACtHR).

[47] For example, ibid, [62].

[48] Ibid, [59].

[49] *Ricardo Canese v Paraguay* 31 August 2004, Series C No. 111 (IACtHR).

fined an exorbitant sum of money, and given a prison sentence. The IACtHR found violations of numerous Articles of the ACHR.[50] The decision provides an explanation of how an aspect of second-order reasoning features in free expression cases:

Democratic control exercised by society through public opinion encourages the transparency of State activities and promotes the accountability of public officials in public administration, for which there should be a reduced margin for any restriction on political debates or on debates on matters of public interest.[51]

In *Ricardo Canese*, the scope for interference with the freedom of expression (which involves second-order reasons, such as the state's ability to assess the requirements best in its society) was reduced, because of the importance of promoting transparency. The consequences of this type of second-order reasoning are discussed elsewhere,[52] but the important point to note at this juncture is that the Court sees a place for there being a margin, based on external factors, to defer to the state, even if in this case the margin is reduced (that is, even if there are grounds for heightened scrutiny of the state's actions).

A final example for now is the case of *Salvador-Chiriboga v Ecuador*,[53] in which the Court was asked to determine whether an expropriation of property was in accordance with the ACHR. The applicants inherited 60 hectares of land in the city, which the authorities seized, declaring it to be of public utility for the Metropolitan Park of Quito, but for which they did not pay compensation. The major issues in the case were related to the delay and quantum required to resolve the dispute. The public utility aspect of the land was not a major issue in dispute.[54] One of the side arguments in the case involved a claim of breach of Article 24 of the ACHR (equal protection), because an adjacent property-owner was allowed to develop the adjoining land. This is where second-order reasoning is most apparent. The state argued that, for 'technical reasons', the other property was treated differently, but details were not provided.[55] The Court decided that there were 'not enough evidentiary elements to determine whether the State, by not granting the authorization to develop a land of property to the alleged victim, has violated [Article 24]'.[56] In deciding thus, the burden of proof favoured the state. It is plausible that, taking into account the arguments of the state, the Court decided the case this way on the basis of a second-order reason that the state is better placed to assess the 'technical reasons' for authorizing development on that land.

---

[50] Including Articles 13, 22(2), 22(3), 8(1), 8(2), 8(2)(f), and 9.
[51] *Ricardo Canese v Paraguay* (n49), [97].
[52] See Chapters 4.6 and 8.3.c.
[53] *Salvador-Chiriboga v Ecuador* Judgment of 6 May 2008, Series C No. 179 (IACtHR).
[54] Ibid, [67].
[55] Ibid, [127].
[56] Ibid.

c. United Nations Human Rights Committee (UN HRC)

While the IACtHR jurisprudence contains fewer instances of deference, the UN HRC has a more varied case law. As with the IACtHR, there are numerous cases that give rise to clear violations, especially often with respect to breaches of Articles 9, 10, and 14 of the International Covenant on Civil and Political Rights (ICCPR) in cases of the treatment of death row detainees in several Caribbean states. However, there are plenty of other cases in which the reasoning is more nuanced and involves the consideration of second-order reasons.

The first case that expressly refers to such second-order reasons is *Hertzberg v Finland*.[57] In that case, the Committee assessed whether the Finnish Broadcasting Company had violated the ICCPR for censoring some programmes that discussed homosexuality to comply with a Finnish law that forbade programmes giving a 'positive picture' of homosexuality. Referring to the fact that 'public morals differ widely', the HRC decided: 'There is no universally applicable moral standard. Consequently, in this respect, a certain margin of discretion must be accorded to the responsible national authorities.'[58] Here, the HRC concluded that there was no breach of Article 19(2) (freedom of expression). The conclusion shows that the HRC took into account the external factor of the lack of universal consensus about how states should respond to this issue. Such reasoning may not have been determinative or correctly applied in that case, but it is evidence of the use of second-order reasons.

In a very interesting case in 1992, the HRC appeared to reject any reliance on a 'margin of appreciation' and potentially therefore the idea of deference. In *Länsman v Finland*,[59] representatives of the Sami people, an indigenous group who live semi-nomadically and for whom reindeer husbandry is a core part of their culture, claimed that a quarry contract endorsed by the state violated their right to enjoy their culture (Article 27 ICCPR). The HRC stated that:

A State may understandably wish to encourage development or allow economic activity by enterprises. The scope of its freedom to do so is not to be assessed by reference to a margin of appreciation, but by reference to the obligations it has undertaken in article 27.[60]

It is apparent here, though, that the HRC has mistaken the way in which a margin of appreciation operates. As discussed above, the margin of appreciation is not determinative, but precisely requires the consideration of all first-order reasons relevant to determining the obligations under Article 27. Although the terminology of the margin of appreciation seems to have been eschewed, the HRC's reasoning appears nevertheless to include consideration of second-order reasons, as can be seen here:

---

[57] *Hertzberg v Finland* CCPR/C/15/D/61/1979 (1982) (HRC).
[58] Ibid, [10.3].
[59] *Länsman v Finland* CCPR/C/52/D/511/1992 (1994) (HRC).
[60] Ibid, [9.4].

Against this background, the Committee concludes that quarrying on the slopes of Mt. Riutusvaara, in the amount that has already taken place, does not constitute a denial of the authors' right, under article 27, to enjoy their own culture. It notes in particular that the interests of the Muotkatunturi Herdsmen's Committee and of the authors were considered during the proceedings leading to the delivery of the quarrying permit, that the authors were consulted during the proceedings, and that reindeer herding in the area does not appear to have been adversely affected by such quarrying as has occurred.[61]

That the state considered the views of the authors and consulted the Sami were second-order reasons that affected the level of deference that the Committee accorded to the state.[62] These were weighed up along with the first-order reasons, and reindeer husbandry was deemed to be not so 'adversely affected' as to constitute a violation of the Covenant. Such consideration of second-order reasons appeared not to be the deliberate application of a doctrine of deference, but, as this case shows, the HRC is nevertheless 'speaking silently the language of the margin'.[63]

States have continued to make the case for deference before the HRC, but have, on the whole, avoided using the terminology of the 'margin of appreciation'. In *Bryhn v Norway*,[64] a woman was sentenced to a year in a rehab clinic for narcotics offences. She appealed on the basis that the sentence was too long and leave to appeal was unanimously rejected. The author took her case to the HRC alleging a violation of Article 14(5) ICCPR for inadequately reviewing her sentence. The state sought a 'certain margin with regard to the implementation of the right to review',[65] on the basis of the external factor that the democratic decision-making process carefully sought to comply with the Article 14(5) standard and for the further external factor that many states have enacted a variety of means to assess applications for review. The HRC responded to this argument as follows:

Although the Committee is not bound by the consideration of the Norwegian parliament, and sustained by the Supreme Court, that the Norwegian Criminal Procedure Act is consistent with article 14(5) of the Covenant, the Committee considers that in the circumstances of the instant case, notwithstanding the absence of an oral hearing, the totality of the reviews by the Court of Appeal satisfied the requirements of article 14, paragraph 5.[66]

Here, the HRC clearly articulates that these factors do not lead to non-justiciability, but it also does not deny the relevance of the democratic process, or the impact of other states' approaches. It is plausible, then, that these arguments impacted the reasoning of first-order considerations.

---

[61] Ibid, [9.6].
[62] Chapter 4.6.b.
[63] Quotation from James Crawford's 'Preface' to Y Arai-Takahashi, *The Margin of Appreciation Doctrine and the Principle of Proportionality in the Jurisprudence of the ECHR* (Intersentia, Antwerpen; Oxford 2002).
[64] *Bryhn v Norway* CCPR/C/67/D/789/1997 (HRC).
[65] Ibid, [4.4].
[66] Ibid, [7.2].

A similar implicit approach to deference can be seen in the case of *Vjatšeslav Borzov v Estonia*.[67] A Russian army retiree residing in Estonia was denied Estonian citizenship even though he was married to a naturalized Estonian. He was denied citizenship on national security grounds—namely that he could become a threat to Estonia by being called up to the Russian army, notwithstanding that he had retired due to illness. The author argued that he could not be called up, and furthermore since he no longer had Russian citizenship he was stateless and could not be a threat to Estonia. The state explicitly sought deference: 'The State party invites the Committee to defer, as a question of fact and evidence, to the assessment of the author's national security risk made by the Government and upheld by the courts.'[68] The HRC responded to this request as follows:

While the Committee recognizes that the Covenant explicitly permits, in certain circumstances, considerations of national security to be invoked as a justification for certain actions on the part of a State party, the Committee emphasizes that invocation of national security on the part of a State party does not, ipso facto, remove an issue wholly from the Committee's scrutiny.... While the Committee cannot leave it to the unfettered discretion of a State party whether reasons related to national security existed in an individual case, it recognizes that its own role in reviewing the existence and relevance of such considerations will depend on the circumstances of the case and the relevant provision of the Covenant.[69]

Here, the HRC makes it clear that a request for deference does not entail any non-justiciability or an abdication of its decision-making responsibility. On the contrary, it considers such arguments and weighs them along with the other considerations in the case. The implication here is that the HRC accepts that the state's assessment of the national security risks may give rise to deference depending on the 'circumstances of the case', and which provision of the ICCPR is in issue.[70] Consequently, the state's assessment will not be determinative of the weight to be applied to national security considerations, but will be considered as a relevant external factor.

The discussion thus far has focused on the fact that, in the Tribunals, the decision-makers take into account factors for a margin of appreciation, and these operate as second-order reasons. The margin of appreciation is not to be understood conceptually as akin to non-justiciability. There may be cases in which the Tribunals mistakenly use arguments for deference as a reason not to engage in a thorough reasoning process, but this would be to produce a poor and unreasoned decision rather than an error attributable to the concept of the margin of appreciation.

---

[67] *Vjatšeslav Borzov v Estonia* CCPR/C/81/D/1136/2002 (HRC).
[68] Ibid, [4.11].
[69] Ibid, [7.3].
[70] The HRC goes on, at [7.3] ibid, to discuss the variable standard of review as follows:

Whereas articles 19, 21 and 22 of the Covenant establish a criterion of necessity in respect of restrictions based on national security, the criteria applicable under article 26 are more general in nature, requiring reasonable and objective justification and a legitimate aim for distinctions that relate to an individual's characteristics enumerated in article 26, including 'other status'.

See further Chapter 8.

6. Conclusion

Commentators often refer to the margin of appreciation descriptively. It is described as the leeway that states enjoy in implementing their international human rights obligations according to local needs and concerns. Factors for deference are listed along with these descriptions, such as the level of state expertise or democratic legitimacy, and extracts from cases discussing such factors are usually set out.

In the face of recent criticism of the margin of appreciation doctrine, discussed in greater detail in the following chapter, an account of deference is required that moves beyond description and explains the practice conceptually. This chapter has intended to provide such an account. Drawing on the theory of second-order reasoning in the philosophy of practical reasoning, it has been argued that deference is the practice of assigning weight to the reasons for a decision on the basis of external factors. These external factors do not prevent the consideration of the reasons related to the case at hand. Instead, all of the reasons, as affected by the external factors, are to be considered at the stage of making a determination. This is commonly known as the 'proportionality assessment' and is discussed in greater detail in Chapter 7.

This chapter has also identified three external factors for a margin of appreciation used by the Tribunals: democratic legitimacy; the common practice of states; and the expertise of states. Having established how such factors operate in the reasoning process, it remains to be determined whether such factors justifiably influence the reasoning of the Tribunals. There are two main approaches to this question both in theory and in practice. The first approach is that the role of the Tribunals is to unify human rights standards and practices, and to police violations. The second is more complex: that the Tribunals' role is to allow the diverse protection of human rights, but to ensure that the diversity allowed does not lead to violations of human rights. These two main approaches are critically assessed in the following chapter, and it is argued that the second approach is to be preferred. The chapter also argues that the second approach best reflects the practice of deference in the Tribunals. That discussion clears the ground for Chapters 4–6, which deal with the external factors in turn, offering a justification for their role in influencing the reasoning of the Tribunals and an exposition of the case law of the Tribunals pertaining to them.

3

Different Approaches to Deference in International Human Rights Law

1. Introduction

The strength of reasons for a margin of appreciation on the basis of external factors depends on one's view of the role of the Tribunals. If one regards the Tribunals as having the primary role of establishing human rights standards, then it is plausible that there ought to be very little scope for a margin of appreciation to states. However, if states are important participants in the interpretation of international human rights standards and their application within their jurisdiction, then there may be reasons to give the state a margin of appreciation. Whilst the external factors themselves provide their own reasons for deference to the state (or stricter scrutiny), this chapter assesses the different general approaches that the Tribunals can take to the margin of appreciation, which affects how significant the external factors are in the deliberative process.

There are two main approaches to the role of the Tribunals in the interpretation and application of human rights. The first is a 'standard-unifying' approach—namely, that the role of the Tribunals is to harmonize human rights standards and practices, and to police violations. On this account, the margin of appreciation is undesirable. The extreme alternative to this approach—namely, the idea that the Tribunals ought to uphold the meaning of the Treaties as understood by the signatory states at the time of their ratification—has been disregarded by the Tribunals and commentators alike,[1] and is consequently not considered here. The second approach to the role of the Tribunals, a 'diversity-permitting' approach, is more nuanced, recognizing that states are the primary protectors of human rights and allowing a limited differential protection of human rights by states, as well as setting standards where appropriate. This involves giving a margin of appreciation where suitable to states' democratically formed fundamental standards, to common trends amongst the practice of contracting states, and to states' greater expertise when setting these standards. Commentators commonly adopt this approach, and it is the approach adopted by the Tribunals themselves. However, it is rarely defended or justified and critics of the margin of appreciation have articulated their positions more coherently.

---

[1] See Chapter 5.3.a.

There are two types of argument advanced in support of the first approach to the role of the Tribunals: the first type of argument is conceptual and the second type of argument is normative. There are (at least) two versions of the conceptual argument and two versions of the normative argument in support of the 'standard-unifying' approach to the role of the Tribunals.

The first version of the conceptual argument complains that the margin of appreciation leads to relativism about human rights and argues that, given that relativism is both undesirable and contrary to the Treaties, the Tribunals should abandon any reliance on the margin of appreciation. There is some evidence in the Tribunals' decisions to suggest that this is not simply a view taken by a minority of commentators, but one supported by a number of judges. However, this argument relies on an overly narrow understanding of universality, one that is both unattractive as a matter of theory and likely to have been far from the minds of the framers of the Treaties. Instead, there is a more promising and richer alternative approach to universality, which is in fact supported by the majority of case law developed by the Tribunals.

The second version of the conceptual argument is not addressed in this chapter, but in Chapter 7. This argument, based on rights theory, is that rights are not to be weighed in the judicial balance along with other interests. Instead, rights trump other interests. Rights are simply to be identified and then applied. This theory is referred to both as the 'rights as trumps' theory and the 'reason-blocking' theory of rights. Some theorists combine this second conceptual argument, based on theories of rights, with the normative arguments in favour of the standard-unifying approach. It seems clear that it is these normative arguments that are most important to these commentators, rather than a commitment to a certain concept of rights. Indeed, the conceptual 'rights as trumps' argument is compatible with the 'diversity-permitting' approach to the role of the Tribunals.[2] Moreover, the 'rights as trumps' argument can be overcome on its own terms: there is an alternative and preferable theory of rights, the 'interest-based' theory, which is clearly compatible with the 'diversity-permitting' approach to the role of the Tribunals reflected in practice.

The two main normative arguments of the first approach are complex. Both are based on the view that it is desirable for the Tribunals to harmonize approaches of states to human rights laws. The first version of the argument is that a margin of appreciation to states jeopardizes the role of the Tribunals as selecting the best human rights standard. This argument is closely connected with the second conceptual argument. Two different commentators, George Letsas and Stephen Greer, have advanced such arguments. Their accounts are considered in this chapter. The second version of the normative argument is based on a combination of factors such as the democratic nature of international treaties, or alternative values that membership of such treaty systems promotes, such as openness to others. This argument is advanced by Neil Walker in the context of European

---

[2] See Chapter 7.4.

human rights law, based on the way in which the European Union (EU) is drawing member states closer together.

There is some case law that supports the arguments of these commentators, but the 'standard-unifying' approach to the Tribunals is ultimately unattractive as a matter of theory and does not best fit the case law of the Tribunals. It is unattractive as a matter of theory because of the normative importance of the role of the state in the protection of human rights, both for democratic and practical reasons, and because human rights instantiations can vary from place to place. Further, the approach fails to reflect the importance of the international context of the Tribunals, and the overlapping responsibilities of states and international institutions in the protection of human rights.

As mentioned, the conceptual and normative versions of the 'standard-unifying' approach are often connected. Sometimes, one mistake leads to another: for example a belief in the importance of uniformity because it is for the Tribunals to find the right moral version of human rights can lead to a view that universality about the morality of human rights has no legitimate variation from time to time or place to place, or vice versa.

The following two sections set out and respond to the first conceptual argument and the normative arguments supporting the 'standard-unifying' approach to the Tribunals. The aim of the discussion is to show the limitations of these views, and to clear the ground for an explanation of the 'diversity-permitting' approach, which is defended in this book as the preferable theoretical justification of the margin of appreciation in the practice of the Tribunals.

2. The margin of appreciation and relativism about human rights

One of the most powerful criticisms of the margin of appreciation doctrine is that it panders to relativist notions of human rights law, which ought to be universal.[3] On this view, the role of the Tribunals is to interpret and substantiate a single, uniform meaning of the human right at issue. But the universality of human rights is compatible with legitimately differential specifications of value, both as a matter of morality and particularly as a matter of law. Thus the margin of appreciation, properly employed, may produce different approaches to the implementation of human rights from place to place, which are nevertheless consistent with the universality of human rights.

It would be helpful at this point to refer to some of the accounts that designate the margin of appreciation as a retreat into relativism. Eyal Benvenisti states that the '[m]argin of appreciation, with its principled recognition of moral relativism, is at

---

[3] This book assumes that fundamental moral values are universal and human rights doctrine is concerned with moral truth. For argument by this author on this point, see A Legg, *Towards a Principled Doctrine of the Margin of Appreciation in International Human Rights Law* (MPhil, University of Oxford 2007) 14–23.

odds with the concept of the universality of human rights'.[4] He goes on to state that he is not 'entering into the well-trodden general debate on universalism versus relativism in human rights jurisprudence', but is instead focusing on institutional arguments about the margin of appreciation, especially arguments concerning 'the inherent deficiencies of the democratic systems'.[5] His initial claim, that the margin of appreciation involves a 'principled recognition of moral relativism', is simply asserted, without any supporting argument. Indeed, by going on to discuss institutional considerations relevant to the margin of appreciation, Benvenisti unwittingly accepts that in fact there are reasons for the doctrine other than (and not reliant upon) the entrenching of moral relativism.

James Sweeney also refers to arguments that suggest that the margin of appreciation has a 'perceived culturally relativist bias'.[6] He refers to the partly dissenting opinion of Judge De Meyer in the case of *Z v Finland*:

In the present judgment the Court once again relies on the national authorities' 'margin of appreciation'. I believe that it is high time for the Court to banish that concept from its reasoning. It has already delayed too long in abandoning this hackneyed phrase and *recanting the relativism it implies.*[7]

There are no clear cases in the Inter-American Court of Human Rights (IACtHR) and the United Nations Human Rights Committee (UN HRC) that reject the margin of appreciation as resulting in relativism about human rights. However, there are cases that rely on the universality of human rights in finding against the state that some might regard as indicative of a narrow approach to universality. In the case of *Raxcacó-Reyes v Guatemala*,[8] the IACtHR decided that the conditions in which the prisoner was kept while on death row violated Article 5 of the American Convention on Human Rights (ACHR), and made reference to the 'universality of the right to decent and humane treatment'. The IACtHR in that case noted that the HRC in *Mukong v Cameroon*[9] had rejected that scarcity of resources as an excuse for failure to respect that right. However, these examples are equally compatible with the broader version of universality developed below.

The literature and the case law do not develop a clear argument about how the doctrine of the margin of appreciation is based on relativism about human rights, although it is clear that there are suspicions that the margin of appreciation betrays universality. But what does 'universality' mean in the context of fundamental values

---

[4] E Benvenisti, 'Margin of Appreciation, Consensus, and Universal Standards' (1999) 31 International Law and Politics 843, 844.

[5] Ibid, 847.

[6] JA Sweeney, 'Margins of Appreciation: Cultural Relativity and the European Court of Human Rights in the Post-Cold War Era' (2005) 54 ICLQ 459, 459. Sweeney's aim is to discount such views and show that the margin of appreciation is based upon institutional subsidiarity.

[7] *Z v Finland* No. 22009/93 (1997) (ECtHR), Part III (emphasis added). See also the footnote to his separate concurring opinion in *Ahmed v UK* No. 22954/93 (1998) (ECtHR). Cases cited in Sweeney (n6) 463, fn21. See further M-B Dembour, *Who Believes in Human Rights? Reflections on the European Convention* (CUP, Cambridge 2006) 159–65.

[8] *Raxcacó-Reyes v Guatemala* Series C No. 133 (15 September 2005) (IACtHR).

[9] *Mukong v Cameroon* CCPR/C/51/D/458/1991 (1994) (HRC).

and human rights? It is only when the meaning of universality has been clarified that it is possible to ascertain whether the margin of appreciation is relativist or whether it is compatible with the universality of human rights. The following sections argue that universality is compatible with diverse instantiations of human rights, and thus that the margin of appreciation is compatible with the universality of human rights.

a. The meaning of universality in moral discourse

Joseph Raz explains that 'what appear to be irreconcilable conflicts, namely the conflicts between diversity and universality of value, and between the social dependence of value and its intelligibility, are not in fact irreconcilable conflicts'.[10] Although he does not claim to reconcile the ostensible conflict, Raz's discussion sheds light on how, while maintaining a commitment to the universality of values, one can also expect these values to be articulated differently according to time and context. Raz's account of universality overcomes the claim that the margin of appreciation succumbs to moral relativism.

It may not be easy for some people to accept the idea of legitimate difference, since it entails 'endorsing affirming, approving attitudes to normative practices which often appear inconsistent, or even positively hostile to each other'.[11] Raz acknowledges that accepting differences may lead to some kind of relativism and is, for those relativists, a rejection of universality, but explains that his purpose is to explore 'the boundaries of coherent relativism',[12] which remains committed to universality.

Raz's explanation of universality can be paraphrased as follows. The fact that something is of value to us requires that which is of value to be identified and extrapolated, and then applied to something else outside of those specific circumstances. This extrapolation objectifies the value making it, in a 'thin' sense, universalizable. Furthermore, the universalizability of values is what makes them intelligible as values. For example, saying that a movie is good today, but was terrible yesterday, obviously lacks intelligibility. This is because we are entitled to assume that any change of value can be explained, and that value explanations depend on universal characteristics: factors such as time and location do not account for varied explanations.[13] A counter-argument might claim that, given the diversity in social practices extant in the world, values are dependent upon a given context for their expression and even for our knowledge of them, and are therefore incapable of universalizability. Raz 'reverses'[14] this argument, by saying that, given that all values are captured within a particular temporal and historical context, this 'takes the sting out of the fact that belief in values is socially

---

[10] J Raz, *Value, Respect and Attachment* (CUP, Cambridge 2001) 74.
[11] Ibid, 11–12.
[12] Ibid, 12.
[13] Ibid, 47–54.
[14] Ibid, 62–76.

dependent'.[15] Friendship, opera, and chess are social creations that came into being at some point in time. Assuming too that these goods could come into being only at a certain point in time, nevertheless 'these goods are universal, for they can in principle be instantiated at any point in time or space'.[16] Given that the 'intelligibility of values requires their universality', it is the case that 'the social dependence of value does not require that it not be universal'.[17]

b. Moral universality and the margin of appreciation

The mistaken understandings of universality and how it operates in moral discourse have caused significant confusion regarding the doctrine of the margin of appreciation. The argument that the universality of values entails their legitimate differential instantiation from place to place means that where a state interprets a human right standard differently within its margin of appreciation, this is not necessarily a reflection of moral relativism. Why should, for example, there be only one right way for a state to decide what a fair trial requires with respect to the anonymity of particular classes of offender, whether they are rapists or children? Why should a uniform approach to free speech be imposed on states that operate in radically different contexts?

The legitimacy of different approaches from state to state can be illustrated in the margin of appreciation context by looking again at the landmark case of *Handyside v UK*.[18] Despite the fact that some countries allowed the publication of *The Schoolbook*,[19] the Court held that:

The Contracting States have each fashioned their approach in the light of the situation obtaining in their respective territories; they have had regard, *inter alia*, to the different views prevailing there about the demands of the protection of morals in a democratic society. The fact that most of them decided to allow the work to be distributed does not mean that the contrary decision of the Inner London Quarter Sessions was a breach of Article 10.[20]

Sweeney's discussion of the margin of appreciation and cultural relativism relies on a conception of morality that, like Raz's discussion of the universality of moral values, acknowledges the role of 'thin' as against 'thicker' conceptions.[21] However, Sweeney relies on Michael Walzer's conception of thick and thin moral values,[22] which differs significantly from Raz's, because Walzer asserts that morality is 'thick from the beginning, culturally integrated, fully resonant and it reveals itself thinly only on special occasions, when moral language is turned to specific purposes'.[23] The better view accepts that it is possible to move from a (thick) culturally

[15] Ibid, 69.
[16] Ibid, 73.
[17] Ibid, 74.
[18] *Handyside v UK* No. 5493/72 (1976) (ECtHR).
[19] Ibid, [11].
[20] Ibid, [57].
[21] Raz (n10) 42–3.
[22] Sweeney (n6), relying on M Walzer, *Thick and Thin: Moral Argument at Home and Abroad* (University of Notre Dame Press, Notre Dame, Ind 1994) 4.
[23] Walzer (n22) 4, cited in Sweeney (n6) 470.

embedded position to reflection upon (thin) universal values.[24] It is problematic for Sweeney that he relies on arguments that reject the universality of values to make the point that a thin conception of morality is able to justify the diversity that the doctrine of the margin of appreciation brings, especially since he claims that this diversity is not the same as moral relativism.[25] To defend the margin of appreciation against charges of moral relativism, it is therefore better to rely on a Razian conception of thin morality, one that is compatible with a universal view of rights.

Universal human rights thus depend on social factors to find expression and realization, and this necessarily differs from place to place and over time. In order more adequately to defend the legal doctrine of the margin of appreciation against charges of moral relativism, it is important to explore some of the legal implications of these arguments that can provide the normative justification for the margin of appreciation.

c. Legal rights that implement moral rights

In different legal systems, decisions on the articulation of rights may vary in a way that is consistent with sharing the same values. Raz discusses an example that shows how laws translated from universal moral principles may differ between legal systems and over time.[26] Although the context here is a discussion of the nature of authority to make laws that have lengthy temporal validity, the focus relevant to this book lies elsewhere, on the nature of translating the 'moral' wrong into law. In this regard, the example that Raz draws about laws against rape is instructive:

The moral wrong committed by rape may involve the violation of a universal moral principle. But the legal regulation of rape may rightly vary from place to place and time to time. To go no further, it is far from a universal principle that rape should constitute a separate offence rather than be assimilated to serious assault . . . Whether and when a sexual motive should determine the character of the offence, rather than be relevant to sentence only, whether or when penetration should single out some sex offences from others, whether or when violence matters or not (it is not a necessary ingredient of rape, according to most jurisdictions) – *all these are questions sensitive to social conditions, to perceived social meanings, to the informal consequences of criminal convictions, and to many other factors that are as variable as any.*[27]

It is the claim in this last emphasized passage that is most relevant. Building on the above argument that expressions of moral value are socially contingent in a way that

---

[24] Legg (n3). The argument deployed there relies on W Kymlicka, *Liberalism, Community and Culture* (Clarendon Press, Oxford 1989), particularly ch 4.

[25] Sweeney (n6) 459 says: 'In responding to these concerns [about the margin of appreciation's perceived culturally relative bias] it is argued that the variations permitted by the use of the margin of appreciation concept do not amount to cultural relativism.' The reliance on Walzer's argument is problematic for the same reason in the chapter on 'Universality' in S Marks and A Clapham, *International Human Rights Lexicon* (OUP, Oxford 2005).

[26] J Raz, 'On the Authority and Interpretation of Constitutions: Some Preliminaries' in L Alexander (ed) *Constitutionalism: Philosophical Foundations* (CUP, Cambridge 1998) 166.

[27] Ibid, 166 (emphasis added).

does not jeopardize their universality, this contingency is augmented when considering the social implications within a particular community's *legal* system. Thus sharing a belief in the universal moral wrong of rape and in the desirability of protection against rape in human rights law is compatible with accepting the legitimacy of differentiation within different societies' human rights laws. Such differentiation does not reject the universal nature of the human right, but does reject an unnatural uniformity of legal expression.

It is important not to take this too far, or to draw hasty conclusions from this discussion. Legal differentiation from place to place *may* rightly vary; the argument is not that it must vary, but simply that uniformity between legal systems ought not be forced. Such uniformity may lead to injustice and a failure to implement human rights, rather than their proper protection.[28] Consequently, there are reasons to consider the external factors for deference because they provide the Tribunals with the opportunity to recognize legitimate diversity. At the same time, there may not be strong reasons to defer in a particular case, it being better to rely on a more uniform legal solution, perhaps based on a common trend among states.[29]

The next section addresses the nature of uniformity between legal orders, drawing on a discussion of comparative legal methodology. The aim is to explore further both reasons in favour of rejecting forced uniformity and reasons in favour of an appropriate level of uniformity in order better to understand the legitimate differentiation that the margin of appreciation entails.

d. Legal orders and comparisons

The necessary connection of law to the society in which it has been formed has attracted debate. Some writers have emphasized the appropriateness on occasions for law to be transplanted into different contexts,[30] whilst others have emphasized the uniqueness of law to their own systems based on their history and culture.[31] It is possible to find within such studies areas of commonality, although the particular projects may have cross-intentions. Alan Watson, despite presenting the transplantability of law and arguing that law from some legal orders has had huge impact on other systems, for example the way in which Roman law and the English common law have been 'exported' to numerous other legal systems to a greater or lesser extent,[32] nevertheless concedes that '[i]t would, I believe, be universally admitted that some degree of correlation *must* exist between law and society'.[33] Watson's purpose in encouraging the finding of legal adoption or transplantation is to urge legal scholars to 'delineate precisely this correlation; and this delineation should be

---

[28] See further the UNESCO Universal Declaration on Cultural Diversity (2 November 2001), in particular Article 4.
[29] See Chapter 6.
[30] For example, A Watson, 'Comparative Law and Legal Change' (1978) 37 CLJ 313.
[31] For example, P Legrand, 'How to Compare Now' (1996) 16 Legal Studies 232.
[32] Watson (n30) 314.
[33] Ibid, 321 (emphasis in original).

in terms of factors that help to bring about legal change'.[34] The idea comes from recognition that law can at times be anachronistic, serving no useful modern purpose. Nevertheless, caution and skill is required for this exercise in transplantation. Hasty comparisons will fail in the allotted aim. Pierre Legrand discusses the techniques of bad comparative law:

[T]he reason why the French have the legislative texts or the judicial decisions they have, say, on a matter of sales law, lies somewhere in their history, in their Frenchness, in their identity. And this is what 'comparatists' do not (want to) see: they stop at the surface, looking merely to the rule or proposition – and they forget about the historical, social, economic, political, cultural and psychological context which has made that rule or proposition what it is.[35]

What can be distilled from the different studies is that it is possible to do improper comparative analysis that undermines the law's particularity and context, but also that legal systems often do deal with similar questions. Comparisons can thus shed light on ways in which to improve the law through legal reform or by the citing of foreign law in judicial decision-making. Whether or not legal systems ought or ought not to rely on comparative law as a matter of legal authority in making judgments depends in the first instance upon each system's rules of legal authority or recognition.[36] Section 39 of the South African Constitution[37] is an example of a provision that explicitly allows reference to other legal orders in the making of constitutional decisions. However, even when it does refer to other jurisdictions, the South African Constitutional Court has been 'careful to underline the fact that foreign legal principles should not be applied blindly'.[38] There has been explicit recognition that foreign law 'will not necessarily offer a safe guide'.[39] Jack Tsen-Ta Lee argues that hitherto the Court 'did not apply foreign or international legal principles unthinkingly, but used them to inform the constitutional law of South Africa and, eventually, to develop its own legal principles',[40] which mirrors the approach that John Bell calls 'cross-fertilization'.[41]

In other constitutions, consideration of foreign law is considered by some as unwarranted as a matter of legal authority, and even as a matter of persuasive

---

[34] Ibid, 321.

[35] Legrand (n31) 236.

[36] This phrase is from HLA Hart, *The Concept of Law* (2nd edn, Clarendon Press, Oxford 1972).

[37] Section 39(1) provides: 'When interpreting the Bill of Rights, a court, tribunal or forum—(a) must promote the values that underlie an open and democratic society based on human dignity, equality and freedom; (b) must consider international law; and (c) may consider foreign law.'

[38] J Tsen-Ta Lee, 'Interpreting Bills of Rights: The Value of a Comparative Approach' (2007) 5 International Journal of Constitutional Law 122, 141, discussing the interpretation of section 35(1) of South Africa's Interim Constitution, which is the precursor to the current section 39, in *State v Makwanyane* (1995) (3) SA 391 (CC).

[39] *State v Makwanyane* (ibid) 414 (Chief Justice Arthur Chaskalson).

[40] Tsen-Ta Lee (n38) 142.

[41] J Bell, 'Mechanisms for Cross-Fertilisation of Administrative Law in Europe' in J Beatson and T Tridimas (eds) *New Directions in European Public Law* (Hart, Oxford 1998).

authority.[42] As well as textual considerations, there are a number of other factors that influence the way in which courts refer to foreign precedent. Chris McCrudden suggests ten such factors, including the type of political regime in which the foreign court is situated, whether there are common alliances between the systems, or whether there is a vacuum of indigenous jurisprudence.[43] While legal approaches to the consideration of legal materials from other jurisdictions differ, it is clear that even where they are most encouraged, for example in the South African context, the courts wisely do not seek to adopt wholesale legal provisions from other contexts. The case referred to above, *State v Makwanyane*,[44] related to the death penalty. Although reference was paid to approaches from numerous other jurisdictions, the Constitutional Court was careful to find a solution that was appropriate to the South African context.

Even in the human rights context therefore, one cannot simply transpose one system's specification of legal norms unthinkingly. Instead, care and skill are cautioned in the study of different countries' approaches to human rights. Foreign case law cannot be transplanted blindly, nor is this the experience of courts dealing with human rights. As McCrudden says: 'Most judges using comparative judicial decisions recognize, indeed *insist*, on the constructed and (to some extent) contingent nature of decision-making on issues of contemporary human rights.'[45] Such judicial practice is consistent with the arguments made above that, notwithstanding the universality of human rights, there is a justifiable moral, and even more so legal, differentiation of these rights from place to place.

e. The margin of appreciation and relativism in practice

The previous sections show theoretically that the margin of appreciation, with its acceptance of legal differentiation, does not simply because of this betray the universality of human rights. This is because moral values rely on social contexts for their expression, and the legal implementation of human rights might also be rightly different from place to place. The discussion has also explained that this argument cannot be taken to mean that law from one system is unable to influence the development of human rights law in other jurisdictions. Both moral discussion and legal development are open to the influence of those outside of one's community.

In addition to being theoretically robust, this broader approach to the universality of human rights is reflected in the practice of the Tribunals, as the following sections demonstrate.

---

[42] For example, Scalia J's dissent in *Thompson v Oklahoma* 487 US 815, 108 S Ct 2687 (SC), in which he argued that it is the US people whose consensus matters, discernible in legislation of the society, which is 'assuredly all that is relevant'.

[43] C McCrudden, 'A Common Law of Human Rights? Transnational Judicial Conversations on Constitutional Rights' (2000) 20 (4) OJLS 499, section 7, 516–27.

[44] *State v Makwanyane* (n38).

[45] McCrudden (n43) 528.

i. European Court of Human Rights (ECtHR)

In *Vo v France*,[46] the Grand Chamber of the ECtHR was asked to decide whether or not Article 2 of the European Convention on Human Rights (ECHR) (right to life) was violated because there was no criminal legislation to prevent and punish the negligent termination of an unborn foetus. In this case, a Vietnamese lady named 'Vo' was due to have a coil removed, and another Vietnamese lady of the same name (the applicant) was due to have a routine pregnancy check-up. The coil-removal procedure was tragically undertaken on the pregnant woman, piercing the amniotic sack and terminating the baby. The applicant argued that the point at which life began, and thus the applicability of Article 2, had a 'universal meaning and definition'.[47] Finding that Article 2 had not been violated, the Grand Chamber stated that:

[C]onsideration [has been] given to the diversity of views on the point at which life begins, of legal cultures and of national standards of protection, and the State has been left with considerable discretion in the matter, as the opinion of the European Group on Ethics in Science and New Technologies at the European Commission appositely puts it: 'the . . . Community authorities have to address these ethical questions taking into account the moral and philosophical differences, reflected by the extreme diversity of legal rules applicable to human embryo research . . . It is not only legally difficult to seek harmonization of national laws at Community level, but because of lack of consensus, it would be inappropriate to impose one exclusive moral code'.[48]

This extract does not mean that the ECtHR has rejected the universality of the right to life, but only that the Court accepts that the articulation of the right can appropriately and legitimately vary under certain circumstances. As Judge Tulkens put this idea in relation to another case, 'the Court must seek to reconcile universality and diversity'.[49]

ii. Inter-American Court of Human Rights (IACtHR)

The IACtHR takes the same approach. In *Herrera-Ulloa v Costa Rica*,[50] the case involving the journalist who was subject to legal proceedings for his writing about honorary diplomatic post-holders, the IACtHR affirmed the universal nature of free speech by recognizing that all human rights systems recognize its 'essential role', but left open the possibility of diverse expressions of free speech, by referring to the importance of effective freedom of expression 'exercised in all its forms'.[51] In

---

[46] *Vo v France* No. 53924/00 (2004) (ECtHR (GC)).
[47] Ibid, [47].
[48] Ibid, [82].
[49] *Leyla Şahin v Turkey* No. 44774/98 (2005) (ECtHR (GC)), [2] of his dissenting opinion, agreeing on this point with the majority.
[50] *Herrera-Ulloa v Costa Rica* Series C No. 107 (2 July 2004) (IACtHR).
[51] Ibid, [116].

another case, *Mayagna v Nicaragua*,[52] the IACtHR explained that the right to property did not only entail a personal, private right to property, but was compatible with a right to property vested in indigenous communities, which was reflective of the unique cultural characteristics that valued property differently from the individual protection of personal interests. A separate opinion in that case stated:

In fact, there are nowadays many multicultural societies, and the attention due to the cultural diversity seems to us to constitute an essential requisite to secure the efficacy of the norms of protection of human rights, at national and international levels. Likewise, we consider that the invocation of cultural manifestations cannot attempt against the universally recognized standards of observance and respect for the fundamental rights of the human person. Thus, at the same time that we affirm the importance of the attention due to cultural *diversity*, also for the recognition of the universality of human rights, we firmly discard the distortions of the so-called cultural 'relativism'.[53]

iii. United Nations Human Rights Committee (UN HRC)

The UN HRC has not thus far explicitly discussed cultural relativism and the universality of human rights in its views. However, given that it does provide for different articulations of rights depending on local considerations in practice,[54] it appears as if the HRC accepts the broader approach to universality. As Jacques Maritain, the influential French philosopher-diplomat involved in the negotiation of the Universal Declaration of Human Rights (UDHR), which along with the International Covenant on Civil and Political Rights (ICCPR) forms part of what is commonly referred to as an 'international Bill of Rights', said of that treaty 'many different kinds of music can be played on the document's thirty strings'.[55]

f. Summary

The arguments thus far made about the nature of universal moral values containing legitimate differences entail that it is implausible to impose uniform approaches to human rights on occasions when it would be appropriate to defer to the state's localized articulation of the right. Arguments about universality and uniformity can sometimes overlap. In a discussion that is ostensibly about the universality of human rights, Anthony Lester argues for greater uniformity of legal approaches to human rights between national legal systems.[56] He argues that, in the Convention's

---

[52] *Mayagna (Sumo) Awas Tingni Community v Nicaragua* Series C No. 79 (31 August 2001) (IACtHR).

[53] Ibid, [14], joint separate opinion of Judges Cançado Trindade, Pacheco Gómez, and Abreu Burelli (emphasis in original).

[54] See, e.g., *Hertzberg v Finland* CCPR/C/15/D/61/1979 (1982) (HRC), and Chapter 2.5.c.

[55] See MA Glendon, *A World Made New: Eleanor Roosevelt and the Universal Declaration of Human Rights* (Random House, New York 2001) 230, fn21.

[56] A Lester, 'Universality versus Subsidiarity: A Reply ' (1998) 1 EHRLR 73, 78. Lester accepts that free speech rights cannot be subject to a unifying principle and requires particularization for different circumstances, and he seems also to accept a limited margin of appreciation. However, the overriding emphasis of his article is on the Court developing a clearer approach that will guide national courts. It is

new legal order, the ECtHR should develop common standards based on the contracting states' shared traditions and that national courts should implement these standards.[57] The implication of this view is that human rights rules are uniform and merely to be implemented by national authorities rather than formed by them in a variety of ways, and that the role of clarification and development of these standards belongs to the ECtHR.

Although this sort of argument impacts discussions about universality, it is better understood as a normative argument that the ECtHR ought to impose uniform human rights standards. This is because whilst the universality of human rights entails their moral and legal differentiation, harmonization of these standards through political or legal development can eliminate what might otherwise be acceptable differences.

The normative claims favouring harmonization need not conflict with accepting that the differentiation of values is compatible with universality. Instead, the corollary of harmonization arguments could be that differentiation should not extend to human rights, for reasons other than fear of relativism. These reasons relate to the institutional interrelationship between states and the Tribunals, and are critically assessed in the following section.

3. Critiques of deference

One argument that it is desirable for the Tribunals to harmonize states' approaches to human rights laws concludes that a margin of appreciation to states jeopardizes the role of the Tribunals to determine the correct human rights standard—that is, that there is 'one right answer'. Another argument in favour of uniformity applies where states are increasingly integrated: that democracy in such circumstances is no longer of prime importance for deciding human rights standards. These arguments are assessed in turn.

a. The 'one right answer' thesis

The most comprehensive argument along the first of these lines has been made by George Letsas in the context of the ECHR system.[58] Letsas argues that judges have a duty to find and implement the best moral understanding of human rights irrespective of the diversity of views or laws within the legal systems of Europe.[59] A disciple of legal philosopher Ronald Dworkin, Letsas adopts a Dworkinian approach to law: that law is an interpretive exercise that finds the best fit of all

---

possible that if only the use of the margin of appreciation doctrine were better reasoned, Lester would be satisfied. However, it appears from his article that he favours the Court setting standards that would apply uniformly across Europe.

[57] Ibid, 75.

[58] G Letsas, *A Theory of Interpretation of the European Convention on Human Rights* (OUP, Oxford 2007).

[59] Ibid, xi.

competing specifications within a legal system. This means that 'states should govern through a coherent set of political principles whose benefit extends to all citizens'.[60] When Letsas applies this to the ECHR system, he takes it to mean that judges should search throughout Europe for coherent principles that furnish the best interpretation of what human rights mean, leading to a uniform legal protection of human rights within Europe, and leaving no room for deference to state conceptions of these standards.

To reach this conclusion, Letsas relies on two main propositions, each of which is problematic. First, he argues that the fact that the ECHR system is based on an international treaty is irrelevant,[61] and that it should be treated in the same way as a state constitution.[62] He argues that reliance on consensus among states is irrelevant[63] and that the evolution of standards based on contemporary state consensus 'smacks of moral relativism'.[64] Instead, Letsas argues that there is one right answer to these matters and that it is the Court's role to discover the moral truth.[65] Letsas' first proposition is problematic because it is not so much established as asserted. There are some scant arguments made about the nature of international legal concepts, but these are vague and misleading.[66] On the contrary, the fact that the ECHR and other human rights treaties are made between states is an important consideration for tribunals when interpreting the values that the treaties enshrine, as discussed in greater depth in Chapter 5.[67]

Letsas' second main proposition is that, when adjudicating about rights, the Court should exclude all considerations involving 'hostile external preferences' of a majority, and thus any balancing or proportionality analysis.[68] Letsas argues that this is an application of a Dworkinian account of 'rights as trumps'. Letsas' second proposition is problematic because it oversimplifies the application of 'rights as trumps' theories. The conceptual argument relied on by Letsas does not lead to the conclusion that there is no room for deference.[69] In addition, it appears that Letsas is leaning on a Dworkinian approach to judicial review,[70] which is criticized in Chapter 4.

---

[60] Ibid, 30.

[61] Ibid, 9.

[62] Ibid, 35.

[63] Therefore Letsas regards what he calls the structural concept of the margin of appreciation to be misplaced: ibid, ch 6.

[64] Ibid, 75.

[65] Ibid, 79.

[66] Ibid, 32.

[67] While the book argues that the international nature of the Treaties affects their interpretation and that the Treaties are not akin to state constitutions, the Treaties may have constitutional qualities. See B Fassbender, *The United Nations Charter as the Constitution of the International Community* (Martinus Nijhoff, Leiden 2009) 48 and 50, but note 103–5.

[68] Letsas (n58) 112–16 and ch 6. This leads to Letsas rejecting what he calls the substantive concept of the margin of appreciation as both superfluous or question begging: ibid, 89.

[69] See Chapter 7.4.

[70] For example, Letsas (n58) 119: '[I]t is natural to assume that courts will normally reach better decisions than legislatures.'

As a result of these arguments, Letsas, ostensibly in a similar way to Lester, is critical of the doctrine of the margin of appreciation and would prefer the ECtHR to develop a uniform conception of human rights law. These mistaken assumptions and unattractive normative commitments lead Letsas to propose an unrealistic and undesirable theory of interpretation of the ECHR.

Stephen Greer, an influential commentator on the ECHR system, appears to share an approach to the role of the ECtHR similar to, although not quite as extreme as, that of Letsas. Greer argues that it is for the courts to select the standards of human rights provisions and to apply them. There is no role for any margin of appreciation to the state on such matters. Greer's position is, however, somewhat ambiguous. He argues that there is no room for deference on the definition of rights, but that there is such 'on the question of whether or not the disputed conduct is compatible with them thus defined'.[71] This presumes a difference between definition and deciding whether conduct is compatible with a right. However, deciding whether or not disputed conduct accords with a right inherently involves the state making a judgment about the scope of the right. This is akin to definition. Similarly, when a tribunal is defining rights in a case, this simultaneously results in a judgment about whether the disputed conduct is compatible with that right. The dispute is precisely about the contours of the relevant right both for the state and the Tribunals. Whether this is called 'definition', or 'balancing', or 'interpretation', or even 'application', is neither here nor there. This problem is discussed further in Chapter 7.

Greer bases his approach on the application of differing levels of what he calls 'constitutional principles'. He argues that the margin of appreciation is one of a number of 'secondary constitutional principles' that are subordinated to what he calls the 'primary constitutional principles'.[72] However, Greer does not explain or substantiate the distinction between primary and secondary constitutional principles. Instead, he asserts that it is 'obvious' that what he calls the primary principles (such as 'democracy', 'effective protection', and 'priority to rights') are more closely connected with the core purpose of the Convention than what he calls the secondary principles (such as 'margin of appreciation', 'evolutive interpretation', 'autonomous interpretation', etc.).[73]

However, Greer's primary principles are abstractions that find their real expression only in what he calls the secondary principles. Thus it does not seem helpful to regard the principles as a hierarchy, when it is only at the level of the secondary principles that the primary principles find their expression as relevant considerations. Rather than being 'disciplined' by primary principles, the margin of appreciation doctrine reveals how the ECtHR shapes the use of what Greer calls the primary principles of 'democracy' and 'priority to rights',[74] and not vice versa. This

---

[71] S Greer, *The European Convention on Human Rights: Achievements, Problems and Prospects* (CUP, Cambridge 2006), 212.

[72] Ibid, 225.

[73] Ibid, 194.

[74] These two principles would be better represented by avoiding this terminology, and instead by examining the relationship between the margin of appreciation and proportionality. See Chapter 7.

also makes greater intuitive sense: vague and abstract principles cannot 'govern' or 'discipline' the exercise of judgment.

Neither Letsas nor Greer envisage their accounts applying beyond the ECHR system.[75] However, it is plausible to extend their ideas to the Inter-American system. The major reason why this might be difficult is that their arguments rely on an assumption that member states regard the decisions of the Strasbourg Court as having binding effect on them. It is difficult presently to apply this general assumption to all states in the Inter-American system, some of which flagrantly disregard the Inter-American Court. However, such a situation may be possible in future. Whilst state compliance does not yet reflect the contracting states' will to abide by decisions of the IACtHR, the approach applies in theory, and will apply in practice if compliance reaches a sufficiently high threshold.

Arguments in favour of creating uniform standards within the UN HRC also necessarily differ from the ECHR context, but Letsas' views that a tribunal's role is to find the best moral version of human rights and Greer's view that it is for the tribunal to define treaty standards could equally apply to the HRC. Such a view is ostensibly taken by Sarah Joseph. She argues that whereas in Europe a margin of appreciation is given when there is sufficient common practice amongst state parties, it would be 'unwise to apply such a doctrine under the ICCPR, where a common practice would rarely be discerned among the very different State Parties to this universal treaty', also claiming that the doctrine 'dilutes human rights protection'.[76] It seems, reading between the lines, that Joseph is arguing that, given the variety of approaches to human rights of the diverse state parties to the ICCPR, the HRC ought to remain clear-minded and make a decision that provides its own authoritative determination, regardless of the diversity of approaches taken by states to the relevant Article around the world.

b. Harmonization and integration

The second normative argument in favour of harmonizing human rights standards applies only in relation to Europe at present, although it might at some future date be relevant for other regional (or indeed universal) human rights systems. This argument favours the harmonization of human rights standards in the context of the closer cooperation and integration of states, particularly in the EU. Neil Walker has made this argument most coherently, arguing that the emergence of an ever-closer EU involves a spur to greater uniformity of human rights within Europe, including in the ECHR context. Walker's main arguments are premised on the view that the new plurality of legal orders requires a rethinking of the moral

---

[75] For example, see Letsas (n58) 38.
[76] S Joseph, J Schultz, and M Castan, *The International Covenant on Civil and Political Rights: Cases, Materials, and Commentary* (2nd edn, OUP, Oxford 2004) [18.24], 527–8.

primacy of democracy; it is no longer possible to rely on democratic methods as being of prime value in the formation of binding legal values.[77]

Moving away from the primacy of democratic involvement in the formation of values is problematic.[78] Walker recognizes some of the difficulties, but nevertheless proposes four joint factors that together might combine to favour harmonizing human rights in Europe at the expense of the self-determination of values represented by the margin of appreciation to states in Strasbourg.[79] He argues, first, that some reflection of the value of democracy in the EU is inherent because it was formed by democracies. Walker accepts that this is a weak democratic argument because: (a) 'constitutional moments'[80] do not validate future actions; (b) the democratic deficit in Europe cannot be assuaged by the existence of failings of democracy in states; and (c) there is no European *demos*, but numerous *demoi*. Nevertheless, he suggests a second factor that might overcome these problems: that the harmonization of human rights is a prudential method of fostering democracy-enhancing rights across Europe, promoting a certain unity within the tessellated European community. This suggestion, though, undermines the democracy that it is seeking to protect by imposing the values by judicial fiat. Walker's third factor is that the supranational harmonization of human rights should occur to compensate for the democratic deficit where there is democratic demand for the protection of rights to spill over from EU rights into other human rights, which is already happening to some extent within Europe. Whilst this has some merit, it relies on some form of growing consensus for uniformity of a certain level of protection, which is already encompassed in the value attributed to common state practice by the approach to deference advocated by this book in Chapter 5. Where such consensus is lacking, the Tribunals should be slow to enforce uniformity. The fourth and final factor presented by Walker he labels 'structural', in that the *Eigenwert* of the old order, democracy, needs to be replaced by something else. Walker nominates Joseph Weiler's ideal of supranationality,[81] which rejects nationalistic biases in favour of other-oriented openness. However, this idea works to promote uniform standards only where a particular human rights standard suggested by a state is closed to consideration of the needs of those beyond the immediate national community.

Much of Walker's argument is premised on the idea that the importance of democratic involvement in the formation of fundamental values is not of the utmost importance in the context of Europe as a whole. He argues that Jeremy

[77] N Walker, 'Human Rights in a Postnational Order: Reconciling Political and Constitutional Pluralism' in T Campbell, KD Ewing, and A Tomkins (eds) *Sceptical Essays on Human Rights* (OUP, Oxford 2001) 138–40.

[78] Walker accepts that the democratic deficit problems within the European Union (EU) are 'notoriously stubborn' and important considerations (ibid, 134), but nevertheless argues that these problems should not prevent the harmonization of rights.

[79] Ibid, 128.

[80] Ibid, 134, quoting from BA Ackerman, *We the People* (Belknap Press of Harv UP, Cambridge, Mass 1991).

[81] J Weiler, *The Constitution of Europe: 'Do the New Clothes Have an Emperor?' and Other Essays on European Integration* (CUP, Cambridge 1999) e.g. 250–2.

Waldron's account of the importance of democratic involvement in the formation of fundamental values is important,[82] but ought to be confined to a domestic national context, and that the fact of the matter is that the world has changed and states no longer provide the archetype; in the absence of the state as a model, the primacy of democracy is to be reconfigured.[83] Whilst the changing prominence of the state is undeniable, Walker's account fails to overcome the powerful Waldronian argument to respect democratically formed fundamental rights. He fails to explain adequately, or at all, why the argument should not operate at the international level. In Chapter 4, it is argued that the importance of democracy in the formation of human rights values is important also in interpreting international human rights norms, and is therefore a reason for deference to the state.

The foregoing discussion outlines the two main types of argument in favour of a uniform conception of human rights and against doctrines of deference; first that this is a reflection of the importance of the Tribunals' role to select or define the one right answer to human rights issues; and secondly, that the system exists in the context of the integration of states and in the plurality of autonomous legal orders that benefit from an 'equalization upward of rights'[84] to reflect the new arrangement. Whilst the theoretical justifications differ significantly, they share the corollary of favouring a harmonization of human rights norms within the system. The discussion turns now to examine to what extent this approach is reflected in the case law of the various tribunals.

c. Supporting case law

i. ECtHR

In Europe, there is certainly some case law showing that certain judges in the ECtHR favour the forging of a uniform approach to the protection of human rights. In *Üner v Netherlands*,[85] the ECtHR considered the discussion by states about how to deal with the deportation of foreign nationals, and did not decide to select a uniform standard for Europe. However, the dissenting judges took a different view. In that case, the majority found that the Netherlands' deportation of a criminal back to Turkey did not violate his Article 8 ECHR rights, notwithstanding that he had a wife and small children who had never left the Netherlands. The majority considered that they could regularly return to the Netherlands if they chose to join him in Turkey, and thus the action was proportionate. The dissenting judges Costa, Zupančič, and Türmen argued that the European-wide discussions on this point had emphasized to varying degrees the same level of protection for third-country nationals as EU citizens, restricting expulsion to matters of national security and bearing in mind particularly the interests of children.[86] Contrary to the

---

[82] Walker (n77) 122.
[83] Ibid, 127.
[84] Ibid, 138.
[85] *Üner v Netherlands* No. 46410/99 (2006) (ECtHR (GC)).
[86] Ibid, [5]–[7], dissenting opinion (Judges Costa, Zupančič, and Türmen).

majority, these judges argued that 'Article 8 of the Convention must be construed in the light of these [international instruments]'.[87] The judges also referred to other states' practices in abolishing such rules as expulsion, because it is like double punishment.[88] These opinions look like they might accord with the sort of approach to unifying human rights that Walker proposes. But this is not obviously the case. It might just be that these judges preferred or gave deference to the EU standard.[89] In another example, *Bosphorus Airways v Ireland*,[90] which involved the impounding of aircraft pursuant to a European Community (EC) Regulation implementing a United Nations Security Council (UNSC) Resolution, the Grand Chamber found that the EC Regulation appropriately standardized the response of EC members to the impounding of the aircraft without paying compensation.[91] This majority decision, on the surface, supports the 'equalisation upward of rights'.[92] However, these decisions do not support that general position, but only that, in some situations, it is appropriate to regard a uniform standard to exist. In this case, the relevant judicial stance is better characterized as deferring to the position of the international body,[93] which in fact accorded with the state's arguments.

There is also case law that, at face value, seems to support the approach that Letsas and Greer advance.[94] In *Martinie v France*,[95] the Grand Chamber of the ECtHR was asked again[96] to assess compliance with Article 6(1) of the role of government commissioners, who were state counsel, in legal proceedings.[97] In that case, a school accountant and principal were charged in their personal capacity for running a sports project that had not been approved by the school's board. The Court of Audit heard the appeal, and the government commissioner was present during the proceedings, having heard the reporting judge's views with the opportunity to address the judge. Whilst he was not a party to the proceedings, the majority of the Grand Chamber found that his presence was enough to violate Article 6(1).[98] The French legal system had, for generations, utilized various forms of state counsel. In this decision, the Grand Chamber ruled this system incompatible with the Convention thereby harmonizing to a greater extent the way in which

---

[87] Ibid, [9].

[88] Ibid, [17].

[89] See Chapter 5.6.b.

[90] *Bosphorus Airways v Ireland* No. 45036/98 (2005) (ECtHR (GC)).

[91] Ibid, [150].

[92] Walker (n77) 138.

[93] See Chapter 5.6.

[94] In the 'Preface' to the paperback version of Letsas (n58), Letsas claims that the following three recent cases support his approach: *EB v France* No. 43546/02 (2008) (ECtHR (GC)); *Dickson v UK* No. 44362/04 (2007) (ECtHR (GC)); and *Hirst v UK (No. 2)* No. 74025/01 (2005) (ECtHR (GC)). These cases, though, fail to support his positions. They are more appropriately analysed as being compatible with the doctrine of the margin of appreciation and indeed as furnishing useful guidance to courts about how the margin of appreciation should operate, as later discussion of these cases shows.

[95] *Martinie v France* No. 58675/00 (2006) (ECtHR (GC)).

[96] See *Kress v France* No. 39594/98 (2001) (ECtHR (GC)) for the earlier occasion on which this issue was considered by the Grand Chamber.

[97] There were a number of other Article 6(1) issues that did not raise issues related to uniformity.

[98] In this way clarifying, and arguably extending *Kress v France* (n96): *Martinie v France* (n95), [53].

states protect fair trial rights within Europe. However, this was in the face of a very strong dissent, and may well have been wrongly decided, as discussed further in section 4.d.i of this chapter.

Even if there are some cases in the ECtHR in which a single standard has been selected, this does not mean that the practice of the ECtHR supports the argument of these commentators. This would require the ECtHR always to produce a uniform solution, and to do so without reference to a margin of appreciation, which is far from the case.

ii. IACtHR

There is also some evidence to support 'standard-unifying' theorists from decisions of the IACtHR.[99] In *Dismissed Congressional Employees v Peru*,[100] which involved the dismissal of employees without any right to complain or be heard, the Court found violations of the right to a fair trial (Article 8) and the right to judicial protection (Article 25) stating that the test was whether Peru had acted 'in keeping with the standards established in the American Convention'.[101] It is unclear from this case whether these standards are intended by the Court to be uniform across all states. It could be interpreted like this. But the standards of the ACHR do not equate to uniformity in all cases before the IACtHR, so such an interpretation is unlikely.

iii. UN HRC

Likewise, in the UN HRC, some cases might appear as if they are developing uniform principles of human rights. In *Toonen v Australia*,[102] the HRC upheld a complaint about Tasmania's prohibition of homosexual sexual activity as a violation of the right to privacy (Article 17). The HRC rejected the view that such moral issues were a matter of concern only to domestic authorities, stating that this would 'open the door to withdrawing from the Committee's scrutiny a potentially large number of statutes interfering with privacy'.[103] However, it is clear that the Committee relied on Australia's commitment to gay rights to reach its decision. While 'standard-unifying' theorists might rely on this case, it is not strong evidence for the proposition that it is the role of the HRC to harmonize human rights.

d. Summary

This section has discussed some case examples that appear to support the 'standard-unifying' theories. Such examples are not sufficient, however, to provide broad

---

[99] See also Chapter 5.3.b and the discussion of 'conventionality control'.
[100] *Dismissed Congressional Employees v Peru* Series C No. 158 (24 November 2006) (IACtHR).
[101] Ibid, [107].
[102] *Toonen v Australia* CCPR/C/50/D/488/1992 (2004) (HRC).
[103] Ibid, [8.6].

support for these theories in the practice of the Tribunals. The following section discusses the 'diversity-permitting' theory, and argues that this approach to the role of the Tribunals is reflected in practice.

4. Justifying the margin of appreciation

The foundation of the theory defended in this book is that the margin of appreciation is, conceptually, the practice of Tribunals assigning weight to reasons for a decision on the basis of certain external factors[104] and is an ordinary facet of legal reasoning. What is yet to be established is why there might be normative reasons for a margin of appreciation. The relevant external factors for deference in international human rights law have been introduced as the democratic legitimacy of the relevantly articulated human right, the expertise of state authorities in reaching that articulation, and the level of international consensus that the articulation receives, either through the practice of states or the activity of other international actors. Each factor provides a normative justification for the margin of appreciation. The margin of appreciation, based on these factors, can therefore lead to the differentiation of human rights standards from place to place and over time, which reflects a proper account of the universality of human rights. More detailed explanation of why a margin of appreciation should be granted on the basis of democratic legitimacy, international consensus, and expertise are found in Chapters 4–6. Two background ideas are discussed in the following sections that form part of the arguments developed in these later chapters, and thus provide normative support for the justification of the margin of appreciation developed in Part Two of the book.

a. The Tribunals as forums for the contestation of sovereignty

Where the Treaties are vague, and the content of a treaty Article is open-textured,[105] this leaves scope for the Tribunals to develop the content of human rights, taking into account the intention of the states. This aspect of treaty interpretation is reflected in Article 31 of the Vienna Convention on the Law of Treaties (VCLT).[106] The Tribunals hear argument on whether they should impose a uniform international standard or whether the states should be able to implement their own approach to that human right. The Tribunals are thus forums for the contestation of sovereignty in the field of human rights. The concept of the margin of appreciation is an adjudicatory technique enabling the Tribunals to navigate a course through the competing considerations, and provides a vehicle through which lawyers for states and applicants can make their claims.

---

[104] See Chapter 2.
[105] See TAO Endicott, *Vagueness in Law* (OUP, Oxford 2000) 31 and 37 for definitions of 'vague' and 'open-textured' respectively.
[106] See Chapter 5.3.

The concept of international organizations providing 'a forum for the contestation of sovereignty'[107] is found in the work of Dan Sarooshi. Sarooshi provides an analytical scheme to distinguish three ways in which powers are conferred by states to international organizations: agency; delegation; and transfer. These three rest on a spectrum of limited to almost total transfer to the organization. Sarooshi discusses two examples of ways in which states are involved in this contestation: first, through their domestic courts (in the case of the 'full transfer' of powers to the EC);[108] and secondly, the role of domestic legislatures (the case of the US 'partial transfer' of powers to the World Trade Organization, or WTO).[109]

The arguments made by states that an international tribunal should defer to the state on the definition of the human rights standard is a further example of how states are involved in the contestation of sovereignty. The Tribunals have the final authority to decide on standards,[110] but the states have the primary task of interpreting and applying the human rights standards. There are consequently overlapping powers between the states and the Tribunals. The Tribunals mediate this tension through their case law, in particular through the doctrines of the margin of appreciation.

This idea has been captured well by John Merrills as follows: '[T]he margin of appreciation is a way of recognising that the international protection of human rights and sovereign freedom of action are not contradictory but complementary. Where the one ends, the other begins.'[111] The same idea has also been expressed in Pieter van Dijk and Godefridus van Hoof's influential work on the European Convention as follows: '[T]he margin of appreciation ... bears witness to the fact that the Convention places the Court at the crossroads of international judicial supervision and national sovereignty.'[112]

This overlapping extent of sovereign powers and consequent plurality of legal orders is an unusual type of legal pluralism. Neil Walker's approach to legal pluralism does not apply in the context of such international human rights systems. Walker's approach to pluralism is that there is 'a provisional and changeable set

---

[107] D Sarooshi, *International Organizations and their Exercise of Sovereign Powers* (OUP, Oxford 2005), ch 1. In this book, Sarooshi uses the notion of sovereignty as an 'essentially contested concept', borrowing it from the work of Samantha Besson, 'Sovereignty in Conflict' in C Warbrick and S Tierney (eds) *Towards an 'International Legal Community'? The Sovereignty of States and the Sovereignty of International Law* (BIICL, London 2006), ch 4, 144. It is true empirically that the meaning and allocation of sovereignty is a contested concept, but it is highly doubtful whether the concept of sovereignty is ontologically contestable, or indeed whether this is required for the work undertaken in the remainder of Sarooshi's work. The argument about contestability of sovereignty works just as well by relying on the empirical contestability of sovereignty, and this notion is preferred.

[108] Sarooshi (n107) ch 6.II.1.

[109] Ibid, ch 6.II.2.

[110] Notwithstanding that, as Sarooshi points out, the views of the HRC do not formally bind: ibid, 60.

[111] JG Merrills, *The Development of International Law by the European Court of Human Rights* (2nd edn, Manchester UP, Manchester 1993) 174–5.

[112] P van Dijk and GJH van Hoof, *Theory and Practice of the European Convention on Human Rights* (3rd edn, Kluwer Law International, The Hague; London 1998) 95.

of relations—putatively authoritative, strategic, and dialogical—between those various and coexisting and overlapping authority sites'.[113] The important thing about this understanding of pluralism is that the legal orders within a territory are both authoritative and 'autonomously grounded, with neither deferring to the other'.[114] Walker does not explain what he means by 'deference'. He is right, of course, that autonomous legal orders do not bow to each other. But on the understanding of deference outlined in Chapter 2, this vision of pluralism is misleading, especially in the context of international human rights law. Deference as the practice of assigning weight to the views of another on the basis of external factors is a plausible and practical response to the fact of legal pluralism, defined as autonomously grounded and separate legal orders with jurisdiction in the same territory.[115]

The approach to legal pluralism espoused by Neil MacCormick[116] is preferable to that advanced by Walker. MacCormick advances the concept of 'pluralism under international law'. According to this approach, the systems are distinct, but only partially independent. Instead, they are 'partially overlapping and interacting'.[117] What is crucial therefore is how the legal orders interact.

How legal orders interrelate of course varies according to which legal orders are at issue. Whilst normative and political issues affect these interrelationships, MacCormick suggests that 'the obligations of international law . . . impose a framework on the interactive but not hierarchical relations between systems'.[118] Deference as an adjudicatory technique in the Tribunals provides an 'interactive' framework, helping to mediate the interaction between them and the states. This practice is an outworking of the principle of subsidiarity,[119] which is discussed further in the next section.

---

[113] Walker (n77) 129.

[114] Ibid, 130.

[115] For an alternative approach that proposes that the legal pluralism in the EU could benefit from deference inspired by the margin of appreciation developed by the Strasbourg Court, see J Gerards, 'Pluralism, Deference and the Margin of Appreciation Doctrine' (2011) 17 ELJ 80.

[116] N MacCormick, *Questioning Sovereignty: Law, State, and Nation in the European Commonwealth* (OUP, Oxford 1999) 118.

[117] Ibid, 119.

[118] Ibid, 118.

[119] This point is made in a similar way by Mireille Delmas-Marty, 'The Richness of Underlying Legal Reasoning' in M Delmas-Marty and C Chodkiewicz (eds) *The European Convention for the Protection of Human Rights: International Protection versus National Restrictions* (Martinus Nijhoff, Dordrecht; London 1992) 333, as follows:

> [T]he doctrine of the margin of appreciation allows a pluralist organisation of the norms. Instead of the traditional conception of norms organised in a uniform manner around a single source of sovereignty, it substitutes norms which one could call 'heterogeneous', because they make possible a certain harmonization without compromising the existence of several sources of sovereignty. Alongside European unification, which would require absolute identity of national norms with European norms, an instrument of harmonization is arising, which requires a degree of similarity or proximity which is sufficient in order to be judged compatible with both European and national norms.

b. Deference and subsidiarity

Doctrines of deference are reflective of the principle of subsidiarity in the international legal order. The margin of appreciation is often described as an expression of the concept of subsidiarity.[120] The principle of subsidiarity in human rights law reinforces the richer notion of universality discussed in sections 2.a and 2.b of this chapter, against those that presume that universality leads to uniformity of human rights protection. The presumption that international human rights law centralizes norms seems to have led Sweeney to describe the margin of appreciation as based upon 'institutional subsidiarity and a form of "ethical decentralisation"'.[121] Despite the oddity of referring to the 'decentralization' of human rights, since human rights find their initial expressions outside of an international context, the phrase 'institutional subsidiarity' does reflect something of the nature of deference in international human rights law. Paolo Carozza similarly sees the margin of appreciation as reflective of subsidiarity:

> The principle of subsidiarity provides an analytically descriptive way to make sense of a variety of disparate features of the existing structure of international human rights law ... [I]t is not surprising to find in the development of human rights law that other doctrines and ideas have arisen that function at least in part as analogues to subsidiarity in addressing the pervasive dialectic between universal human rights norms and legitimate claims to pluralism. The doctrine of the 'margin of appreciation', first developed by the European Court of Human Rights (ECHR), is the most notable example.[122]

Subsidiarity as a general concept involves a complex tension designed to enhance the freedom of smaller groupings of people to act (down to individuals). It operates as a presumptive theory, described by Finnis as a principle that 'larger associations should not assume functions which can be performed efficiently by smaller associations'.[123]

In the context of the Treaties, a primary role is envisaged for states.[124] This means that, in the first instance and on the whole, it is for the state to interpret and implement its human rights obligations, and the Tribunals operate as a check and balance on this process. Where the Tribunals give appropriate deference to the state, their decisions uphold comity, which is the duty of an authority to respect

---

[120] For example, '...the notion of subsidiarity—in the form of the doctrine of the margin of appreciation in the Strasbourg system—...' from P Mahoney, 'Universality versus Subsidiarity in the Strasbourg Case Law on Free Speech: Explaining Some Recent Judgments' (1997) 4 EHRLR 364, 369. See also E Benvenisti, 'Margin of Appreciation, Consensus, and Universal Standards' (1999) 31 International Law and Politics 843, 846 and T Endicott, '"International Meaning": Comity in Fundamental Rights Adjudication' (2001) 13 (3) IJRL 280, 283.

[121] Sweeney (n6).

[122] PG Carozza, 'Subsidiarity as a Structural Principle of International Human Rights Law' (2003) 97 (1) AJIL 38, 40.

[123] J Finnis, *Natural Law and Natural Rights* (Clarendon Press, Oxford 1980) 146–7.

[124] For example, Article 2 ICCPR, Article 1 ECHR, Article 1 ACHR. See D McGoldrick, *The Human Rights Committee: Its Role in the Development of the International Covenant on Civil and Political Rights* (Clarendon Press, Oxford 1991) 13: 'There was general agreement during the drafting that the primary obligation under the ICCPR would be implementation at the national level.'

the role of institutional authorities, in this case for the Tribunals to respect the primary role of states in implementing their human rights obligations.

It might be said that recognizing the primary role of states in the protection of human rights perpetuates a dated primacy of the state polity in international relations. But this is not necessarily the case at all. The arguments of the book are neutral in the debate about the continuing pervasiveness of the nation state. Indeed, they are consistent with ideas that discuss the changing nature and role of the state in international affairs, such as Susan Marks' arguments about rethinking international perspectives on democracy to pursue the ideal of democracy rather than a statist version of it. She calls her approach the 'principle of democratic inclusion' in international law.[125] This principle entails including 'a bias in favour of popular self-rule and equal citizenship'[126] where the traditional principles of international law, such as sovereign equality, may have excluded such considerations. Indeed, the arguments of the book share Marks' bias in favour of the participation of individuals in the formation of fundamental values that affect their community. Whilst the arguments of this book could apply to other groups[127] that exercise democratic participation, and also groups that form international legal norms, the state is the object of such deference because of its continuing importance in international relations as a matter of fact and recognition as such before international tribunals.

c. Views of commentators

Many commentators appear to agree with the idea that the margin of appreciation is an important and legitimate concept in the reasoning of the Tribunals.[128] Other writers note the significance of the margin of appreciation, and discuss its relevance in the jurisprudence without objecting to it, ostensibly acquiescing in its use.[129] However, there are two main difficulties with the accounts of commentators who

---

[125] S Marks, *The Riddle of All Constitutions: International Law, Democracy and the Critique of Ideology* (OUP, Oxford 2000) 109.

[126] Ibid, 111.

[127] A good example of this is the Awas Tingni Community discussed in this chapter at section 2.e.ii in relation to *Mayagna (Sumo) Awas Tingni Community v Nicaragua* (n52).

[128] Especially Dijk and Hoof (n112), Merrills (n111), P Mahoney, 'Marvellous Richness of Diversity or Invidious Cultural Relativism?' (1998) 19 HRLJ 4, Sweeney (n6), RSJ Macdonald, 'The Margin of Appreciation' in RSJ Macdonald, F Matscher, and H Petzold (eds) *The European System for the Protection of Human Rights* (Martinus Nijhoff, Dordrecht; London 1993), Y Arai-Takahashi, *The Margin of Appreciation Doctrine and the Principle of Proportionality in the Jurisprudence of the ECHR* (Intersentia, Antwerpen; Oxford 2002), HC Yourow, *The Margin of Appreciation Doctrine in the Dynamics of European Human Rights Jurisprudence* (DPhil, University of Michigan 1995; Kluwer Law International, The Hague 1996), and H Waldock, 'The Effectiveness of the System Set Up by the European Convention on Human Rights' (1980) 1 HRLJ 1, 9.

[129] For example, DJ Harris, M O'Boyle, C Warbrick, and E Bates, *Harris, O'Boyle & Warbrick: Law of the European Convention on Human Rights* (2nd edn, OUP, Oxford 2009) 11–14, AR Mowbray, *Cases and Materials on the European Convention on Human Rights* (2nd edn, OUP, Oxford 2007) 629–33, M Janis, R Kay, and A Bradley, *European Human Rights Law: Text and Materials* (3rd edn, OUP, Oxford 2008) 242–4, and P Leach, *Taking a Case to the European Court of Human Rights* (2nd edn, OUP, Oxford 2005) 163–4, 284.

are broadly supportive of the margin of appreciation. First, they do not provide an account of how deference operates (see Chapter 2 for such an account), without which it is unclear to what they are referring. Secondly, these accounts do not provide detailed enough arguments for the various reasons for a margin of appreciation (discussed in Part Two), or how the margin of appreciation affects the reasoning of the Tribunals (discussed in Chapters 7–8).

It is a contention of this book that not only is the approach to the margin of appreciation advanced herein the strongest conceptually, but that it is also the account that best reflects the decisions of the Tribunals. The remainder of this chapter sets out decisions that show how on occasion the Tribunals, in exercising their role in the protection of human rights, permit and value the diverse understanding of human rights standards by states.

d. The practice of the Tribunals

i. ECtHR

In Europe, it is clear that the Strasbourg Court accepts the diversity of protection of human rights. For example, in *Leyla Şahin v Turkey*,[130] the Grand Chamber of the ECtHR explained as follows, citing other cases to support its position:

It is not possible to discern throughout Europe a uniform conception of the significance of religion in society[131]... and the meaning or impact of the public expression of a religious belief will differ according to time and context[132]... Rules in this sphere will consequently vary from one country to another according to national traditions and the requirements imposed by the need to protect the rights and freedoms of others and to maintain public order[133].... Accordingly, the choice of the extent and form such regulations should take must inevitably be left up to a point to the State concerned, as it will depend on the domestic context concerned.[134],135

Judge Martens made a similar observation in his dissenting opinion in *Borgers v Belgium*:[136]

[T]he Convention does not aim at uniform law but lays down directives and standards, which, as such, imply a certain freedom for member states. On the other hand, the Preamble to the Convention seems to invite the Court to develop common standards. These contradictory features create a certain internal tension which requires... the Court to act with prudence and to take care not to interfere without a convincing justification.[137]

---

130 *Leyla Şahin v Turkey* (n49).
131 *Otto-Preminger-Institut v Austria* Series A No. 295-A (2004) (ECtHR), [50].
132 *Dahlab v Switzerland* No. 42393/98 (2001) (ECtHR).
133 *Wingrove v UK* No. 17419/90 (1996) (ECtHR), [57].
134 *Gorzelik v Poland* No. 44158/98 (2004) (ECtHR (GC)), [67]: 'It is not for the Court to express a view on the appropriateness of methods chosen by the legislature of a respondent State to regulate a given field. Its task is confined to determining whether the methods adopted and the effects they entail are in conformity with the Convention.' The Court also cited *Murphy v Ireland* No. 44179/98 (2003) (ECtHR), [73], which related to the sensitivity of religious broadcasting in Ireland.
135 *Leyla Şahin v Turkey* (n49), [109].
136 *Borgers v Belgium* No. 12005/86 (1991) (ECtHR), [4.2].   137 Ibid, [4.2].

In *Martinie v France*,[138] there was a strong dissenting opinion arguing that the approach of the majority created an 'abstract procedural uniformity' in finding the role of the state counsel, the General Commissioner, to violate Article 6(1). The dissenting judges regarded the majority to have 'succumbed to the temptations of uniformity whereas what the judicial institutions of democratic Europe need is to be able to function smoothly, constantly, foreseeably and in conformity with the spirit of the Convention, rather than uniformity'.[139] These judges opined that 'fairness' would be better served by allowing diversity:

It is better to accept certain national judicial features and concentrate on harmonizing the guarantees which States must provide in respect of substantive rights and liberties: the necessary dialogue between judges will, we think, be greatly facilitated by this, in the interests of all, domestic courts and European Court alike, and will promote justice that is truly 'fair'.[140]

ii. IACtHR

Similarly before the IACtHR, it is clear that states can, in diverse ways, implement the human rights protections envisaged by the ACHR. The best example of this can be seen in the following excerpt from an Advisory Opinion of the Court:

[T]he Commission [does not have] the authority to rule as to how a legal norm is adopted in the internal order. That is the function of the competent organs of the State. What the Commission should verify, in a concrete case, is whether what the norm provides contradicts the Convention and not whether it contradicts the internal legal order of the State.[141]

In *Yatama v Nicaragua*,[142] Judge Sergio García-Ramírez, in his separate concurring opinion, expressed the following view:

The Court has not established, nor would it have to, the characteristics of a system of laws – and, in general, public action, which is more than general norms – favorable to the exercise of the political rights of members of indigenous communities, so that they are, truly, 'as much citizens as the other citizens.' The State must examine the situation before it in order to establish the means to allow the exercise of the rights universally assigned by the American Convention, precisely in those situations. *The fact that the rights are of a universal nature does not mean that the measures that should be adopted to ensure the exercise of the rights and freedoms has to be uniform, generic, the same, as if there were no differences, distances and contrasts among their possessors.* Article 2 of the Pact of San José should be read carefully: the States must adopt the necessary measures to give effect to the rights and freedoms. The reference to 'necessary' measures that 'give effect' to the rights refers to the consideration of particularities and compensations.[143]

---

[138] *Martinie v France* (n95), [8], joint partly dissenting opinion of Judges Costa, Caflisch, and Jungwiert.
[139] Ibid, [9].
[140] Ibid, [8].
[141] *Certain Attributes of the Inter-American Commission on Human Rights (Arts 41, 42, 44, 46, 47, 50 and 51 of the American Convention on Human Rights)* Advisory Opinion OC-13/93 Series A No. 13 (16 July 1993) (IACtHR), [29].
[142] *Yatama v Nicaragua* Series C No. 127 (2005) (IACtHR).
[143] Ibid, [31], concurring opinion of Judge Sergio García-Ramírez (emphasis added).

Judge García-Ramírez interprets Article 2 ACHR to recognize state variations in human rights as required by the very terms of the treaty. Whilst not always based on Article 2, it is clear that other decisions of the IACtHR affirm this approach to the role of the court. This is confirmed by the following dictum:

No one questions the principle of the subsidiarity of the international jurisdiction, which refers specifically to the *mechanisms* of protection; nor should one lose sight that, at substantive level, in the present domain of protection, the norms of the international and domestic legal orders are in constant *interaction*, to the benefit of the protected human beings.[144]

iii. UN HRC

The UN HRC similarly supports this approach to the legitimate variety of forms of protection of human rights. In *Kavanagh v Ireland*,[145] the HRC found that Ireland had violated Article 26 (equality before the law) because it had failed to justify the trial of the communicant before a separate criminal court designed for trying insurgents. The separate court did not have the guarantees of trial by jury or other safeguards, and there was no suggestion by the state that the communicant was linked to insurgency. In finding against the state, however, the HRC made it clear that separate systems of justice for insurgency were not a violation of Article 26 per se: '[D]ifferent trial systems may exist, and the mere availability of different mechanisms cannot of itself be regarded as a breach.'[146] It is clear that the HRC is open to states pursuing the protection of human rights in ways that fit within their cultures and societies, tempered always by requirements of proportionality.[147]

e. Summary

Whilst there are some indications in each of the Tribunals' bank of decisions of a judicial desire for uniformity, they cannot be taken to be indicative of a general approach to human rights adjudication, and are better seen as specific examples of where a move towards a uniform international minimum standard is required, which is compatible with the approach to deference taken in this book.[148] It seems

---

[144] *Las Palmeras v Colombia* Series C No. 90 (2001) (IACtHR), [6], joint separate opinion of Judges Cançado Trindade and Pacheco Gómez. See also *Enforceability of the Right to Reply or Correction (Arts. 14(1), 1(1) and 2 American Convention on Human Rights)* Advisory Opinion OC-7/86, Series A No. 7 (1986) (IACtHR), which says, at [27]: 'The contents of the law may vary from one State to another, within certain reasonable limits and within the framework of the concepts stated by the Court.'

[145] *Kavanagh v Ireland* CCPR/C/71/D/819/1998 (2001) (HRC).

[146] Ibid, [7.2].

[147] *Sprenger v The Netherlands* CCPR/C/44/D/395/1990 (HRC), [7.4]–[7.5], and *Marshall v Canada* CCPR/C/43/D/205/1986 (1991) (HRC), [5.4]–[5.5]. See also Chapter 7.

[148] Even where the dissenting opinion in *A, B and C v Ireland* No. 25579/05 (2010) (ECtHR (GC)) referred to a 'harmonizing' role of the Convention's case law, this was limited to situations that were supported by consensus amongst European states and did not apply where there was a clear difference of approach taken by European states: see [5], joint partly dissenting opinion of Judges Rozakis, Tulkens, Fura Hirvelä, Malinverni, and Poalelungi.

that most judges would rather regard their role as being to supervise what is in the first instance the state's responsibility to implement and protect shared human rights norms, accepting that such implementation appropriately differs from place to place.

5. Conclusion

This chapter has assessed the conceptual argument that the margin of appreciation leads to relativism about human rights and concluded that such an argument misconstrues the nature of universality, leaving out the necessary legitimate instantiation of value that universality requires. Consequently, the differentiation of human rights standards resulting from the margin of appreciation can be compatible with the universality of human rights, and indeed can provide strong conceptual grounds on which to justify the margin of appreciation.

The chapter has also addressed the normative arguments against the margin of appreciation, concluding that they do not afford sufficient primacy to the democratic formation of fundamental norms and rely on weakly argued suppositions about majority decision-making, moral relativism, and an alleged distinction between definition and application of human rights in the Tribunals. Instead, the chapter introduces the argument that there are sound and sensible reasons for the Tribunals, as a matter of deference and not authority, to extend a margin of appreciation to national parties in the determination of human rights. This is because the Tribunals mediate between the allocation of sovereignty in the determination of human rights standards and because the Tribunals play a subsidiary role to states. The chapter has merely introduced the arguments justifying deference; more needs to be said about why deference on the basis of democratic legitimacy, the current practice of states, and state expertise is acceptable. These justifications are explored in the following three chapters in Part Two. In addition, those chapters expound and assess the way in which the Tribunals in practice are influenced by these external factors for deference.

PART II

PRACTICE: FACTORS AFFECTING THE MARGIN OF APPRECIATION

Three factors for a margin of appreciation have been identified: first, democratic legitimacy; secondly, the current practice of states (consensus); and thirdly, expertise. Part Two explores each of these factors in Chapters 4, 5, and 6.

Each chapter in Part Two begins with a discussion exploring the justification for a margin of appreciation on the basis of each of these factors. This continues the justification of the margin of appreciation that began in Part One. In addition, each chapter in Part Two provides a detailed discussion of the case law of the Tribunals, which explains how these factors affect the operation of the margin of appreciation in practice. These chapters are likely to be of particular interest to lawyers making or considering arguments for or against extending a margin of appreciation to the state.

Part Two does not attempt to explain how these three factors interrelate with other factors in human rights cases (for example the 'nature of the right'). Such factors may impact the margin of appreciation by affecting how weighty arguments must be before the Tribunals will defer to the states as part of the proportionality assessment. Such matters are explored in Part Three.

4

Democracy and Participation

1. Introduction

The Tribunals often regard reasons for a margin of appreciation to the state as strengthened on the basis that a decision has democratic legitimacy or was taken following widespread public participation. The sorts of considerations relating to this second-order reason for deference vary from case to case. There are a number of questions about the relevant considerations for deciding the strength of such second-order reasons and how much they should influence the first-order reasoning. But this is jumping ahead. There is a prior question to be dealt with about whether the margin of appreciation on this basis is justifiable at all.

There are numerous theories relevant to the question: 'Is a margin of appreciation justifiable on the basis of democratic legitimacy?' These theories are commonly found in arguments about the legitimacy of judicial review of legislative action in domestic constitutional theory. These domestic constitutional theories can be adjusted to relate to international human rights law on the basis that both contexts involve an assessment of the importance of democratic institutions compared with courts in relation to the definition of fundamental rights.

The various theories of judicial review discussed in this chapter are intended to be mutually exclusive. In other words, the aim of these theories is to discredit and replace the others. None of the theories in this debate consider deference as a form of second-order reasoning. Even where these debates concern supposed 'theories of deference',[1] they do not consider how the concept of deference operates, or what factors justify and affect deference in the context of fundamental rights adjudication. If these constitutional theories were to consider the concept of deference in greater depth, as the practice of assigning weight on the basis of external factors, they would be able to develop more nuanced and less controversial theories. Such theories could focus on the factors that should lead courts to give deference to or heighten scrutiny of the views of the state as part of the judicial review of government action. Theories of judicial review could move beyond a 'black and white' approach of assessing whether tribunals should review fundamental rights standards at all.

---

[1] R Dworkin, *Taking Rights Seriously* (Duckworth, London 1978) 138.

The concept of judicial deference consequently provides the basis for a different approach to theories of judicial review. This new approach focuses on how, by relying on the concept of judicial deference, courts are able to mediate between the various strengths of the traditional theories of judicial review on a case-by-case basis, without having to be entirely committed to one account. This approach is supported by the practice of courts, as demonstrated in this chapter by drawing on examples from the case law of the Tribunals.

The primary aims of this chapter are both: (i) to argue that a margin of appreciation on the basis of democratic legitimacy is justified by drawing on and developing theories of judicial review (section 2 of this chapter); and (ii) to show that the Tribunals do in fact give a margin of appreciation to the state on the basis of this external factor (section 4). A secondary aim of the chapter is to establish that, when the Tribunals give a margin of appreciation on the basis of democratic legitimacy, they thereby contribute to the development of theories of democratic governance in international law (section 3). The reasons that the Tribunals give for extending a margin of appreciation or applying heightened scrutiny on the basis of democratic legitimacy (sections 5 and 6, respectively) form the substance of the Tribunals' contribution to democratic theories. It is not the aim of this chapter to develop a theory of democracy or to map the Tribunals' contribution to democratic theory. Rather, the later sections of this chapter expound the doctrine of the margin of appreciation on the basis of democratic legitimacy in the Tribunals. A by-product of this discussion is that it demonstrates the Tribunals' contributions to wider notions of democratic theory in international governance. This doctrinal exposition shows how the Tribunals give deference to conceptions of human rights advanced by states, which have been formed following widespread public participation, and which provide particular examples of such a margin of appreciation.

2. Theories of judicial review and the justification of the margin of appreciation for democratic reasons

Judicial deference on the basis that public participation is valuable in the formation of rights is far from unproblematic. There is serious debate about the level of importance of democratic processes vis-à-vis judicial review. Some of these ideas were discussed in the previous chapter, for example Neil Walker's claim that the moral primacy of democracy in forming human rights norms can be replaced. What are the arguments in favour of democratic or participatory instantiations of human rights? Why might courts defer to democratic organs? What are the arguments against this?

These are familiar questions in the domestic constitutional context that have culminated in solutions based on a number of different theories. Whilst these theories were developed primarily for the domestic constitutional context, with some minor adjustment they are applicable in the context of international human rights law. The organs of government being compared in the domestic constitutional framework are national constitutional or supreme courts and democratic organs. In the international human rights context, the comparators are the Tribunals and the same domestic organs. The theories require modification only in so far as the nature of international adjudication relevantly differs from adjudication by domestic courts.

There is significant overlap between the roles that national constitutional or supreme courts and the Tribunals play. Both are authoritative bodies that resolve disputes relating to their founding texts (either constitutions or the Treaties). They employ judicial decision-making techniques. The differences, whilst significant, do not affect the nature of the exercise. Rather the differences relate to treaty interpretation (discussed in Chapter 5) and concerns about the protection of cultural diversity (discussed in Chapter 3). These limited differences do not significantly affect the relevance of the theoretical issues discussed in this chapter.

There are three important theories. The first, by Jeremy Waldron,[2] is pro-participatory and critical of the judicial formation of rights.[3] The second theory, by Ronald Dworkin,[4] favours the judiciary shaping rights standards. The third, by John Hart Ely,[5] promotes review where this bolsters participatory rights. Each of these theories highlights important issues that require consideration in the adjudication of fundamental rights, but the theories are mutually exclusive and consequently none of them provides adequate scope for the strengths of the other theories to feature in its account of judicial review.

Waldron argues as follows: given that there is disagreement over the content and meaning of basic rights, public debate should be encouraged, and a democratic procedure of participation, representation, and voting should be adopted as the only authoritative decision-making process, since giving each person involvement more accurately respects the dignity and autonomy of citizens than relying on a tribunal's robed elite.

Although promoting individual engagement is an important consideration, it does not lead to a convincing denial of a judicial role in the formation of basic rights.[6] As Dworkin argues, the primacy of democratic processes per Waldron does not rule out the possibility of substantive injustice or democratic error where a hostile majority is able to dictate the terms of fundamental rights in their favour.[7]

---

[2] J Waldron, *Law and Disagreement* (Clarendon Press, Oxford 1999).

[3] It is noteworthy that Walker discusses Waldron's view and regards it as a good theory for domestic polities, but asserts that it is not applicable in an international or supranational context, without substantiating this position: N Walker, 'Human Rights in a Postnational Order: Reconciling Political and Constitutional Pluralism' in T Campbell, KD Ewing, and A Tomkins (eds) *Sceptical Essays on Human Rights* (OUP, Oxford 2001) 122 and 127.

[4] R Dworkin, *Freedom's Law: The Moral Reading of the American Constitution* (Harv UP, Cambridge, Mass 1996), R Dworkin, *Law's Empire* (Hart, Oxford 1998), especially ch 10. Dworkinian theory seems to be followed by Letsas and Greer: see Chapter 3.3.a.

[5] JH Ely, *Democracy and Distrust: A Theory of Judicial Review* (Harv UP, Cambridge, Mass 1980).

[6] A Kavanagh, 'Participation and Judicial Review: A Reply to Jeremy Waldron' (2003) 22 (5) Law and Philosophy 451.

[7] Some interpretations of Dworkin's theory have argued that democratic involvement per se involves the solidification of majoritarian prejudices. Such a view is an oversimplification of the

Instead, Dworkin argues that a court, which is not driven by pressure to satisfy majoritarian sentiment, can produce more principled decisions. The danger of taking Dworkin's view too far is its failure to overcome the reproach of elitism, despite his claims of a court's democratic credentials,[8] and also of not giving enough weight to the importance of democratic processes.

The third theory is that the judicial role acts as a check on democratic powers, ensuring representation for minorities and enabling procedural participation, per Ely. The weakness of this approach is that limiting review on the basis of the primacy of process rights is a substantive value that requires justification as part of a broader substantive vision, especially where it is used as justification for limiting the role of the judiciary in a non-process context[9] in which it might be appropriate for the judiciary to correct imbalances in legislative reasoning.

Each of these theories emphasizes important considerations. Waldron eloquently and convincingly articulates the importance of participation in the formation of rights as a means of respecting persons and autonomy. Ely justifies review of democratic action where participation is at risk. And Dworkin goes further, justifying judicial involvement on occasions when democratic procedures have led to substantive injustice.[10] When analysing the case law in the subsequent discussion, these considerations are identified and discussed, with a view to seeing how they affect the operation of deference.

The practice of judicial deference is able to mediate between the above theoretical debates so that each theory's strength can be taken into consideration in relevant cases. The practice of deference as assigning weight on the basis of second-order reasons enables judges to consider whether a case raises particular concerns that Ely or Dworkin emphasize so as to heighten scrutiny of a state's arguments rather than to give deference to the state on the basis of the value of participation that Waldron articulates. Reasons in favour of valuing participation thus provide grounds for deference on the basis of democratic legitimacy. The strength of these reasons for deference depends on the participatory pedigree entailed by the decision under review. Where it appears that majoritarian prejudices have been enforced by a legislature rather than an objective reasoning process, there are grounds for greater scrutiny. Similarly, there are grounds for increased scrutiny where a minority has not had adequate opportunity to engage in the decision-making process or have its

---

legislative reasoning process. See R Ekins, *Legislative Intent and Group Action* (MPhil, Oxford University 2005). Whilst the central case of the legislative process is to deliberate on the basis of right reason, in practice (and history shows this) there are occasions on which majorities are able to ensure that their prejudices and/ or preferences become law without a fair hearing and without discussion of all relevant considerations.

  [8] For example, by offering a platform for otherwise excluded minorities to participate in the formation of rights.

  [9] L Tribe, 'The Puzzling Persistence of Process-Based Theories' (1980) 89 Yale LJ 1063.

  [10] Of course, such a claim is controversial. Dworkin seeks to sanitize the controversy through a theory of adjudication that claims that controversial decisions are based on the objective principles inherent in a system of law, rather than on a judge's personal values. This ingenious approach unconvincingly perpetuates the myth that judges discover the law, whilst offering valuable guidance about how to make decisions in hard cases. See further Dworkin (n1) ch 4.

concerns taken into account by the legislature. But where such dangers are absent, the importance of democracy as articulated by Waldron provides grounds for deference to democratically decided rights standards. This deference is not determinative, but is to be weighed along with first-order reasons that affect a case. Consequently, Dworkin's concern that judges should ensure principled standards that accord with substantive justice can be taken into account along with Waldron's compelling account of the importance of democracy. The argument that judicial deference provides a pragmatic resolution of these debates is further explored in section 7 of this chapter, following exposition of the relevant case law showing that the Tribunals in fact give deference on the basis of democratic legitimacy.

3. The contribution of the Tribunals to theories of democracy in international law

The case law exposition that follows shows how the Tribunals accord weight to democratic factors in their decision-making. In according this weight, the Tribunals indicate what they consider to be valuable aspects of democratic decision-making in the formation of human rights and regard it as part of their role to protect effective political democracy.[11] This practice contributes to discussions about democratic theory in international law. There are important ongoing conversations about what democracy should entail as a norm in international relations. These conversations are conducted by state governments, international organizations, and various civil society participants.[12]

It is important to note the differences between the Tribunals with respect to their approach to democratic norms. The European Council requires that states reach certain democratic standards prior to admission, which may include future democratic and human rights commitments. Consequently, whilst there are a variety of approaches to it among the contracting states, democracy is a core purpose of the European Convention on Human Rights (ECHR) system as demonstrated in the Convention's Preamble.[13] There is a clear mandate for the European Court of Human Rights (ECtHR) to favour democratic political arrangements. Similarly within the American Convention on Human Rights (ACHR) system, the treaty explicitly favours democratic arrangements.[14] The same cannot be said of the

---

[11] P Gallagher, 'The European Convention on Human Rights and the Margin of Appreciation' (UCD Working Papers in Law, Criminology and Socio-Legal Studies Research Paper No. 52/2011 2012) [11]–[12].

[12] A helpful collection of various discussions of democratic norms in the international arena is found in Part 1 of GS Goodwin-Gill, *Free and Fair Elections* (Inter-Parliamentary Union, Geneva 2006).

[13] 'Reaffirming their profound belief in those Fundamental Freedoms which are the foundation of justice and peace in the world and are best maintained on the one hand by an effective political democracy...'

[14] Preamble ACHR: 'Reaffirming their intention to consolidate in this hemisphere, *within the framework of democratic institutions*, a system of personal liberty and social justice based on respect for the essential rights of man...' (emphasis added).

International Covenant on Civil and Political Rights (ICCPR) or the Optional Protocol system, which encompasses a broader range of governments.[15] In this context, it might be said that there is less scope for the United Nations Human Rights Committee (UN HRC) to give deference on the basis of democratic legitimacy, but the ICCPR does contain references to standards that are 'necessary in a democratic society', as do the other Treaties.[16]

It is increasingly accepted that there is an entitlement of democratic governance in international law.[17] There are, however, competing arguments about the nature of democratic ideology in international law.[18] Formal or procedural democracy may exist in a state, but it might be arguable that the state is not properly democratic according to a richer, substantive sense of democracy.[19] Likewise, a contextualized substantive approach to democracy may be a better factor for deference, which might warrant the label 'public participation'. This criterion could be analogous to (although weaker than) the factor 'democratic legitimacy', but be considered in contexts in which there is not a formal democratic system of governance. Without formal democratic processes, it is likely to be difficult for a state to demonstrate the broad public participation in the formation of a standard necessary to warrant deference. However, the argument remains available for an appropriate case. Such cases have not arisen to date; all discussions of deference that follow have occurred within the context of generally (or formally) democratic states.

The Tribunals, as forums for the contestation of sovereignty in human rights,[20] hear competing accounts of the concept of democracy and are required to make decisions that reveal their preferences. Decisions of the Tribunals that involve deference to states (or heighten scrutiny of states) on the basis of democratic legitimacy consequently contribute to the content of democratic theory in international law. The assessment of the decisions of the Tribunals in the following sections shows to a limited extent what content the Tribunals contribute to theories of democracy, and how they defer to states by giving them leeway to 'mould their own democratic vision'.[21] For example, there is greater deference to states when democratically legislating the allocation of private rights, or laws that uphold moral requirements of the society (section 5 of this chapter), and there is greater scrutiny relating to rights that protect democracy (such as free speech or electoral rights), where minority rights are at risk, where the level of democratic participation (for example the level of societal or parliamentary debate) is inadequate, or where there are rule of law concerns such as an indiscriminate or sweeping limitation of freedoms (section 6).

---

[15] No mention is made in the Preamble of the ICCPR to democratic government.
[16] Articles 14, 21, and 22 ICCPR.
[17] TM Franck, *Fairness in International Law and Institutions* (Clarendon Press, Oxford 1995) ch 4.
[18] S Marks, *The Riddle of All Constitutions: International Law, Democracy and the Critique of Ideology* (OUP, Oxford 2000).
[19] Ibid, chs 3 and 4.
[20] D Sarooshi, *International Organizations and their Exercise of Sovereign Powers* (OUP, Oxford 2005). See Chapter 3.4.a.
[21] *Hirst v UK (No. 2)* No. 74025/01 (2005) (ECtHR (GC)), [61].

One of the challenges facing democratic theory in international law is the extent to which democratic decision-making and principles can be reflected in international forums. David Beetham argues that there is a universalism inherent in democracy in that there is an assumption that all adults everywhere can be involved in their governance, although democracy seems to have stopped at national borders.[22] Beetham argues that international human rights law can therefore speak to notions of cosmopolitanism. Cosmopolitanism involves overlapping sites of democratic power, and the development of involvement in decision-making at various levels: local; national; and international. In making decisions that both strengthen and weaken deference to states depending on their democratic pedigree, international tribunals are thereby: (i) promoting the engagement of individuals in their governance at an international level; (ii) enabling individuals to shape the standards that affect their understanding of democracy; (iii) allowing individuals to participate in the formation of the rights at issue in the case at hand; and (iv) giving greater weight to decisions that are democratically formed.

It might be said that the shaping of meanings of democracy by the Tribunals is relevant to discussions about whether democracy is itself a human right. Whilst aspects of democracy are protected by human rights, none of the Treaties describes democracy per se as a human right. Instead, democracy is regarded as a value or principle in the decision-making of the Tribunals.

4. Democratic legitimacy as an external factor for the margin of appreciation in practice

It is apt to begin expounding the relevant case law by considering decisions that reveal how the Tribunals give a margin of appreciation to states on the basis of democratic legitimacy or popular participation. There is a plethora of evidence that shows the ECtHR deferring to states on the basis of democratic legitimacy. Thus far there have been fewer cases in the Inter-American Court of Human Rights (IACtHR) that have warranted deference to the democratic interpretations of ACHR standards, but there is some evidence of a margin of appreciation on this basis. In the UN HRC context, there is good evidence of a margin of appreciation to democratic participation.

a. European Court of Human Rights (ECtHR)

The ECtHR has shown in numerous cases that it recognizes the special role of the legislature. From early on in the Court's jurisprudence, this has led to deference, showing the value placed on participation in the formation of rights. The ECtHR in *Handyside* stated, in the context of Article 10(2), that the margin of appreciation

   [22] D Beetham, 'Human Rights as a Model for Cosmopolitan Democracy' in D Archibugi, D Held, and M Köhler (eds) *Re-imagining Political Community: Studies in Cosmopolitan Democracy* (Polity Press, Cambridge 1998) 58.

was to be 'given to both the domestic legislator ("prescribed by law")', as well as to other bodies that interpret and apply the law.[23] The Court thus singled out the legislature as worthy of a margin of appreciation in its own right, not to be lumped together with all national bodies claiming deference. Likewise in *Dudgeon v UK*, the ECtHR, in the context of legislation criminalizing certain homosexual activities in Northern Ireland said to impugn Article 8, affirmed that the national authorities had a margin of appreciation,[24] and explained that reasons for deference were strengthened because of the democratic character of the legislation. This can be seen in the following passage:

Without any doubt, faced with these various considerations, the United Kingdom Government acted carefully and in good faith; what is more, they made every effort to arrive at a balanced judgment between the differing viewpoints before reaching the conclusion that such a substantial body of opinion in Northern Ireland was opposed to a change in the law that no further action should be taken.[25]

This case goes on to show how deference operates in the ECtHR. Notwithstanding the second-order reasons to strengthen deference to the state's first-order reasoning because of the importance of its democratic handling of the legislation,[26] 'this cannot of itself be decisive as to the necessity for the interference with the applicant's private life resulting from the measures being challenged',[27] since these reasons need to be considered alongside others (other second-order reasons and first-order reasons) that may override the reasons to defer on the basis of democratic legitimacy. The Court went on to find that the legislation was disproportionate to the aims pursued. Thus from the earliest case law of the Court can be seen a recognition that the Court 'cannot assume the role of the competent national authorities', who 'remain free to choose the measures which they consider appropriate'.[28] Recognition of the competence of the national authorities is based on the high importance placed on democracy by the Convention system and an understanding that the Court should consequently find reasons for deference in the democratic nature of the national authorities. At this early stage, these indications were somewhat simplistic, but in later cases the Court explains further the doctrine of deference on the basis of democratic legitimacy.

---

[23] *Handyside v UK* No. 5493/72 (1976) (ECtHR), [48].
[24] *Dudgeon v UK* No. 7525/76 (1981) (ECtHR), [52].
[25] Ibid, [59].
[26] See further on this point the dissenting opinion of Judge Walsh ibid, who, at [18] of his dissenting judgment, noted the approach of the Court in recognizing the importance of the legislature's role:

> I venture the view that the Government concerned, having examined the position, is in a better position to evaluate [the effect on Northern Ireland of a change of law] than this Court, *particularly as the Court admits the competence of the State to legislate in this matter* but queries the proportionality of the consequences of the legislation in force. [Emphasis added]

[27] Ibid, [59]. Note that the Court engages in substantive legislative review, which is somewhat reflective of the Dworkinian approach to the judicial role.
[28] *Belgian Linguistics Case* No. 1474/62 (1968) (ECtHR), [10].

By the time of *Hirst v UK (No. 2)*,[29] the Grand Chamber is able to articulate in greater depth the Court's doctrine of deference on the basis of democratic legitimacy.[30] The case concerned an applicant who was convicted of manslaughter on grounds of diminished responsibility, who, subsequent to his admission to prison, was prevented from voting, and thus claimed that he had suffered a violation of Article 3, Protocol 1, ECHR, amongst other claims. The UK courts deferred to Parliament on the question of whether a blanket legal provision denying all inmates the right to vote was proportionate. The case raises multifaceted challenges in deciding how much deference to give on the basis of democratic participation, and reveals the ECtHR's participation in the development of what democracy entails. On the one hand, the legislature seeks deference on the basis of its role in creating the law regulating voting rules, but the applicant seeks judgment for the denial of participation.[31] It is noteworthy that in this context, in which the Court is being asked to heighten scrutiny because the legislature is limiting suffrage, the Court affirms as follows that it is nevertheless appropriate to find reasons for deference on the basis of the democratic nature of the institutions:

> 60. ... [T]he rights bestowed by Article 3 of Protocol No. 1 are not absolute. There is room for implied limitations and Contracting States must be allowed a margin of appreciation in this sphere.

> 61. There has been much discussion of the breadth of this margin in the present case. The Court reaffirms that the margin in this area is wide (see *Mathieu-Mohin and Clerfayt*[32] [52], and, more recently, *Matthews v the United Kingdom* [GC], no. 24833/94, [63], ECHR 1999-I; see also *Labita v Italy* [GC], no. 26772/95, § 201, ECHR 2000-IV, and *Podkolzina v Latvia*, no. 46726/99, [33], ECHR 2002-II). There are numerous ways of organising and running electoral systems and a wealth of differences, *inter alia*, in historical development, cultural diversity and political thought within Europe which it is for each Contracting State to mould into their own democratic vision.

The variety of ways in which a legislature could organize its electoral systems is discussed by Waldron in the context of arguing that we should rely on democratic processes to determine which democratic processes to use. His argument on this question is shaky: we should resort to such a procedure since it is the only one available.[33] As a reason to rely exclusively on the role of the legislature, the non-availability of other options is weak. Consequently, exclusive reliance on democratic processes is not appropriate,[34] but there is still a role for deference based on

---

[29] *Hirst v UK (No. 2)* (n21).

[30] See also *Hatton v UK* No. 36022/97 (2003) (ECtHR (GC)), [97].

[31] This is exactly the sort of right that Ely (n5) had in mind to defend, and where consequently there should be less deference and greater judicial scrutiny. See section 6.b of this chapter.

[32] *Mathieu-Mohin and Clerfayt v Belgium* Series A No. 113 (1987) (ECtHR), 23. This case and those cited with it show the overlap of the consideration of democratic legitimacy with the 'nature of the right' as a ground for deference, discussed in Chapter 8.

[33] Waldron (n2) 300–1.

[34] *Hirst v UK (No. 2)* (n21) [62], in which the Court affirms its role in checking the legislature as follows: 'It is, however, for the Court to determine in the last resort whether the requirements of Article 3 of Protocol No. 1 have been complied with.'

democratic legitimacy, allowing the states to 'mould...their own democratic vision'.[35] Indeed, in line with this assertion, one of the dissenting opinions expressed forcefully in this case that 'it is essential to bear in mind that the Court is not a legislator and should be careful not to assume legislative functions'.[36] The majority judgment emphasized that any 'departure from the principle of universal suffrage risks undermining the democratic validity of the legislature thus elected and the laws it promulgates',[37] and that the legislature and its laws have 'democratic validity', notwithstanding that it goes on to find for the applicant.

In *Hirst (No. 2)*, then, the ECtHR confirmed that it was appropriate to find reasons for deference on the basis of the democratic credentials of the UK, notwithstanding that the context (in which voting rights were at risk) meant that such reasons were weakened, and in this case did not prevent the finding of a violation. In other contexts in which there may be additional second-order reasons for deference to be considered along with democratic legitimacy, the effect of reasons to defer on the basis of democratic legitimacy might be strengthened. An example of this can be seen in *Jahn v Germany*,[38] in which the ECtHR considered whether a land law passed in 1992 violated Article 1, Protocol 1, because it did not pay compensation to those who lost title granted in a 1990 law passed by the transitional government. The Court reiterated its approach that, notwithstanding the fact that other considerations would need to be taken into account (such as the proportionality of the legislation), because of the direct knowledge of the society and its needs (in particular the challenges of introducing post-reunification Germany into a market economy),[39] the role of the legislature, and the nature of the rights involved, the state would enjoy a margin of appreciation.[40] Furthermore the Grand Chamber, finding it natural that 'the margin of appreciation available to the legislature in implementing social and economic policies should be a wide one, will respect the legislature's judgment as to what is "in the public interest" unless that judgment is manifestly without reasonable foundation'.[41]

Two comments should be noted regarding the concept that legislation will not be in violation of the Convention unless it is 'manifestly without reasonable foundation'. The first is that this should be regarded as the high-water mark of deference. In order to reach this level of deference, a number of factors (such as the nature of the case involving social and economic policies,[42] along with the special importance of democratic institutions) will come together to bolster the reasons for deference. Indeed, one need only look back at *Hirst* to see that this level of deference is not given in all cases. Even in *Jahn*, in which the majority did defer

---

[35] Ibid, [61].
[36] Ibid, [6], dissenting opinion of Judges Wildhaber, Costa, Lorenzen, Kovler, and Jebens.
[37] Ibid.
[38] *Jahn v Germany* No. 72552/01 (2005) (ECtHR (GC)).
[39] This is a reflection of the expertise of the state authorities. See Chapter 5.
[40] *Jahn v Germany* (n38) [91].
[41] Ibid.
[42] See Chapter 6.4.f.

to Germany, the decision to do so was controversial within the Court.[43] Furthermore, deference did not replace an assessment of all reasons, but rather the majority decided the case after close scrutiny of all of the relevant criteria.

The second comment is a concern that it will be very difficult to meet the 'manifestly without reasonable foundation' test. Given that there was a large dissenting minority in *Jahn*, this concern does not appear to hold much water. Even stronger proof of this, though, is found in taking an example of a case[44] in which the Court found the legislature to have acted manifestly without reasonable foundation.[45] In *Chassagnou v France*,[46] the Grand Chamber found that the national legislature had advanced reasons that seemed only 'artificial'[47] and which led the Court to reject the legislative regime set up to coordinate hunting activities in a number of *départements*—a regime that required these landowners to become members of a hunting association and for their land to be available for hunting against their will. The finding against the legislation shows the Court willing to engage in direct assessment of a state's reasoning as manifestly without reasonable foundation, notwithstanding the margin of appreciation.[48] One dissenting opinion disagreed with the majority that there was a violation of Article 1, Protocol 1, and Article 11, standing alone without Article 14, because it took a different view of the importance of the margin of appreciation, based here on 'the importance of the objective pursued by the *Loi Verdeille*, which goes beyond the mere regulation of a leisure activity, having economic and ecological aspects', and the 'absence of any obvious disproportion between the objective concerned and the means adopted to attain it'.[49] The majority[50] found rather that the reasons adduced by the state legislature were 'not sufficient'.

b. Inter-American Court of Human Rights (IACtHR)

In the IACtHR, there are no obvious cases of a margin of appreciation to democratic bodies. However, this cannot be interpreted as meaning that the IACtHR will not give a margin of appreciation on the basis of democratic legitimacy in appropriate cases. There is implicit evidence of this in a number of cases.

---

[43] The decision split the Court eleven to six that there had been a violation of Article 1, Protocol 1, ECHR.

[44] *Chassagnou v France* Nos 25088/94, 28331/95, 28443/95 (1999) (ECtHR (GC)).

[45] This language was used only by a dissenting judge in holding that the test had not been met. It appears that the majority decided, in coming to the contrary view, that it was unnecessary to use such condemnatory language and so employed softer rhetoric, noting how the states' argument 'seems artificial', at [111]. Using softer language is reflective of the institutional comity and respect that exists between the tribunal and the states even when there is an adverse finding against the state. For more on comity as respect despite judicial disagreement, see T Endicott, ' "International Meaning": Comity in Fundamental Rights Adjudication' (2001) 13 (3) IJRL 280, 286–8.

[46] *Chassagnou v France* (n44).

[47] Ibid, [111].

[48] Which was articulated clearly at [113] for Article 11, and at [75] for Article 1, Protocol 1, ECHR.

[49] Ibid, partly dissenting, partly concurring opinion of Judge Caflisch, joined by Judge Pantiru.

[50] Twelve to five finding a violation of Article 1, Protocol 1, and Article 11.

One such example is found in the case of *Kimel v Argentina*,[51] in which a well-known journalist wrote a book called *The San Patricio Massacre* that implicated a number of people in positions of authority, including a judge, who brought defamation proceedings. The author was convicted and fined, and claimed that Argentina had violated Article 13 (free expression) and Article 8 (to a fair trial) ACHR. On the facts of this case, the IACtHR did not give a margin of appreciation. This is because the state accepted that it was responsible for violating the ACHR. Nevertheless, the Court went on to provide reasons for its decision and, in doing so, discussed reasons to give a margin of appreciation on the basis of the state's democratic legitimacy:

Every fundamental right is to be exercised with regard for other fundamental rights. This is a reconcilement process in which the State has a key role in trying to determine responsibilities and impose sanctions as may be necessary to achieve such purpose.[52]

Recognizing the 'key role' that the state plays in trying to implement and shape human rights standards within its own jurisdiction implies that the IACtHR is likely to defer in appropriate circumstances on the basis of a state's democratic legitimacy.

c. United Nations Human Rights Committee (UN HRC)

There is a different story apparent in the UN HRC context. There are numerous examples of the HRC deferring to the democratically made decisions of legislatures. A case that exemplifies such a margin of appreciation well is *Vos v The Netherlands*.[53] In this case, a woman claiming disability benefits was transferred to widows' benefits after her ex-husband died. Men did not automatically get transferred and so she claimed that she had suffered discrimination, because the transfer reduced her income contrary to Article 26 (equality and non-discrimination) ICCPR. The state argued that the majority of women were better off with the change, and that it needed a clear system to reduce wastage through double taxation and additional administrative costs. The Committee decided the case as follows:

In the light of the explanations given by the state party with respect to the legislative history, the purpose and application of the [relevant Acts], the Committee is of the view that the unfavourable result complained of by Mrs Vos follows from the application of a uniform rule to avoid overlapping in the allocation of social security benefits. This rule is based on objective and reasonable criteria, especially bearing in mind that both statutes under which Mrs Vos qualified for benefits aim at ensuring to all persons falling thereunder subsistence level income.[54]

This decision relies on the 'light' of the state's explanations. Just how much of a margin of appreciation was involved is difficult to determine, but it does appear that the Committee scrutinized the logic of the legislature at least to some degree. In

---

[51] *Kimel v Argentina* Series C No. 177 (2008) (IACtHR).
[52] Ibid, [75].
[53] *Vos v The Netherlands* CCPR/C/35/D/218/1986 (1989) (HRC).
[54] Ibid, [12].

Stalla Costa v Uruguay,[55] a lawyer's application to work in public service was rejected on the basis that only former government employees were subject to appointment. He argued that this was discriminatory, but the state argued that the legislature was unanimous that this was a necessary means of reuniting the country following arbitrary acts of the military dictatorship. The HRC did not agree with the state that the agreement of all political parties in Uruguay made this issue inadmissible, which supports the argument that a margin of appreciation is not akin to a doctrine of non-justiciability. However, the Committee did seem to give a margin of appreciation to the state, without explicitly using that terminology. Furthermore, the HRC supported the approach of the legislature, stating that these provisions were akin to remedies for violations of human rights during military rule.[56] This case was a radical realigning of the relationship between Uruguay and the HRC to one of cooperation in the endeavour of protecting human rights, whereas previously the military government had been found in violation of human rights in numerous cases and had treated the HRC with contempt.

It cannot be said, though, that the HRC defers on all occasions to democratic bodies. There is evidence too of a more Dworkinian approach to testing the substantive correctness of the state's decision. In *Tae-Hoon Park v Korea*,[57] a student was arrested and imprisoned on her return to Korea because, when she studied in the US, she had joined a student organization opposed to the Korean and US governments' stance on North Korea. The state argued that the law authorizing this was democratically legitimate and in effect that the Committee should defer on this basis, claiming additionally that national security was at stake.[58] There were reasons to heighten scrutiny on the basis that her free speech was at risk[59] and the HRC paid close attention to the first-order reasons in the case, scrutinizing all court decisions and finding that, because none of the state actions were necessary, there was a violation of the student's rights to free speech (Article 19 ICCPR).[60]

d. Giving state legislatures time to change the law

Claims for deference to democratic bodies are sometimes made to allow the state to proceed with its review of current law through the ordinary legislative and parliamentary processes. Such claims are like requests to allow the democratic bodies a reasonable time in which to deal with the issue without the pressure of an international human rights court ruling against them. In *Jahn*,[61] the Grand Chamber found that, given the enormous complexity of the reunification of Germany, 'the German legislature can be deemed to have intervened within a reasonable time to correct the—in its view unjust—effects of the Modrow Law'.[62]

---

[55] *Stalla Costa v Uruguay* CCPR/C/30/D/198/1985 (1987) (HRC).
[56] Ibid, [10].
[57] *Tae-Hoon Park v Korea* CCPR/C/64/D/628/1995 (1998) (HRC).
[58] Chapter 6.4.a.
[59] See section 6.a of this chapter.
[60] *Tae-Hoon Park v Korea* (n57) [10.3]–[10.4].
[61] *Jahn v Germany* (n38).
[62] Ibid, [116].

Although the reasonableness of time that it took for the legislature to act was not decisive on its own, it was one of three major considerations in the case, along with the lack of democratic credibility of the Modrow Law and the need to correct legal uncertainty.[63] A similar approach to allowing legislatures reasonable time in which to change the law can be seen in *Pye (Oxford) Ltd v UK*.[64] In that case, the Grand Chamber found that although landowners were less likely to lose title to their land under claims of adverse possession under the new Land Registration Act 2002 and that, had this law been implemented earlier, the claimants would have been unlikely to fall foul of the adverse possession rules in place at the time (which had themselves been criticized by English courts), nevertheless 'legislative changes in complex areas such as land law take time to bring about, and judicial criticism of legislation cannot of itself affect the conformity of the earlier provisions with the Convention'.[65] In *Sheffield and Horsham v UK*,[66] the Court indicated that deference to allow for legislative change would not extend beyond a reasonable time. In that case, the Court reiterated that it had highlighted the need for legislative review of laws relating to the recognition of the post-operative gender status of transsexuals in previous cases,[67] but that 'it would appear that the respondent State has not taken any steps to do so'.[68] The continued unresponsiveness of the UK government to review these laws gave the Court greater confidence in finding breaches of Articles 8 and 12 in *Christine Goodwin v UK*.[69] Indeed, the Court cited this consideration as crucial in finding that the 'Government can no longer claim that the matter falls within their margin of appreciation, save as regards the appropriate means of achieving recognition of the right protected under the Convention'.[70]

There are examples also of the HRC allowing the state time in which to implement appropriate human-rights-compliant legislation or conduct. In *Hartikainen v Finland*,[71] a Finnish humanist school teacher complained that children who were exempt from religious education were required to learn about the history of religion and ethics, claiming that this violated Article 18(4) ICCPR (parental

---

[63] Ibid.

[64] *Pye (Oxford) Ltd v UK* No. 44302/02 (ECtHR (GC)). Another case exemplifying this approach is *Stec v UK* No. 65731/01 (2006) (ECtHR (GC)), in which, at [64]–[65], the Court explained that the UK 'cannot be criticised for not having started earlier on the road towards a single pensionable age', and that:

> the Court does not consider it unreasonable of the Government to carry out a thorough process of consultation and review, nor can Parliament be condemned for deciding in 1995 to introduce the reform slowly and in stages. Given the extremely far-reaching and serious implications, for women and for the economy in general, these are matters which clearly fall within the State's margin of appreciation.

[65] Ibid, [81].

[66] *Sheffield and Horsham v UK* No. 22885/93, 23390/94 (1998) (ECtHR).

[67] *Rees v UK* No. 9532/81 (1986) (ECtHR), [47]; *Cossey v UK* No. 10843/84 (1990) (ECtHR), [42].

[68] *Sheffield and Horsham v UK* (n66) [60].

[69] *Christine Goodwin v UK* No. 28957/95 (ECtHR (GC)). See in particular [92], which noted that there had been reports, but that '[n]othing has effectively been done to further these proposals and in July 2001 the Court of Appeal noted that there were no plans to do so'.

[70] Ibid, [93].

[71] *Hartikainen v Finland* CCPR/C/12/D/40/1978 (1981) (HRC).

liberty regarding religious and moral education). The Committee in this case recognized that coming up with appropriate plans was proving difficult for the state, but that 'appropriate action is being taken to resolve the difficulties and it sees no reason to conclude that this cannot be accomplished, compatibly with the requirements of article 18 (4) of the Covenant, within the framework of the existing laws'.[72]

The IACtHR has also noted that the adjustment of domestic legislation may take time, and thus may warrant a measure of leeway. Nevertheless, the Court will monitor the time it takes to update legislation and rule accordingly.[73]

5. Cases in which democratic legitimacy is a factor in favour of granting the state a margin of appreciation

Democracy or participation is used as a factor to strengthen reasons for a margin of appreciation in two main areas: first, where there are conflicting private rights and the legislature has decided the policy of the law, and the international tribunal is called upon to examine the compliance of this policy with international human rights standards; and secondly, where there are conflicting personal and public freedoms, the resolution of which is often controversial within the state, and the international court is invited to assess the state's response.

a. Conflicting private rights: testing the choice of the legislature

i. ECtHR

Where legislation seeks to strike a balance between two competing private human rights, the ECtHR has given a margin of appreciation to states on the basis of their democratic legitimacy in finding a solution. *Odièvre v France*[74] involved French legislation that denied children knowledge of who their parents were when the parents had requested anonymity and had abandoned their children. The Court noted that the case involved the evaluation of conflicting private rights as follows:

The expression 'everyone' in Article 8 of the Convention applies to both the child and the mother. On the one hand, people have a right to know their origins... On the other hand, a woman's interest in remaining anonymous in order to protect her health by giving birth in appropriate medical conditions cannot be denied.[75]

In this case, the ECtHR found that the state legislature sought exactly to strike a balance between these and the other interests involved (for example the public

---

[72] Ibid, [10.5]. For a case in which neither the state nor the HRC considered the question of timing, but it appears that they could have done, see *Pauger v Austria* CCPR/C/44/D/415/1990 (1992) (HRC).

[73] *Barreto-Leiva v Venezuela* Series C No. 206 (2009) (IACtHR), [108]–[109].

[74] *Odièvre v France* No. 42326/98 (2003) (ECtHR (GC)).

[75] Ibid, [44].

interest in avoiding abortions, particularly illegal abortions),[76] and that in these circumstances 'the States must be allowed to determine the means which they consider to be best suited to achieve the aim of reconciling those interests'.[77]

The case of *Evans v UK*[78] required the Court to decide on the legislature's approach to in vitro fertilization (IVF) treatment for which the male had withdrawn consent. As the Court explained:

The dilemma central to the present case is that it involves a conflict between the Article 8 rights of two private individuals: the applicant and J. Moreover, each person's interest is entirely irreconcilable with the other's, since if the applicant is permitted to use the embryos, J will be forced to become a father, whereas if J's refusal or withdrawal of consent is upheld, the applicant will be denied the opportunity of becoming a genetic parent.[79]

In this context, the Court made it clear that the margin of appreciation applied both on the basis of the legislature's role in deciding whether or not to enact laws governing the use of IVF treatment and also, where it decides to enact the laws, to the outcome that those laws achieve in balancing the competing interests.[80] Likewise, in *Pye (Oxford) Ltd v UK*,[81] the Grand Chamber found, whilst reiterating that 'the margin of appreciation available to the legislature in implementing social and economic policies should be a wide one',[82] that this 'is particularly true in cases such as the present one where what is at stake is a longstanding and complex area of law which regulates private law matters between individuals'.[83]

Noteworthy too is the fascinating decision in *SH v Austria*.[84] This case involved two married couples who suffered from infertility and sought medically assisted procreation techniques involving donors. Both couples could not receive such IVF treatment under the Austrian Artificial Procreation Act, which prohibited donor-assisted pregnancies. The Grand Chamber noted that the use of IVF treatment 'continues to give rise to sensitive moral and ethical issues against a background of fast-moving medical and scientific developments',[85] and went on to affirm the approach taken in *Evans*[86]—that the role of the Court in such cases in which there is a wide margin of appreciation such as this is not to second-guess the approach of the legislature, but to ensure that it is within the range of appropriate responses that would be consistent with the state's obligations under Article 8. *SH v Austria* provides as follows:

The Court accepts that the Austrian legislature could have devised a different legal frame-work for regulating artificial procreation that would have made ovum donation permissible. It notes in this regard that this latter solution has been adopted in a number of member States of the Council of Europe. However, the central question in terms of art 8 of the Convention is not whether a different solution might have been adopted by the legislature

---

[76] Ibid, [45].   [77] Ibid, [49].
[78] *Evans v UK* No. 6339/05 (2007) (ECtHR (GC)).   [79] Ibid, [73].
[80] Ibid, [82].   [81] *Pye (Oxford) Ltd v UK* (n64).
[82] Ibid, [71]. This phrase will be assessed in greater detail in the following chapter.
[83] *Pye (Oxford) Ltd v UK* (n64), [71].
[84] *SH and others v Austria* No. 57813/00 (2011) (ECtHR (GC)), [94] and [106].
[85] Ibid, [97].   [86] *Evans v UK* (n78).

that would arguably have struck a fairer balance, but whether, in striking the balance at the point at which it did, the Austrian legislature exceeded the margin of appreciation afforded to it under that Article.[87]

ii. IACtHR

Examples from the IACtHR include *The Yakye Axa Indigenous Community v Paraguay*,[88] in which the indigenous community claimed ancestral rights to property that had become subject to ownership by various agricultural corporations. In recognizing the role of the state to govern legal relations to property,[89] the IACtHR indicated that deference might be given in an appropriate case as a result. Deference was not the main emphasis of the IACtHR's decision in that case, but rather proportionality. Given the facts, this is hardly surprising. In seeking to assert their property rights, the indigenous people suffered greatly. Without any alternative accommodation, they camped by the roadside of the property without access to education or health care. Some members died as a result. In addition to finding a breach of the right to property (Article 21 ACHR), the IACtHR also found violations of the rights to judicial protection (Article 25) and a fair trial (Article 8).[90]

In a similar case on the facts, the IACtHR asserted that it was not its role to mediate disputes between private parties; this was for the state. Rather, 'the Court has competence to analyze whether the State ensured the human rights of the members of the Sawhoyamaxa [indigenous] Community'.[91] The Court's analysis implies that had the state considered the rights of the indigenous community in its approach to the dispute, then this would have led to deference. The reasoning of the state, however, instead sought to justify the denial of the property from the perspective of the private companies, and its international relationship with Germany (with which the state had signed a bilateral investment treaty relating to the property). In such circumstances, the IACtHR paid close attention to the first-order reasoning, and intervened with less deference than it might have done had the state paid closer attention to the conflicting private rights.

iii. Summary

It might be thought that, in these sorts of situations,[92] it would be better for the Tribunals not to give a margin of appreciation to states, since legislation is unable to individualize solutions to the private conflicts. However, this perspective overlooks

---

[87] *SH v Austria* (n84) [106].
[88] *The Yakye Axa Indigenous Community v Paraguay* Series C No. 125 (2005) (IACtHR).
[89] Ibid, [66]–[71].
[90] Article 4 (the right to life) was not found to be violated in this case, but the Court did find such a violation in the later case of *The Sawhoyamaxa Indigenous Community v Paraguay* Series C No. 146 (2006) (IACtHR).
[91] Ibid, [136].
[92] For a further example, see *Fretté v France* No. 36515/97 (2002) (ECtHR), e.g. [42]: 'As the Government submitted, at issue here are the competing interests of the applicant and children who are eligible for adoption.'

the fact that many laws govern the interaction of private individuals, and their *raison d'être* is to consider the variety of ways in which interactions between individuals are regulated, and in doing this such legislation determines the contours of what is most appropriate in the general interest. It is thus appropriate for a margin of appreciation to be given, whilst the application of the law in a particular case must be proportionate to the aims of the legislation.[93] Thus if the legislature were to overlook a matter that causes particular hardship, the Tribunals would, whilst remaining cognizant of the margin of appreciation on the democratic basis of the legislation, be able to find a violation of human rights where appropriate.

b. Conflicting personal–public freedoms: questions of moral or political controversy

i. ECtHR

Where legislation seeks to implement general policies that are considered to be in the interests of society, notwithstanding their impact on private freedoms, the ECtHR has given a margin of appreciation to states on the basis of their democratic legitimacy in striking the balance between public and private rights.[94] In *Folgerø v Norway*,[95] in which the Grand Chamber was called upon to assess whether the educational system in Norway violated the rights of some parents to educate their children according to their own philosophical convictions (in accordance with Article 2, Protocol 1) because of the Christian emphasis in their state school's national religious education curriculum, the importance of the state in setting the curriculum was affirmed, including that parents are not permitted to 'object to the integration' of religious or philosophical teaching.[96] Notwithstanding the need to give leeway to the state's general role in this regard, the Court went on to declare: 'The State is forbidden to pursue an aim of indoctrination that *might be considered as not respecting parents' religious and philosophical convictions*. That is the limit that must not be exceeded.'[97] The state had a margin of appreciation for setting the curriculum[98] when the limits of these public policies conflicted with the private rights of parents who did not share the Christian thrust of the curriculum. Likewise, in *Sheffield and Horsham v UK*,[99] in which the Grand Chamber was required to review UK laws relating to the recognition of the post-operative gender status of transsexuals, the Court referred to the 'complex scientific, legal, moral and social issues'.[100] Along with the lack of consensus amongst states about how to deal with this issue,[101] the Court found that the decision was within the state's margin of appreciation. Because the legislature was dealing with complex moral and social issues, reasons for deference were found in this case.

---

[93] See Chapter 7.
[94] See, e.g., *A, B and C v Ireland* No. 25579/05 (2010) (ECtHR (GC)), [233] and [239].
[95] *Folgerø v Norway* No. 15472/02 (2007) (ECtHR (GC)).
[96] Ibid, [84][g]. [97] Ibid, [84][h] (emphasis added).
[98] Ibid, [89]. [99] *Sheffield and Horsham v UK* (n66).
[100] Ibid, [58]. [101] See Chapter 6.

A further relevant case is *Burden and Burden v UK*.[102] Two sisters who had lived together for several decades and acquired a substantial estate complained that they would be subject to high inheritance tax on the death of either of them, resulting in the forced sale of their property, whereas same-sex couples who were registered as civil partners would not be so liable, and the sisters did not have the option of registering as civil partners. The exclusion of siblings under the Civil Partnership Act 2004 was consequently at issue, and the private rights of these sisters contrasted with the public interest. The Grand Chamber stated that:

The Contracting State enjoys a margin of appreciation in assessing whether and to what extent differences in otherwise similar situations justify a different treatment, and this margin is usually wide when it comes to general measures of economic or social strategy.[103]

The Grand Chamber went on to find that there was no violation of Article 14 in conjunction with Article 1, Protocol 1, ECHR. Some of the reasoning that the Court employed was circular in this case:[104] it found that because the sisters did not take on the burdens of a legal relationship, they could not be compared to civil partners, notwithstanding that their exclusion from this formal procedure was the very matter at issue. The majority pitched these reasons along with the various reasons for deference (in addition to social policy, there was mention of a wide margin of appreciation in taxation policy,[105] and the lack of international consensus in dealing with such matters).[106]

The Court did not expressly set out the reasons affecting why homosexual relationships were deserving of greater tax protection than committed sibling relationships like that of the Misses Burden, and on what basis the differentiation was legitimate, and nor did the state. Nor did the Court apply to these first-order reasons what it was about reasons for deference that caused the ECtHR to go along with the UK's approach to the problem. In this context, one can understand the sarcastic remark made by Judge Zupančič that 'needless to say . . . reference to margins of appreciation makes all other argumentation superfluous'. This phrase reveals frustration with how the margin of appreciation is sometimes invoked along with a paucity of reasoning. Whilst reasons for deference were given in this case, they were not applied clearly in the context of the proportionality exercise, which assesses first-order reasons to more or less exacting levels of scrutiny.[107] It would have been better if the first-order reasons had been set out with greater transparency, and then the decision made having discussed both the second-order and first-order reasons.

What is clear, though, is that where the state is involved in considering the interrelationship between individual rights and the wider public interest, the European

---

[102] *Burden and Burden v UK* No. 13378/05 (2008) (ECtHR (GC)).
[103] Ibid, [60], citing *Stec v UK* (n64) [51]–[52].
[104] See further the dissenting opinion of Judge Borrego Borrego for arguments about how the decision involves circular reasoning.
[105] See Chapter 6.4.f.   [106] See Chapter 5.   [107] See Chapter 7.

Court defers to the state organs on the basis of their democratic legitimacy in dealing with such complex social matters.[108] This is context-specific and these reasons for deference are not determinative; they can be overridden during the assessment of first-order reasons in the proportionality exercise. This is shown in the case of *Tyrer v UK*,[109] in which the corporal punishment of 'birching' on the Isle of Man was found to be contrary to Article 3, notwithstanding that the island's community supported its use. But here the government was not requesting deference on the relevant basis that the local community held such practices to be humane and non-degrading, but rather that they did not 'outrage public opinion'. Indeed, the Court noted that 'it might well be that one of the reasons why they view the penalty as an effective deterrent is precisely the element of degradation it involves'.[110] In such circumstances, deference to any democratic decision-making would be overridden by the first-order reasoning for holding such practices to be contrary to Article 3.[111]

ii. UN HRC

In the UN HRC context,[112] the case of *Wackenheim v France*[113] exemplifies the HRC showing deference where the state balances private rights with societal standards. This case involved the prohibition of dwarf tossing in France. The communicant, a dwarf, argued that the prohibition was discriminatory, violated his rights to freedom and employment, and, contrary to the state's assertion that the practice was an affront to his dignity, the communicant argued that his resulting unemployment was an affront to dignity. The HRC discussed only the discrimination claim (Article 26 ICCPR), agreeing with France that the other arguments were not relevant (that there has been a deprivation of liberty and denial of legal personality, contrary to Articles 9 and 16 respectively). The HRC found that the decision was based on objective and reasonable differences between dwarves and non-dwarves, since tossing could not physically be accomplished with non-dwarf adults. The HRC showed deference in this case. The deference is seen in the way in which they handled the communicant's argument that other similar practices had not been banned and thus the treatment was discriminatory. The HRC left the legislature plenty of room for manoeuvre. The Committee reasoned as follows:

The Committee is aware of the fact that there are other activities which are not banned but which might possibly be banned on the basis of grounds similar to those which justify the ban on dwarf tossing. However, the Committee is of the opinion that, given that the ban on dwarf tossing is based on objective and reasonable criteria and the author has not established that this measure was discriminatory in purpose, the mere fact that there may be other

---

[108] See also *Hatton v UK* (n30) [76], [103], and [123].
[109] *Tyrer v UK* No. 5856/72 (1978) (ECtHR).   [110] Ibid, [31].
[111] Another example is the case of *Dudgeon v UK* (n24).
[112] See further *Vos v The Netherlands* (n53), *Althammer v Austria* CCPR/C/78/D/998/2001 (2003) (HRC), and *X v Colombia* CCPR/C/89/D/1361/2005 (2007) (HRC).
[113] *Wackenheim v France* CCPR/C/75/D/854/1999 (2002) (HRC).

activities liable to be banned is not in itself sufficient to confer a discriminatory character on the ban on dwarf tossing.[114]

The HRC has also considered the balance between public and private rights involving a politically sensitive issue in relation to the compulsory spelling of a name in the case of *Leonid Raihman v Latvia*.[115] The majority in this case acknowledged that, in cases involving the impact on one's private rights for societal reasons, there is a margin of appreciation. However, on the facts and having undertaken an assessment of the proportionality of the interference, the Committee found a violation of Article 17 ICCPR for, inter alia, the following reasons:

While the question of legislative policy, and the modalities to protect and promote official languages is *best left to the appreciation of State parties*, the Committee considers that the forceful addition of a declinable ending to a surname, which has been used in its original form for decades, and which modifies its phonic pronunciation, is an intrusive measure, which is not proportionate to the aim of protecting the official State language.[116]

It is noteworthy that there was a dissenting opinion in this case, which 'stresses' that such matters of policy are 'best left to the appreciation of States'. It appears that the same factors were considered, but that these two Committee members considered there to be stronger grounds for deference than the majority.

iii. IACtHR

The propensity for deference when dealing with the impact that the public interest has on individual rights is seen in the IACtHR in the case of the *The Girls Yean and Bosico v Dominican Republic*.[117] The IACtHR had to determine whether the state's application of its nationality laws had violated the applicants' rights to a nationality (Article 20 ACHR) and equality (Article 24), amongst other rights. The children had Dominican mothers and Haitian fathers, which led to numerous obstacles to their registration as nationals, and consequently they lacked access to social services and education. The Court assessed the state's approach to the problem of balancing individual interests with those of the wider community through assessing the legislation in place at the time. The Court explained that:

The determination of who has a right to be a national continues to fall within a State's domestic jurisdiction. However, its discretional authority in this regard is gradually being restricted with the evolution of international law, in order to ensure a better protection of the individual in the face of arbitrary acts of States.[118]

Whilst there is scope for deference to the state's discretion, then, this deference is limited by the state's human rights obligations, as well as by other international obligations such as avoiding and reducing statelessness.[119] In assessing the first-order

---

[114] Ibid, [7.5].
[115] *Leonid Raihman v Latvia* CCPR/C/100/D/1621/2007 (2010) (HRC).
[116] Ibid, [8.3] (emphasis added).
[117] *The Girls Yean and Bosico v Dominican Republic* Series C No. 130 (2005) (IACtHR).
[118] Ibid, [140].   [119] Ibid. See Chapter 5.6.d.

reasons in this case, the IACtHR found violations of the Convention. The margin of appreciation, then, did not play a large role in this decision, and rightly so on the facts. However, the IACtHR indicated that it would consider the role of deference in a suitable case.

6. Cases in which democratic legitimacy issues heighten scrutiny

The Tribunals also heighten scrutiny of state action, or limit the margin of appreciation, on the basis of various democratic considerations. Some such issues are reminiscent of Ely's theory justifying review on the basis of promoting participation in the political process. There are cases in which state action has limited electoral participation, or affected minorities. In both of these sorts of cases, the Tribunals have heightened scrutiny of state action. Similarly, where there has not been much societal debate, the values defended by Waldron in favour of democratic procedures lose their potency. In these sorts of cases, there is likewise a more limited margin of appreciation. There are also cases in which the Tribunals have given reasons related to the protection of the rule of law to increase scrutiny of state action and to keep a check on the democratic process.

The reasoning in cases from the above categories sheds light on the ways in which the Tribunals contribute to democratic theory. Where cases lead to greater scrutiny of state action, this is tantamount to an exhortation to states to make efforts to improve their processes or to face more exacting examination before the Tribunals. There are noticeably greater numbers of IACtHR cases in this section. This shows that even where there are not many opportunities to defer to states, the IACtHR nevertheless offers guidance to states about the democratic standards it deems worthy of deference.

a. Democratic rights: the example of electoral participation

Some of the rights in the Treaties are designed specifically to protect democracy. Consequently, where there are complaints that state authorities are violating these rights, there is less reason to defer on democratic grounds. The pedigree of democratic protection is precisely the matter at issue on these occasions. Free speech cases are prominent examples of this.[120] Another example of rights that protect democracy is the body of rights that seek to ensure electoral participation, such as the right to vote, to stand in elections, or the freedom of association for political parties. There is evidence that the Tribunals heighten scrutiny where there is a risk that electoral participation has been reduced, for the sorts of reasons that Ely encouraged judicial review of state action.[121]

---

[120] See Chapter 8.3.c.   [121] Ely (n5) chs 5 and 6.

i. IACtHR

In the IACtHR case of *Yatama v Nicaragua*,[122] the Court makes clear that there are grounds for deference to the state for how it organizes its electoral system.[123] In that case, a number of indigenous political groups, including Yatama, had sought to stand in an election, but were hampered by requirements that all parties represent at least 3 per cent of the population. This requirement led to the formation of various coalitions in the run-up to registration. Yatama, which did in fact comply with the requirement to represent 3 per cent of the population, was refused registration on the mistaken ground that it was connected to a smaller group that did not have 3 per cent support. When the mistake was discovered, Yatama did not have enough time to campaign and refused to stand, and consequently claimed a violation of Article 23 ACHR (right to participate in government) amongst other violations. Although the laws requiring 3 per cent support were later declared unconstitutional, the IACtHR went on to confirm that the actions of the state violated Article 23. In making this finding, the Court emphasized the importance of enabling participation in the electoral process, including that there ought not be requirements for candidates to be part of a political party.[124]

ii. UN HRC

The UN HRC has similarly handled cases that affect electoral participation, and has modified the level of deference accordingly. There have been a number of cases before the HRC in which the Committee has shown deference notwithstanding that a denial of participation can be seen in the case, but this has first required the state to make a convincing case for how its actions are actually bolstering the protection of democracy. In *Debreczeny v The Netherlands*,[125] a police officer was denied the right to stand for election to the municipal council. The rationale was that because police officers report to the mayor, there would be a conflict of interest for one to sit on the council; thus refusing serving police officers access to political office would further democracy. Whilst the reasoning in the decision was somewhat thin, there appears to have been deference given to the state's reasoning. The HRC specifically mentions that the state's reasoning 'to guarantee the democratic decision-making process by avoiding conflicts of interest'[126] leads it to find the position acceptable. Thus it appears as if the HRC is more willing to defer in circumstances

---

[122] *Yatama v Nicaragua* Series C No. 127 (2005) (IACtHR).

[123] Ibid, [206]–[207]. Affirmed in *Castañeda Gutman v México* Series C No. 184 (2008) (IACtHR), [149], [155], and [162]–[173]. In this case, the IACtHR found in favour of the state that there was no violation of Article 23, notwithstanding the heightened scrutiny that arises from the importance of democratic rights, as affirmed by the Court at [140]–[143].

[124] *Yatama v Nicaragua* (n122) [218]–[219]. See also *Ricardo Canese v Paraguay* 31 August 2004, Series C No. 111 (IACtHR), in which the IACtHR scrutinized the state closely where the applicant had stood as a presidential candidate (and failed to win) prior to the legal action taken against him.

[125] *Debreczeny v The Netherlands* CCPR/C/53/D/500/1992 (1995) (HRC).

[126] Ibid, [9.3].

that bolster the democratic nature of decision-making even if participation for one individual is thereby reduced.[127]

iii. ECtHR

The ECtHR Grand Chamber, in the case of *Hirst v UK (No. 2)*,[128] whilst articulating grounds for a margin of appreciation on the basis of the democratic legitimacy of the authorities, appears to heighten scrutiny on the basis of promoting participation in the political process. The judgment articulates the promotion of participation as a factor to heighten scrutiny in an apparently self-conscious way, but not using this explicit terminology. Rather, the deference is evidenced by phrases such 'while the margin of appreciation is wide, it is not all-embracing',[129] and by referring to the right to vote as 'vitally important'.[130]

Heightening scrutiny on the basis of promoting political participation is more clearly seen in the case of *Refah Partisi (the Welfare Party) v Turkey*.[131] In that case, the Grand Chamber assessed whether the dissolution of the Refah Partisi political party was compatible with the ECHR. This party was extremely popular in Turkey, but was accused of intending to implement religious fundamentalism that would undermine Convention rights, democratic processes, and secularism. The ECtHR made clear that there was only a 'limited margin of appreciation' in the context of dissolving a political party, and that the exceptions to Article 11 were 'to be construed strictly'. The Court states that '[d]rastic measures, such as the dissolution of an entire political party and a disability barring its leaders from carrying on any similar activity for a specified period, may be taken only in the most serious cases'.[132]

The ECtHR has emphasized in decisions related to Article 3, Protocol 1, ECHR (free elections) that the rights are subject to a margin of appreciation, but will also be scrutinized carefully by the Court.[133] The same can be said for cases relating to the right of individuals to stand for political office.[134]

In such cases, it is clear both that there are reasons in favour of deference here articulated, allowing states to forge their own democratic vision,[135] and yet that

---

[127] See also *Gillot v France* CCPR/C/75/D/932/2000 (2002) (HRC), in which the HRC seemed to defer to France's approach to limiting the enfranchisement of New Caledonian residents for a referendum on the future of the island's connection with France on the basis that this furthered the self-determination of the peoples of New Caledonia (see [13.4]–[13.8]). At the same time, the HRC considered whether the standards used disproportionately denied the involvement of relevant parties.

[128] *Hirst v UK (No. 2)* (n21).

[129] Ibid, [82].

[130] Ibid.

[131] *Refah Partisi (the Welfare Party) v Turkey* Nos 41340/98, 41342/98, 41343/98, 41344/98 (2003) (ECtHR (GC)).

[132] Ibid, [100].

[133] For example, *Ždanoka v Latvia* No. 58278/00 (2006) (ECtHR (GC)), [103].

[134] Ibid, [115]. See also *Podkolzina v Latvia* No. 46726/99 (2002) (ECtHR), [33]–[38]; *Melnychenko v Ukraine* No. 17707/02 (2004) (ECtHR), [53]–[67].

[135] For example, *Marshall v Canada* CCPR/C/43/D/205/1986 (1991) (HRC), [5.4], in the context of assessing rules of participation at a constitutional conference, the HRC decided: 'It is for the legal and constitutional system of the State party to provide for the modalities of such participation.'

where there is a risk that certain elements of participation are inappropriately being hampered, such as the right to vote, or to stand in elections as a political party or candidate, then less deference and greater scrutiny will result.

b. Minorities and vulnerable groups

Similarly, in cases in which minorities and vulnerable groups are involved, the Tribunals seem to defer less to states. Such deference may be needed, in Ely's words, to ensure 'the effective protection of minorities whose interests differ from the interests of most of the rest of us'.[136] Consequently, where the human rights of minorities are concerned, the Tribunals can be less deferential. The reasons for this are based on the shortcomings of democratic government to represent the interests and views of minorities properly. This approach could be criticized by Waldronians on the basis that when legislatures make laws relating to minorities, they do so on the basis of what would be right, proper, and appropriate, and not on the basis of what is in the best interests of the majority. Whilst this works theoretically, it does not take into account human weakness and vice, which are prone to corrupt the purity of the idea. It is hardly surprising to find that greater scrutiny is given when minorities' rights are concerned.

i. ECtHR

In *Chassagnou v France*,[137] the landowners who objected to hunting were a minority. In this context, the ECtHR made clear that it would be careful to assess the balance of first-order reasons (without, of course, using this terminology). It reasoned as follows:

[P]luralism, tolerance and broadmindedness are hallmarks of a 'democratic society'. Although individual interests must on occasion be subordinated to those of a group, *democracy does not simply mean that the views of a majority must always prevail: a balance must be achieved which ensures the fair and proper treatment of minorities* and avoids any abuse of a dominant position.[138]

This passage shows the ECtHR clearly contributing to democratic theory by stating what it regards as required by democracy. The same passage was cited in the case of *Sørensen and Rasmussen v Denmark*.[139] In this case, the applicants were required to enter into closed-shop agreements with trade unions when they began employment. Neither applicant wanted to enter into such an agreement because they disagreed with the political stance of the trade unions. The ECHR did not explicitly exclude closed-shop trade union agreements[140] and they were legal in Denmark.

---

[136] Ely (n5) 78. See also Ely (n5) 78–87 and ch 6.

[137] *Chassagnou v France* (n44).

[138] Ibid, [112] (emphasis added).

[139] *Sørensen and Rasmussen v Denmark* Nos 52562/99, 52620/99 (2005) (ECtHR (GC)).

[140] At the time the ECHR was signed, the issue was debated, but there was insufficient agreement to exclude these provisions.

Whilst the changing attitudes of European states to such agreements are an important factor in the level of deference in this case,[141] another issue was the fact that employees who disagreed with the trade unions would be a minority. Having cited the passage set out above, the Court went on to explain that greater scrutiny would result:

In assessing whether a Contracting State has remained within its margin of appreciation in tolerating the existence of closed-shop agreements, particular weight must be attached to the justifications advanced by the authorities for them and, in any given case, the extent to which they impinge on the rights and interests protected by Article 11.[142]

The impact of this factor was stated plainly in the partly concurring and partly dissenting judgment of Judge Sajó in *MSS v Belgium and Greece*,[143] as follows:

The concept of a vulnerable group has a specific meaning in the jurisprudence of the Court. True, if a restriction on fundamental rights applies to a particularly vulnerable group in society who have suffered considerable discrimination in the past, such as people with mental disabilities, *then the State's margin of appreciation is substantially narrower* and it must have very weighty reasons for the restrictions in question . . . [144]

ii. IACtHR

In *The Sawhoyamaxa Indigenous Community v Paraguay*,[145] the IACtHR was assessing whether the land rights of the indigenous community had been adequately protected vis-à-vis private landowning companies, which had exploitation rights. Less deference was granted to the democratic bodies since they had failed to respect adequately the views of this minority community. The Court found that the state's arguments viewed 'the indigenous issue exclusively from the standpoint of land productivity and agrarian law, something which is insufficient for it fails to address the distinctive characteristics of such peoples'.[146]

   Similarly, in *Yatama v Nicaragua*,[147] the IACtHR pointed out, in the course of its judgment against the state, that the fact that Yatama was a minority was a consideration to take into account in its electoral law, and the fact that the state did not provide for this became a relevant factor in finding the state's actions to be in violation of the ACHR.[148]

---

[141] See Chapter 5.
[142] *Sørensen and Rasmussen v Denmark* (n139) [58]. For another case evidencing heightened scrutiny on the basis that the case involved a minority (Roma children), see *Oršuš and others v Croatia* No. 15766/03 (2010) (ECtHR (GC)), [181]–[182]. See also the strong dissenting judgment in *Oršuš* for an alternative approach, which emphasized the margin of appreciation at [8], and the fact that the Grand Chamber was overruling a well-reasoned Constitutional Court judgment and a unanimous Chamber judgment: see [19].
[143] *MSS v Belgium and Greece* No. 30696/09 (2011) (ECtHR (GC)).
[144] Ibid, section II, partly concurring and partly dissenting judgment of Judge Sajó (emphasis added).
[145] *The Sawhoyamaxa Indigenous Community v Paraguay* (n90).
[146] Ibid, [139].
[147] *Yatama v Nicaragua* (n122).
[148] Ibid, [223].

In *Saramaka People v Suriname*,[149] the IACtHR was asked by the state for clarification of the requirement to allow minority groups to participate in decisions affecting them. In particular, the state asked whether it was required to speak with every individual or group, and asked what should be done in the event that the minority group had internal divisions and different views.[150] The Court explained that representatives must be consulted, and that those representatives must be chosen by the minority group itself. Any discrepancies between views of the minorities should be resolved by that minority, and the state must not select one particular group with which to deal over another.[151]

iii. UN HRC

Before the UN HRC, there are numerous examples of heightened scrutiny relating to the protection of minorities. An early example can be seen in the case of *Ibrahima Gueye v France*.[152] A Senegalese national, whose French army pension was frozen whilst the same pensions held by French nationals continued to increase, complained that this practice was discriminatory contrary to Article 26 ICCPR. The Senegalese communicant and others in his position were not represented, nor were they given the opportunity to participate in the decision-making on pensions, and for this reason they were particularly vulnerable. The HRC consequently closely scrutinized the reasoning of the state. Previously, pensions had been awarded on the basis of service rendered and not on the basis of nationality, and so the state's reasons for differential treatment were not regarded as sound.

In another case, the HRC shows clearly that it heightens scrutiny when the case involves minorities, but gives greater deference when there is evidence that the state has carefully considered the requirements and representations of the minority group. In *Länsman v Finland*,[153] the Sami people complained that their culture and way of life (Article 27 ICCPR) was under threat by nearby quarrying activities. In finding that there was no violation of the Covenant, the HRC explicitly discussed the level of participation that the Sami people had as follows:

[The Committee] notes in particular that the interests of the Muotkatunturi Herdsmens' Committee and of the authors were considered during the proceedings leading to the delivery of the quarrying permit, that the authors *were* consulted during the proceedings, and that reindeer herding in the area does not appear to have been adversely affected by such quarrying as has occurred.[154]

In the case of *Ángela Poma Poma v Peru*,[155] the HRC found that affording genuine participation to the members of the minority community, whose livelihood and

---

[149] *Saramaka People v Suriname* Series C No. 185 (Interpretation of a previous judgment) (2008) (IACtHR) (referring to *Saramaka People v Suriname* Series C No. 172 (2007) (IACtHR)).
[150] Ibid, [11].
[151] Ibid, [22] and [25]–[27].
[152] *Ibrahima Gueye v France* CCPR/C/35/D/196/1985 (1989) (HRC).
[153] *Länsman v Finland* CCPR/C/52/D/511/1992 (1994) (HRC).
[154] Ibid, [9.6] (emphasis in original).
[155] *Ángela Poma Poma v Peru* CCPR/C/95/D/1457/2006 (2009) (HRC).

way of life (alpaca farming) was at stake as a result of the government's water diversion programme, was a core part of ensuring compliance with the Covenant.[156] For additional examples expressly discussing the level of participation of minorities, see *Länsman (No. 2) v Finland*[157] and *Apirana Mahuika v New Zealand*.[158]

c. A lack of societal/parliamentary debate

Where the democratic process works well, or at least ordinarily, there are sound reasons to give a margin of appreciation to the decision-makers on that basis, as the foregoing demonstrates. We have just discussed practical difficulties related to the effectiveness of democracy relating to minorities. However, there are other problems not related to minorities that nevertheless affect representation and the appropriateness of the democratic process. If a case raises problems showing that there has not been appropriate societal debate to produce an adequately reasoned legal solution, then less deference will be given to the decision-makers on that basis.[159] This aspect of the margin of appreciation is also seen where a tribunal offers less deference on the basis that there has been insufficient parliamentary debate when developing a legislative position.

i. ECtHR

In *Hirst v UK (No. 2)*,[160] the ECtHR discussed the level of parliamentary debate in some detail, along with other relevant factors. The majority stated:

As to the weight to be attached to the position adopted by the legislature and judiciary in the United Kingdom, there is no evidence that Parliament has ever sought to weigh the competing interests or to assess the proportionality of a blanket ban on the right of a convicted prisoner to vote. It is true that the question was considered by the multi-party Speaker's Conference on Electoral Law in 1968 which unanimously recommended that a convicted prisoner should not be entitled to vote. It is also true that the working party which recommended the amendment to the law to allow unconvicted prisoners to vote recorded that successive governments had taken the view that convicted prisoners had lost the moral authority to vote and did not therefore argue for a change in the legislation. It may be said that, by voting the way they did to exempt unconvicted prisoners from the restriction on voting, Parliament implicitly affirmed the need for continued restrictions on the voting rights of convicted prisoners. Nonetheless, it cannot be said that there was any substantive debate by members of the legislature on the continued justification in light of modern-day penal policy and of current human rights standards for maintaining such a general restriction on the right of prisoners to vote.[161]

---

[156] Ibid, [7.6].
[157] *Länsman (No. 2) v Finland* CCPR/C/58/D/671/1995 (1996) (HRC), [10.5].
[158] *Apirana Mahuika v New Zealand* CCPR/C/70/D/547/1993 (2000) (HRC), [9.6].
[159] The opposite is also true. Where there has been a strong and vibrant societal debate leading to a clear democratic choice, this provides a basis for a wider margin of appreciation. See *A, B and C v Ireland* (n94) [239]; read with [233].
[160] *Hirst v UK (No. 2)* (n21).
[161] Ibid, [79].

This excerpt shows the majority contributing to understandings of democracy by highlighting the importance of parliamentary debate. Where such debate is present, it appears that greater deference will be accorded to the legislature. This shows the importance that the ECtHR attributes to ensuring that legislation is reflective of a societal debate. Of course, whilst there are grounds in this case for heightened scrutiny of the state's approach, this alone does not lead to the majority's finding of a violation of the Convention, which appears to stem from a strongly held view by the majority about the voting rights of prisoners.

The dissenting judgment also discussed the impact that the level of debate should have and the way in which the majority handled it. The dissenting judges said 'it is not for the Court to prescribe the way in which national legislatures carry out their legislative functions'.[162] This approach may regard the ECtHR's heightened scrutiny on the basis of low societal debate as inappropriate. The better view is that increasing scrutiny of the state's actions is appropriate where the law impacts a minority group or there is an issue that does not give rise to substantial discussion in society or parliament, because there is less chance in such circumstances that the state has adequately assessed all of the competing considerations.

The approach of the majority in *Hirst* was followed in *Dickson v UK*,[163] another case involving the rights of prisoners. In this case, a prisoner and his wife wanted the right to undertake an artificial insemination procedure. These procedures were permitted only in exceptional circumstances and the Secretary of State ruled that the prisoner's wife likely being too old to conceive when the prisoner was released was not a sufficiently strong factor to grant them permission because, amongst other matters, his was a serious crime, the relationship had formed while he was in prison, and there had been no stable relationship in which a child might grow up. Finding in favour of the prisoner, the Grand Chamber discussed the level of deference as a result of societal debate as follows: '[S]ince the Policy was not embodied in primary legislation, the various competing interests were never weighed, nor were issues of proportionality ever assessed, by Parliament.'[164] The Grand Chamber went on to find that the decision fell outside of the margin of appreciation.[165]

ii. UN HRC

The UN HRC has also included the relative strength of societal debate as a factor for deference. In the case of *Faurisson v France*,[166] the communicant denied the existence of gas chambers at Auschwitz, and was convicted of an offence under

---

[162] Ibid, [7], dissenting opinion of Judges Wildhaber, Costa, Lorenzen, Kovler, and Jebens.

[163] *Dickson v UK* No. 44362/04 (2007) (ECtHR (GC)).

[164] Ibid [83]. See further *Evans v UK* (n78) [86]–[89], in which the Grand Chamber found that the stark and absolute nature of the law provided legal certainty, and that the legislation reflected a detailed examination of the social implications. This is in contrast to *Hirst* (n21) and *Dickson* (n163), which both contained stark provisions, but were not the result of a careful discussion by Parliament.

[165] *Dickson v UK* (n163) [85].

[166] *Faurisson v France* CCPR/C/58/D/550/1993 (1996) (HRC).

French law. The complaint argued that the law was shoddy and not reflective of a decent societal debate, as evidenced by the fact that it was rejected when it was first introduced and passed only upon reintroduction following some high-profile anti-Semitic violence.[167] The HRC referenced the parliamentary criticisms of the law within France, and the lack of international consensus on how to deal with Holocaust denial, and reached the conclusion that the finding of an offence did not violate freedom of expression (Article 19 ICCPR). The reasoning is somewhat opaque, but it appears that the HRC does not, in this case, find the lack of wide-ranging societal debate to be enough of a problem to result in a violation. However, after mentioning the lack of debate, the HRC paid greater attention to the application of the law in the context of the particular case,[168] noting that there would certainly be occasions on which the law might fall foul of the Covenant.[169]

d. The application of legal formulae where the provisions are too broad-brush

In some cases, the Tribunals heighten scrutiny of state action where the legislative provisions appears too sweeping and ill-considered to provide an adequate solution to the problems intended by the legislation. This is not to say that the Tribunals take upon themselves the role of legislative review, but simply that less deference to the state is given and more close scrutiny taken of the first-order reasons than if the outcome were more discriminating.

i. ECtHR

In *Chassagnou v France*,[170] in which certain landowners were automatically made to become members of hunting associations notwithstanding their opposition to hunting, the blanket requirement itself seems to have heightened scrutiny. Whereas the Parliament would ordinarily have been granted deference in this sort of situation, the fact that it employed such a broad-brush solution appears to reduce this deference. The Court stated: 'It should be pointed out that the French parliament chose to provide for the compulsory transfer of hunting rights over land by means of compulsory membership of an association responsible for the management of the properties thus pooled.'[171]

Similar reasoning can also be seen in the case of *Hashman and Harrup v UK*.[172] In this case, two hunting protestors were required to pay £100 to keep good behaviour and not to breach the peace. They had previously sabotaged hunts, although had not yet been found to breach the peace. The protestors claimed that their free speech rights were violated contrary to Article 10 ECHR. Whilst Article

---

[167] *Faurisson v France* CCPR/C/58/D/550/1993 (1996) (HRC), [8.7].
[168] Ibid, [9.3]–[9.7].   [169] Ibid, [9.3].
[170] *Chassagnou v France* (n44).   [171] Ibid, [111].
[172] *Hashman and Harrup v UK* No. 25594/94 (1999) (ECtHR (GC)).

10 cases often involve consideration of a margin of appreciation,[173] the ECtHR found that there was a violation of Article 10 because the term *contra bonos mores* was not clear enough for the applicants to know how they could protest without being subject to further legal action by the state. The catch-all nature of the provision made the ECtHR suspicious and less inclined to defer to the state.[174]

In *Sommerfeld v Germany*,[175] a father was denied access to his daughter because she was born out of wedlock. Whilst the ECtHR made clear that it did not review legislation in the abstract,[176] it was nevertheless unconvinced by the government's arguments, which were 'based on general considerations that fathers of children born out of wedlock lack interest in contact with their children'.[177]

ii. IACtHR

In the case of *Dismissed Congressional Employees v Peru*,[178] the IACtHR showed similarly that applying legal solutions that are far-reaching and which appear arbitrary will raise the issue of whether deference on the basis of democratic legitimacy is appropriate, or whether close scrutiny of the state's first-order reasoning is required. In this case, the democratic organs of government had been dissolved and congressional employees dismissed without due process. In this context, there was no room for deference on the basis of democratic legitimacy. Nevertheless, the state explained how the principles would operate in a suitable case as follows:

The Court considers that States evidently have discretionary powers to reorganize their institutions and, possibly, to remove personnel based on the needs of the public service and the administration of public interests in a democratic society; however, these powers cannot be exercised without full respect for the guarantees of due process and judicial protection.[179]

In situations in which there are 'blanket and indiscriminate' measures adopted by the state, or broad-brush legal mechanisms, the Tribunals defer less on democratic grounds to the state and instead pay closer scrutiny to the state's reasoning.[180]

---

[173] Chapter 8.3.c. In the present case, the ECtHR recalls that prior restraint of free speech is subject to the 'most careful scrutiny': [32].

[174] It is unsurprising that this case led to a dissenting opinion since, in the context of heightened scrutiny, there is scope for disagreement on the first-order reasons. Judge Baka, in his short dissenting opinion, argued that 'the "keep the peace or be of good behaviour" obligation has to be interpreted in the light of the specific anti-social behaviour committed by the applicants. In this context, I think that the binding-over requirement was foreseeable and enabled the applicants to a reasonable extent to behave accordingly'.

[175] *Sommerfeld v Germany* No. 31871/96 (2003) (ECtHR (GC)).

[176] Ibid, [86].

[177] Ibid, [87], citing the Chamber decision at [55]. For other examples, see *Hirst v UK (No. 2)* (n21), which says at [82] 'The provision [denying the vote] imposes a blanket restriction on all convicted prisoners in prison', and *S and Marper v UK* No. 30562/04 (2008) (ECtHR (GC)), [119] and [125].

[178] *Dismissed Congressional Employees v Peru* Series C No. 158 (24 November 2006) (IACtHR).

[179] Ibid, [110].

[180] Also see *Baena-Ricardo v Panama* Series C No. 72 (2001) (IACtHR).

e. Other rule of law concerns

Sometimes, democratic procedures appear to undermine the requirements of the rule of law.[181] They may not be inappropriate decisions, but on such occasions the Tribunals rightly have reason to pay closer attention to the first-order reasoning in the case, and not to defer too much to states.

i. ECtHR

In Europe, such cases have arisen infrequently. The clearest example of the narrowing of the margin of appreciation on this basis can be seen in the case of *Zielinski and Pradal v France*.[182] In that case, a group of French nationals, born in and around the 1950s who worked for social security bodies, complained that they had not received wages due to them for work that they had done. The claims took over a decade to fight in the courts. They finally received judgment in their favour before the legislature passed a law determining a payment settlement. On appeal to the French *Cour de Cassation*, the state won on the basis that the new law should be followed. Before the ECtHR, the individuals claimed that the actions of the legislature in passing the new arrangements only after an adverse court decision interfered with their right to a fair trial. Whilst the margin of appreciation was not explicitly discussed in this case, it is clear from the following excerpt that, as a result of the potential impact of the legislature's actions on the principles of the rule of law, less deference was granted to the legislature than would ordinarily be the case:

The Court reaffirms that while in principle the legislature is not precluded in civil matters from adopting new retrospective provisions to regulate rights arising under existing laws, the principle of the rule of law and the notion of fair trial enshrined in Article 6 preclude any interference by the legislature – other than on compelling grounds of the general interest – with the administration of justice designed to influence the judicial determination of a dispute.[183]

ii. IACtHR

In the IACtHR, actions of democratic bodies appearing to impinge the rule of law have been given less deference. This can be seen in the case of *Baena-Ricardo v Panama*,[184] in which many public sector employees were dismissed, allegedly for involvement in a governmental coup attempt, but without any recourse to an appeal. A retroactive law was passed legalizing the dismissals, and whilst aspects of the law were held to be unconstitutional, there was no domestic recourse to

---

[181] For helpful accounts of what the rule of law requires, see J Raz, *The Authority of Law: Essays on Law and Morality* (Clarendon Press, Oxford 1979) ch11 and J Finnis, *Natural Law and Natural Rights* (Clarendon Press, Oxford 1980) 270–3.

[182] *Zielinski and Pradal v France* Nos 24846/94; 34165/96–34173/96 (1999) (ECtHR (GC)).

[183] Ibid, [57].

[184] *Baena-Ricardo v Panama* (n180).

reinstatement or compensation. In this case, the IACtHR noted that the state has appropriate discretion to handle public services.[185] However, there was little scope for deference to this discretion in the present case. The decisions were justified only retroactively and on the basis of very shaky reasoning. In this context, the Court explained its exacting scrutiny of the case as follows: 'In sum, under the rule of law, the principles of legality and non-retroactivity govern the actions of all bodies of the State in their respective fields of competence.'[186]

7. Conclusion

This chapter has argued that the practice of judicial deference on the basis of democratic legitimacy contributes to general theories that justify the judicial review of democratic action. The chapter has also argued that giving a margin of appreciation on this basis results in the Tribunals contributing to theories of democratic governance in international law. The remaining sections of the chapter expounded the relevant case law of the Tribunals that supports these arguments.

The first of these arguments was that the practice of judicial deference on the basis of democratic legitimacy mediates between the main theoretical debates about the nature of judicial review. In the case law of the Tribunals, it can be seen that each of these theories provides important considerations for the Tribunals depending on the context. Where Waldron's theory eloquently articulates the importance of participation in the formation of rights, instead of moving from this position to criticize judicial review, it is more appropriate to argue that the value of participation provides a reason to strengthen grounds for deference to state entities. Where Ely's theory justifies the review of democratic action only where it bolsters participation itself, it is much more convincing to argue instead that where process rights are at stake, there should be stricter scrutiny, as is reflected in the practice of the Tribunals. Where Dworkin's approach justifies judicial review in order to overcome substantive injustice, rather than argue that the problems with judicial review outlined by Waldron are overridden, it would be better to argue instead that where there is substantive injustice (for example if state action is disproportionate), then reasons for deference have less impact on the deliberative process because the first-order reasons against the state will be stronger.[187] The practice of judicial deference is thus able to employ the best aspects of the theoretical debate about democracy and judicial review, and to rearticulate them so that each of them can be considered in appropriate cases.

This approach is reflected in the practice of the Tribunals. There is not a general reluctance by the Tribunals to assess democratically made decisions as a pure Waldronian theory might produce, nor is there a practice of judicial legislation pronouncing the Tribunals' approach on each question as a wholly Dworkinian tribunal might do. Rather the Tribunals weigh relevant factors. Reasons for

---

[185] Ibid, [131]. [186] Ibid, [107]. See also [108]–[109] and [172]–[173].
[187] See Chapter 7.

deference are strengthened in cases that involve democratic decision-making processes, and reasons for stricter scrutiny exist in cases in which the democratic
pedigree of the state's decision is at stake.

The chapter has also argued that the sorts of reasons that the Tribunals use to
strengthen reasons for deference or to heighten scrutiny affect international discussions about theories of democracy. This can be seen in cases related to the
democratic rights of free speech and electoral participation, by cases that emphasize
the protection of minorities, the encouragement of societal debate and engagement
in decision-making, and the protection of the rule of law. The cases in these areas
show the various ways in which the Tribunals reveal their preferences about what
democratic governance requires.[188] In this way, the Tribunals are contributing to
the international development of democratic theory.

Democratic legitimacy is only one of the factors for a margin of appreciation.
The next chapter goes on to explore the way in which common practice amongst
states in a particular case affects arguments for a margin of appreciation.

---

[188] Another example is seen in *Tănase v Moldova* No. 7/08 (2010) (ECtHR (GC)), [168]–[170], in
which the Grand Chamber makes it clear that an electoral system might legitimately require loyalty to
the state, but not to a particular government.

5

Treaty Interpretation, Current State Practice, and Other International Law Influences on the Practice of Deference

1. Introduction

One of the more controversial aspects of the reasoning employed in the Tribunals is the role that the current practice of contracting states should have in the interpretation of the Treaties and in particular in relation to the margin of appreciation to be given to the state. It is argued in this chapter that current practice is and ought to be a relevant external factor for a margin of appreciation. When the scope and meaning of a human rights treaty standard is unclear, the intention of the contracting states as evidenced by their current practice is relevant to defining the legal standard. This argument draws on discussions that international agreements derive their legality from the agreement of states (section 2 of this chapter) and discussions about treaty interpretation (section 3), in particular Article 31 of the Vienna Convention on the Law of Treaties (VCLT) and the special nature of human rights treaty interpretation.

Section 4 addresses the views of the main sceptics. Section 5 discusses the extent to which the Tribunals rely on such reasoning in practice and expounds the criteria that influence the operation of this external factor for deference.

Section 6 goes on to discuss whether the Tribunals should consider reasons for deference to the actions of other international tribunals, norms, institutions, or organizations. There are a number of recent cases that raise this relatively new area of concern, and the law is somewhat undeveloped. Where the arguments and decisions of such international actors provide reasons for deference, this impacts the margin of appreciation accorded to states.

2. State consent and the legality of international agreements

The main reason why a margin of appreciation on the basis of the current practice of states is justifiable (either where there is a common trend or narrowing the margin where there is a lack of consensus) is based on the importance of the state in the formation of international obligations. The relationship between the role of state consent and international tribunals generally is discussed in this section, and it is argued that tribunals balance their role in setting international standards with upholding the intention of states. In the context of the Tribunals, this balance is reflected well by the impact of the current practice of states on the margin of appreciation given to states.

The sovereign equality of states is one of the fundamental principles governing international relations.[1] In this society of legal equals, authoritative norms are established primarily through the consensus of states. One important source of legal norms is the consent of states recorded in a multilateral treaty. Another source of international legal obligations is customary international law, which Finnis describes as 'a substitute for unanimity under conditions which require a substantial degree of unanimity'.[2] Human rights in international law, although protected by customary international law,[3] are protected principally through treaties. As founding members of the treaty, the states themselves have influenced the wording of the text. All signatory states determine as a matter of volition that it is in their interests to sign up to the treaty rather than to stay out of it.[4] States can amend these obligations, exit the treaty regime as individuals,[5] or collectively dissolve the treaty system and replace it or live without it. The willingness of states to be bound is a prerequisite of the system's existence.

The role of consent in the international legal system gives rise to some theoretical problems. When consensus is used as an argument by a tribunal to weaken reasons for deference, this undermines the ongoing consent of the state that disputes the legal position. This problem captures in an unorthodox setting the dilemma of using consent as a source of international law. The debate and literature surrounding this problem is vast.[6] Martti Koskenniemi's writing in *From Apology to Utopia*[7] brilliantly encapsulates the difficulties of consent within theories of international law. Grossly simplified, he argues that whilst international norms are supposed to be derived from state consent, this leads to apologism on the basis that the law is not really a constraining force on the actions of states, but rather a means of legitimizing what states do. Whenever lawyers try to show that international law is a meaningful constraint on state behaviour despite state consent, then they are open to the charge of utopianism—the states are constrained by natural law or simply the views of the writer or the court in question. One tactic often used by theoreticians to explain

[1] A Cassese, *International Law* (2nd edn, OUP, Oxford 2005) ch 3.2. See also I Brownlie, *Principles of Public International Law* (6th edn, OUP, Oxford 2003) 287: 'The sovereignty and equality of states represent the basic constitutional doctrine of the law of nations.'

[2] J Finnis, *Natural Law and Natural Rights* (Clarendon Press, Oxford 1980) 238.

[3] One oft-cited recognition of the customary international law of human rights is found in American Law Institute, *Restatement of the Law, the Third, the Foreign Relations Law of the United States* (American Law Institute Publishers, St Paul, Minn 1987) vol 2, 161, [702].

[4] AV Lowe, *International Law* (Clarendon Press, Oxford 2007) 19–20.

[5] As Peru did from the American Convention on Human Rights (ACHR) from 1999 to 2001.

[6] See, e.g., the extensive footnotes to 'The Sources of International Law' in D Kennedy, *International Legal Structures* (Nomos, Baden-Baden 1987) ch 1.

[7] M Koskenniemi, *From Apology to Utopia: The Structure of International Legal Argument* (CUP, Cambridge 2005).

this sort of behaviour is tacit consent, which was used for example by the International Court of Justice (ICJ) in the *Anglo-Norwegian Fisheries* case[8] to explain that the UK's inactivity in responding to Norway's maritime delimitation amounted to acquiescence. Tacit consent, as Koskenniemi argues, is an incoherent means of constraining state activity: states do not consent to the disputed action, which is why they are disputing it.[9] Koskenniemi's argument elucidates a fundamental theoretical dilemma at the heart of international legal theory. Vaughan Lowe argues that nevertheless the account will not cause international law to grind to a halt.[10] Lowe argues that when states submit voluntarily to international tribunals, they submit also to the judges of these tribunals resolving any indeterminacy of the rules according to principles. But this view does not seem to give enough weight to the problematic fact that the principles on which judges rely in resolving the indeterminacies emanate from a system based on state consent.

Given the consent-based context within which they operate, international tribunals then have to cautiously navigate the need to resolve a dispute involving a state with the fact that the state may not in fact consent to the proposed resolution. In the case of a treaty system, this can sometimes be easier than a case involving customary international law because there is a text from which to work—a text that clearly stems from the consent of the relevant state. Nevertheless, the dispute involves interpretation of the text, and it may be that the interpretation is difficult and there is no clear idea of what the framers of the text intended for the meaning; at times, the text may have been purposefully vague or the result of compromise. It may be that a uniform international standard was intended, or it may have been that there was to be room for manoeuvre by states in the application of that standard. As Susan Marks argues in the context of international human rights tribunals ruling on derogations:

[I]f the organs are too demanding...they risk being dismissed as utopian.... If, on the other hand, they are too cautious, they expose themselves to a charge of apologism.... [I]t is commonly argued that this is to be resolved by maintaining a balance between the two competing interests.[11]

In exercising this balance from case to case in the context of human rights, the tribunals 'endow...the rather abstract and generally formulated provisions...with substance and shape'.[12] In this way, the international court is developing the obligations of sovereign nations. It is in this context that the margin of appreciation is so crucial. Merrills argues that:

---

[8] *Anglo-Norwegian Fisheries* (*UK v Norway*) 1951 ICJ Rep 116, 121 (ICJ), 121.

[9] Koskenniemi (n7) 325–33. An application of this discussion to treaty interpretation generally is at 333–45.

[10] AV Lowe, 'Book Review of *From Apology to Utopia: The Structure of International Legal Argument*' (1990) 17 Journal of Law and Society 384, 386.

[11] S Marks, 'Civil Liberties at the Margin: The UK Derogation and the European Court of Human Rights' (1995) 15 OJLS 69, 92.

[12] F Matscher, 'Methods of Interpretation of the Convention' in RSJ Macdonald, F Matscher, and H Petzold (eds) *The European System for the Protection of Human Rights* (Martinus Nijhoff, Dordrecht; London 1993) 63.

[T]he margin of appreciation is a way of recognising that the international protection of human rights and sovereign freedom of action are not contradictory but complementary. Where the one ends, the other begins. In helping the international judge to decide how and where the boundary is to be located, the concept of the margin of appreciation has a vital part to play.[13]

This extract captures something of the essence of deference in international human rights law: it is a practice that informs the limits of state sovereignty in human rights decision-making. As already discussed, the Tribunals are forums for the contestation of sovereignty in the field of human rights law.[14] Once a decision is made delimiting sovereignty in a new way, the reactions and responses of experts, public opinion, and governments can inform the way in which the Tribunals respond in future— revealing the complex dialogue over the values that form the rights in the Treaties.[15]

This section has argued that the nature of international agreements as emanations of state consent explains why current state practice remains such a pervasive influence in the interpretation of international obligations. The Tribunals have the task of balancing the views of states with the role of developing the international standards, which is reflected in doctrines of deference. The following section explores in greater detail how the nature of interpretation of human rights treaties informs this balance.

3. Treaty interpretation: Article 31 of the Vienna Convention on the Law of Treaties (VCLT) and the special status of human rights treaties

Much of this book relates to interpretation of the Treaties. This section addresses the general legal guidance to the interpretation of treaties found in the VCLT, linking previous discussions to it. The reason why it is raised here for the first time is that the practice of states is explicitly mentioned in Article 31(3)(b) VCLT as a factor relevant to the interpretation of treaties. This section argues that it is desirable, and that a correct understanding of what Article 31 requires, that the current practice of states be taken into account in deciding whether to give deference to the views of the respondent state.

The rules under Article 31 should not be applied dogmatically or mechanistically. Richard Gardiner explains this as follows:

---

[13] JG Merrills, *The Development of International Law by the European Court of Human Rights* (2nd edn, Manchester UP, Manchester 1993) 174–5.

[14] See Chapter 3.4.a for discussion of D Sarooshi, *International Organizations and their Exercise of Sovereign Powers* (OUP, Oxford 2005).

[15] See also Lowe (n10) 387 for a discussion of the way in which dialogue informs such fundamental values as *jus cogens* norms. For a commentary on the fascinating 'dialogue' between the German Constitutional Court and the ECtHR, see M Andenæs and E Bjorge, '*Preventive Detention No. 2 BvR 2365/09*' (2011) 105 (4) AJIL 768. See further *Cabrera García and Montiel Flores v Mexico* Series C No. 220 (2010) (IACtHR), [31]–[32] and [88], concurring opinion of Judge Ad Hoc Eduardo Ferrer MacGregor Poisot on the concept of 'jurisprudential dialogue' between national and Inter-American judges.

A key to understanding how to use the Vienna rules is grasping that the rules are not a step-by-step formula for producing an irrebuttable interpretation in every case. They do indicate what is to be taken into account . . . [16]

Each of the relevant elements of the Vienna rules are thus to be considered together.

Article 31(1) VCLT reads: 'A treaty shall be interpreted in good faith in accordance with the ordinary meaning to be given to the terms of the treaty in their context and in light of its object and purpose.' Where the ordinary meaning of the language of the treaty provides a clear answer, there is very rarely any scope for deference to the views of the states. Arguments of deference arise when the ordinary meaning of the language nevertheless remains ambiguous. It is clear here that the arguments about the object and purpose of human rights treaties and the role of the Tribunals discussed in Chapter 3 are of the utmost importance. It was argued there that the international systems for the protection of human rights complement, as subsidiary organs, the protection given in the first instance by the state systems. It is not the purpose of the Tribunals to harmonize the legal approaches to human rights protection across all states, but to provide guidance to states about when and how to exercise their discretion in the protection of human rights standards, and to intervene on behalf of individuals when the state fails to uphold these standards. It is for these reasons that the consent of states is relevant to the second-order reasoning of the Tribunals. Furthermore, Article 31(3)(b) also requires it.

Article 31(3)(b) states that there 'shall be taken into account, together with the context . . . any subsequent practice in the application of the treaty which establishes the agreement of the parties regarding its interpretation'. Article 31(3)(b) features explicitly in the reasoning of a number of cases in the European Court of Human Rights (ECtHR),[17] and there is frequent reliance on the provisions of Article 31 generally.[18] Given the expertise in public international law that the judges of the Tribunals tend to have, it is unsurprising that the practice of states is of relevance to the Tribunals in their interpretation of the Treaties. It appears that the most common way in which the practice of states impacts the decision-making of the Tribunals is by considering deference to states where there is a lack of consensus amongst states or the emergence of a common trend amongst states, as set out in section 5 of this chapter. A strict application of Article 31(3)(b) would not lead to the doctrine of deference on the basis of a lack of consensus, since it requires practice[19] that evinces the agreement of all states parties and it is clear that the Tribunals are persuaded to give deference where there is less pervasive agreement (or lack of consensus) than this. However, rather than applying this provision formulaically, Article 31(3)(b) shows the importance and relevance of state practice

---

[16] RK Gardiner, *Treaty Interpretation* (OUP, Oxford 2008) 9.

[17] For example, *Banković v Belgium* No. 52207/99 (2001) (ECtHR (GC)), [56], and *Loizidou v Turkey (Preliminary Objections)* No. 15318/89 (1995) (ECtHR (GC)), [73].

[18] *Saadi v UK* No. 13229/03 (2008) (ECtHR (GC)), [61]: 'In ascertaining the Convention meaning of [the relevant] phrase [in Article 5(1)], [the Court] will, as always, be guided by Articles 31 to 33 of the Vienna Convention on the Law of Treaties', referencing a number of other cases. See also *Roger Judge v Canada* CCPR/C/78/D/829/1998 (2003) (HRC), [10.4].

[19] Although not necessarily of all states: see Gardiner (n16) 239.

in the interpretation of treaty rights, because it 'constitutes objective evidence of the understanding of the parties as to the meaning of the treaty'[20] to be considered along with the object and purpose of the Treaties.

Why is deference to states on the basis of current state practice desirable? It is here that the special nature of human rights treaties becomes relevant. In ordinary treaties that contain reciprocal arrangements between states, the practice of states under Article 31(3)(b) can be employed as an interpretative tool to elucidate the meaning intended to be attributed to the obligations by the states. However, human rights treaties are different. As the ECtHR stated in *Ireland v UK*,[21] '(u)nlike international treaties of the classic kind, the Convention comprises more than mere reciprocal engagements between contracting States'. The Inter-American Court of Human Rights (IACtHR) went further in an Advisory Opinion, saying that:

Modern human rights treaties in general ... are not multilateral treaties of the traditional type. ... Their object and purpose is the protection of the basic rights of individual human beings. ... In concluding these human rights treaties, the States can be deemed to submit themselves to a legal order which they, for the common good, assume various obligations, not in relation to other States, but towards all individuals within their jurisdiction.[22]

The fact that human rights treaties do not merely represent reciprocal arrangements for the mutual benefit of states, but instead show submission by states to standards for the protection of all individuals, could be interpreted as meaning that there should not be any role for the Tribunals to consider the current practice of states in the interpretation of human rights norms. Such arguments are assessed in section 4 of this chapter. However, the special nature of human rights treaties instead means that any consideration of state practice should be towards the end of interpreting the content of these standards and not towards the end of upholding state consent. Whilst there is increased scope for the Tribunals to imbue the vague provisions of the Treaties with content without relying on state practice, it can nevertheless help in this task. Where states act intending to uphold their international human rights obligations, state practice can provide the Tribunals with guidance in situations of ambiguity about what the international standard should be and whether there should be scope for some differentiation by states in their implementation of the standard.

a. Original intent or 'evolutive' interpretation

Often, current state practice as an external factor for deference raises discussion about whether the Treaties should be subject to strict textual interpretation, sometimes referred to as 'original intent' interpretation, or instead an 'evolutive' or 'living tree' interpretation. Such debate is rich in the context of interpretation of the US Constitution in which there are vocal opponents on both sides. In

---

[20] [1966] 2 YILC 221, [15].
[21] *Ireland v UK* No. 5310/71 (1978) (ECtHR).
[22] *The Effect of Reservations on the Entry into Force of the American Convention on Human Rights (Arts 74 and 75)* Advisory Opinion OC-2/82 of 24 September 1982, Series A No. 2 (1982) (IACtHR), [29]. For a similar comment by the UN HRC, see General Comment 24(52), [17].

international human rights law, the matter is more or less decided by the fact that Article 31 VCLT makes clear that Treaties are not solidified as historic records of their drafter's intentions, but can change where there is evidence that signatory states have modified their approaches to the issues, and share a common interpretation of the requisite treaty standards.

The discussion is thus something of a non-debate in the context of international human rights law. The few early calls for originalism in the ECtHR, for example the dissenting opinion of Fitzmaurice in *Golder v UK*,[23] were not sustained once more flexible approaches to interpretation became widely accepted. Whilst Article 31 makes clear that a strict textual originalism will not be acceptable when interpreting international treaties, Article 32 makes it clear that the original intent of the drafters can remain relevant when an interpretation under Article 31 leaves the meaning obscure, ambiguous, or manifestly absurd or unreasonable. Article 32 explains that '[r]ecourse may be had to supplementary means of interpretation, including the preparatory work of the treaty and the circumstances of its conclusion'. This method of interpretation is secondary to ascertaining the states' current interpretations, but it remains of relevance. In the case of *Banković v Belgium*,[24] the ECtHR recalled that the *travaux préparatoires* of the European Convention on Human Rights (ECHR) can be used under Article 32, and applied this to the facts of the case, which raised the issue of whether the ECHR applied to actions of Belgium and other North Atlantic Treaty Organization (NATO) states when the relatives of those killed by NATO's bombing of a radio and television station during the Kosovo war brought a claim to the ECtHR. The applicants argued that the contracting states had brought their relatives 'within their jurisdiction'[25] by undertaking the bombing. The Court found that the *travaux préparatoires* confirmed the 'ordinary meaning' of the words as territorial jurisdiction,[26] and that any recognition of extraterritorial jurisdiction by the Court would be exceptional, and would have to fit within the 'effective control' test developed by the Court.[27] The use of the original intention of the founders by the Court here is not best regarded as an example of originalism, since it formed only part of the reasoning, confirming what was otherwise determined to be the purpose of the treaty.[28]

---

[23] *Golder v UK* No. 4451/70 (1975) (ECtHR).
[24] *Banković v Belgium* (n17).
[25] Article 1 ECHR.
[26] Article 31 VCLT. See *Banković v Belgium* (n17) [65]:

> the extracts from the *travaux préparatoires* detailed above constitute a clear indication of the intended meaning of Article 1 of the Convention which cannot be ignored. The Court would emphasise that it is not interpreting Article 1 'solely' in accordance with the *travaux préparatoires* or finding those *travaux* 'decisive'; rather this preparatory material constitutes clear confirmatory evidence of the ordinary meaning of Article 1 of the Convention as already identified by the Court.

[27] Ibid, [71].
[28] For a compelling alternative approach to this issue, see A Orakhelashvili, 'Restrictive Interpretations of Human Rights Treaties in the Recent Jurisprudence of the European Court of Human Rights' (2003) 14 EJIL 529, 536–51.

Since the case of *Tyrer v United Kingdom*[29] in 1978, the ECtHR has clearly not adhered to an original intent interpretational methodology and the other Tribunals have followed suit.[30] The debate instead has been directed towards the type of evolutive interpretation that the Tribunals undertake, whether or not current state practice has an appropriate part to play, or whether the Tribunals should simply direct themselves to what is the best moral reading of the Treaty text.[31] In the case of *Öcalan v Turkey*,[32] the ECtHR reaffirmed that current state practice can steer evolutive interpretation.[33] Nevertheless, critics have argued that there are alternative ways of construing the role of interpretation and deny that there is an appropriate role for consensus. These views are discussed in section 4 of this chapter.

b. Treaty provisions with autonomous meanings

Some cases raise the question of how to interpret aspects of the Treaties that have differing definitions between domestic systems. For example, if a state decides that a disciplinary procedure is not to be classified as a 'criminal charge', is this determinative of that matter for the purpose of applying criminal procedural rights in the Treaties? If there are diverse ways of dealing with the matter amongst states, does this provide grounds for deference to the state? In the case of *Engel v Netherlands*,[34] four conscripted soldiers complained that the discipline they faced violated provisions of fair trial rights (Article 6 ECHR). The state argued that military discipline did not come within the Article 6 concept of the determination of a 'criminal charge' and was therefore not applicable. Accepting the distinction

---

[29] *Tyrer v UK* No. 5856/72 (1978) (ECtHR), [31]:

> The Court must also recall that the Convention is a living instrument which, as the Commission rightly stressed, must be interpreted in the light of present-day conditions. In the case now before it the Court cannot but be influenced by the developments and commonly accepted standards in the penal policy of the member States of the Council of Europe in this field.

[30] For example, *Claude-Reyes v Chile* Series C No. 151 (2006) (IACtHR), separate opinion of Sergio García-Ramírez.

[31] G Letsas, *A Theory of Interpretation of the European Convention on Human Rights* (OUP, Oxford 2007) 74–9.

[32] *Öcalan v Turkey* No. 46221/99 (2005) (ECtHR (GC)).

[33] Ibid, [163]–[164], citing the following statement of the Chamber with approval:

> It is recalled that the Court accepted in *Soering* [*v UK* No. 14038/88 (1989) (ECtHR), [103]] that an established practice within the member States could give rise to an amendment of the Convention. Subsequent practice in national penal policy, in the form of a generalised abolition of capital punishment, could be taken as establishing the agreement of the Contracting States to abrogate the exception provided for under Article 2 § 1 and hence to remove a textual limit on the scope for evolutive interpretation of Article 3. However, Protocol No. 6, as a subsequent written agreement, shows that the intention of the Contracting Parties as recently as 1983 was to adopt the normal method of amendment of the text in order to introduce a new obligation to abolish capital punishment in time of peace and, what is more, to do so by an optional instrument allowing each State to choose the moment when to undertake such an engagement. In these conditions, notwithstanding the special character of the Convention . . . Article 3 cannot be interpreted as generally prohibiting the death penalty.

[34] *Engel v The Netherlands* No. 5100/71 (1976) (ECtHR).

between the two concepts of 'disciplinary matters' and 'criminal charges', the ECtHR proceeded to determine itself whether the matter should be classified as disciplinary or criminal.

It is hardly surprising that the ECtHR defers very little to the state on such matters.[35] In this sort of case, relating to legal procedure, the Tribunals themselves have expertise and this would reduce reasons for deference to the state.[36] But this does not mean that there are never grounds for deference on autonomous concepts to the state. In the more recent case of *Chassagnou v France*,[37] the question of what the ECHR meaning of 'association' was raised. France advanced two types of argument to say that Article 11 had not been violated, the first of which was that the organizations that farmers had to join were not in fact associations, but 'para-administrative' institutions.[38] Unsurprisingly, the Court gave such arguments short shrift, explaining that states cannot merely attach their own labels to squirm out of their treaty obligations.[39] It was for the ECtHR to ensure that it can assess whether ECHR standards apply to relevant cases, and thus to determine the extent of its jurisdiction. But this is not the end of the matter.[40] The second type of argument that the state advanced was that the protection of Article 11 applied only both if membership was compulsory and also there were negative consequences to such membership.[41] Here, the Court clearly considered arguments about deference.[42] This shows the limits of what have become known as 'autonomous concepts'. This case is a strong example that autonomous concepts do not, as some commentators have argued,[43] show that the Court's role is simply to select the appropriate human rights standards uninfluenced by state views. The Tribunals have to ensure that the state does not merely circumvent treaty protections by making an arbitrary

---

[35] See also in the ECtHR, *Frydlender v France* No. 30979/96 (2000) (ECtHR (GC)), [30]–[41], and *Ezeh and Connors v UK* Nos 39665/98, 40086/98 (2003) (ECtHR (GC)), which was a decision split eleven to six (with strong dissents siding with Lord Woolf's interpretation of Articles 5 and 6 ECHR, over the majority's). For examples from the UN HRC, see *De Montejo v Colombia* CCPR/C/ 15/D/64/1979 (1982) (HRC), [10.4]:

> It is true that the Spanish text of article 14 (5), which provides for the right to review, refers only to 'un. delito', while the English text refers to a 'crime' and the French text refers to 'une infraction'. Nevertheless the Committee is of the view that the sentence of imprisonment imposed on Mrs. Consuelo Salgar de Montejo, even though for an offence defined as "contravencion" in domestic law, is serious enough, in all the circumstances, to require a review by a higher tribunal as provided for in article 14 (5) of the Covenant.

See also *A v Australia* CCPR/C/59/D/560/1993 (1997) (HRC), in particular the concurring opinion of PN Bhagwati. See also *Serena and Rodriguez v Spain* CCPR/C/92/D/1351-1352/2005 (2008) (HRC), [9.3]. For further examples, see D McGoldrick, *The Human Rights Committee: Its Role in the Development of the International Covenant on Civil and Political Rights* (Clarendon Press, Oxford 1991) 159.

[36] See Chapter 6.5.a.
[37] *Chassagnou v France* Nos 25088/94, 28331/95, 28443/95 (1999) (ECtHR (GC)).
[38] Ibid, [98].
[39] Ibid, [100]. And indeed such arguments were contentious even within France: ibid, [99].
[40] As Letsas supposes: Letsas (n31) 46–8.
[41] *Chassagnou v France* (n37) [110].
[42] Ibid, [112]–[117].
[43] Letsas (n31) 79.

reclassification, but when determining the substance of the treaty obligations, the Tribunals will give deference to the state when there are appropriate grounds.

A similar, although arguably more ambitious, approach to standard-setting can be seen in the IACtHR's development of its 'conventionality control' doctrine. This judicial doctrine maintains that national judges are required to implement international human rights standards, whether encompassed in treaty or decisions of the IACtHR, even where this requires them to overturn domestic legislation to do so. It will be interesting to see the extent to which domestic judges will accept this doctrine. The development of this doctrine and detailed commentary on it can be found in the concurring opinion of Judge Ad Hoc Eduardo Ferrer MacGregor Poisot in *Cabrera García and Montiel Flores v Mexico*.[44]

It might be thought that the 'conventionality control' doctrine is supportive of the 'standard-unifying' approach to the role of the Tribunals discussed in Chapter 3. However, it is clear that this doctrine is likewise compatible with the margin of appreciation. The focus is on ensuring that where there are shared regional human rights standards, these should be widely implemented within domestic legal systems, resulting in a constitutional *'Ius Constitutionale Commune* in the Americas'* as Judge Ad Hoc Eduardo Ferrer MacGregor Poisot has described it.[45] Ultimately, this is likely to be a matter of how the state constitutional mechanisms respond to the doctrine. Nevertheless, any development of these common standards by the IACtHR 'should be . . . fully aware of the standards that will be constructed through the use of its jurisprudence, considering also the "national discretion" that nation-States have to interpret the Inter-American *corpus juris'*. Here, Judge Ad Hoc Eduardo Ferrer MacGregor Poisot refers to the margin of appreciation in a footnote,[46] thereby affirming the relevance and importance of this doctrine, alongside any development of the 'conventionality control' doctrine by the IACtHR.[47]

c. Summary

This section has argued that, in the international legal system, the current practice of states (or 'consensus') is a relevant external factor for a margin of appreciation to states. Where there is a common trend amongst states on the meaning of a human right in a particular context, then reasons for deference to alternative definitions are weakened, but where there is a lack of consensus, reasons in favour of deference are

---

[44] *Cabrera García and Montiel Flores v Mexico* (n15).

[45] Ibid, [85]–[88], concurring opinion of Judge Ad Hoc Eduardo Ferrer MacGregor Poisot.

[46] The publication referred to is J García Roca, *El Marge de Apreciación Nacional en la Interpretación del Convenio Europeo de Derechos Humanos: Soberanía e Integración* (Civitas, Madrid 2010).

[47] See C Binder, 'The Prohibition of Amnesties by the Inter-American Court of Human Rights' (2004) 12 German Law Journal 1203, 1216 (emphasis in original):

> . . . the need for an effective implementation of the Convention at the national level does not necessarily give the Inter-American Court the competence to determine *how* this is to be done. Rather, it would be up to the respective state to decide how best to comply with its obligations under the ACHR in accordance with the specificities of its domestic legal system.

strengthened. This is because greater consistent practice by states implies that the respondent state is closely aligned with what the contracting states regard as their obligations. Where there is ambiguity about the meaning of human rights treaty obligations and a diversity of practice amongst states, the Tribunals should be cautious in finding a violation of the treaty, since the international obligations themselves are derived from a treaty text to which all states have voluntarily submitted. Furthermore, Article 31 VCLT envisages that the current practice of states continues to be relevant in the interpretation of treaties.

4. Other approaches to the role of current state practice

This chapter has argued that current state practice is an important and valid factor for the courts to consider when interpreting human rights. It is a second-order reason or external factor for a margin of appreciation because it provides reasons to reach a determination on interpretation outside of the factual matrix of the dispute and the content of the right itself. This consensus can change over time. The consent-based source of the obligations in international law and Article 31 VCLT ensure that the practice of states continues to have relevance in the interpretation of the Treaties.

The Tribunals share this approach to current state practice, as seen in discussion of the relevant case law in section 5 of this chapter. However, this approach to consensus is not universally approved, and some scholars argue that to rely on it as a justification for a margin of appreciation is illegitimate. Eyal Benvenisti argues that consensus prevents the court from using its jurisdiction to decide the case, and results in a 'breach of duty by the international human rights organs'[48] and an unwelcome reliance on state sovereignty that he seems to claim is outmoded.[49] It is mistaken to claim that state consent, as a feature of international norm making, is outmoded. Whilst theories of sovereignty continue to become increasingly complex in an interdependent global world in which states transfer sovereign powers to international organizations, it is hyperbolic to claim that state consent is a relic of the past. And to claim that consensus is used as a means of denying jurisdiction is to misrepresent how consensus features as part of the reasoning of the Tribunals.

Benvenisti also claims that the role of consensus in the reasoning of the Tribunals is otiose and does not add anything; rather, it 'is but a convenient subterfuge for implementing the court's hidden principled decisions'.[50] The same sort of critique is made by George Letsas. He argues that instead of relying on detailed exposition of domestic legislation to provide evidence of a consensus, the ECtHR instead makes fleeting mention of consensus. Letsas argues, in the context of *Marckx v*

---

[48] E Benvenisti, 'Margin of Appreciation, Consensus, and Universal Standards' (1999) 31 International Law and Politics 843, 854.

[49] Ibid, 852: 'From a theoretical perspective, this doctrine can draw its justification only from nineteenth-century theories of State consent.'

[50] Ibid.

Belgium,[51] that 'such assertion was a mere addition to a chain of substantive reasoning'.[52] Letsas argues that this is a pattern of how the ECtHR has used consensus reasoning: it is mentioned as a means of bolstering reasoning that is otherwise substantive, or first-order reasoning. Letsas argues that the evolutionary interpretation seen in the case law is not in correspondence with current consensus, but towards moral truth.[53] Moreover, Letsas argues that consensus ought to have no place, for it 'smacks of moral relativism'.[54] It has been argued earlier in this book that such a view misunderstands the role of differential speciation of value in international human rights law, and the importance of allowing diversity where appropriate.[55] In addition, these critics do not accept the legitimate nature of the treaty systems as emanations of international law, and reflective of state consent to be bound. In this context, there is a proper place for deference to the consensus of states in the interpretation of ambiguous or vague textual provisions in the Treaties. Such deference does not necessarily lead to moral relativism, since there cannot be relativism where there is no norm requiring uniformity. And where uniformity is not required, there can be legitimate differentiation in the legal protection of universal values.

The main argument expounded by these authors against the use of consensus as a factor relates to the role of the Tribunals in treaty interpretation as the pursuit of moral truth. The argument can be summarized in the following stages:

(i) international human rights law treaties incorporate important moral values;

(ii) such values are necessarily vague, and thus require careful interpretation to flesh them out;

(iii) signatory states have transferred responsibility to the Tribunals to undertake this interpretation and to determine authoritatively how the Treaty standards should be developed; and

(iv) therefore, in this context, any reference to consensus is irrelevant, unless and in so far as it simply affirms the reasonableness of the correct moral stance.[56]

Whilst it is true that the Treaties incorporate moral values that are necessarily vague and require interpretation this argument is objectionable at stages (iii) and (iv). The problem with (iii) is that it does not explain how the Tribunals should develop standards—how should they determine moral truth? On Letsas' approach, the Tribunals should rely on a Dworkinian theory of 'law as integrity', and develop a coherent system of human rights protection based on moral principles. Where these principles are uncertain, the Tribunals ought to select the best possible answer. But this approach is not consonant with international legal reality, particularly where there is much controversy and disagreement. In other international law contexts, in

---

[51] *Marckx v Belgium* No. 6833/74 (1979) (ECtHR).   [52] Letsas (n31) 78.
[53] Ibid, 79, using *Dudgeon v UK* No. 7525/76 (1981) (ECtHR), [60], as an example, in which the Court referred to an increased tolerance of homosexual behaviour in the great majority of Council of Europe states, but also referred to it as a 'better' understanding.
[54] Letsas (n31) 75.   [55] See Chapter 3.2.   [56] See Letsas (n31) 79.

which there is no clear answer and in which it is not necessary for a tribunal to make a determination in the resolution of the dispute, the tendency is to say that states retain the sovereign freedom to resolve the problem as they see fit. Letsas thus either needs to modify the theory of law as integrity for the international context of interpretation of treaties,[57] for example by accepting that it will not be uncommon for there to be no international solution, or he needs to abandon his application of the law as integrity theory altogether.[58]

It has been argued in sections 2 and 3 of this chapter that the critics are mistaken in saying that the role of the Tribunals is to develop interpretations of the treaty toward moral truth and thus there is no role for consensus. However, notwithstanding that there is a role for considering the extent of consensus among states in the interpretation of the Treaties, it is also part of the role of the Tribunals, through careful interpretation of the Treaties, to develop the standards of rights protection. In resolving a dispute, the Tribunals have the opportunity to clarify states' human rights obligations. However, the Tribunals ought to exercise this opportunity cautiously. They have been entrusted by contracting states to interpret the Treaties, and they should take into account state practice in their interpretation. Furthermore, in making decisions where there are a number of morally good options, or even where there are conflicting outcomes and people differ in terms of morality, whose understanding of moral truth counts? The Tribunals would face a problem of legitimacy if they were to claim for themselves the status of philosopher kings with ultimate moral authority. Thus the Tribunals face an epistemological quandary about how to make judgments that have profound moral and legal implications. It is for this reason that, as well as exercising their own moral judgments, the courts do well to derive guidance from current state practice and, as argued in Chapter 4, to give deference to determinations made democratically. This approach furnishes substantive guidance about the content of moral norms, but also addresses the legitimacy problems raised by interpretations of the Treaties that result in new moral guidelines for signatory states. Where there is not sufficient clarity or impetus for the Tribunals to produce a uniform solution, then deference resulting in a diversity of state approaches may be the most appropriate outcome.

---

[57] Ibid, 35–6, where Letsas equates interpretation of the ECHR with the interpretation of municipal constitutional rights. His two-pronged argument—that (i) the nature of the ECHR is between individuals and their own states, and (ii) states regard ECHR judgments as like those of a constitutional supreme court—is unconvincing. States do not regard the Court has having full authority to determine every possible human rights question in accordance with its own view of moral truth. Indeed, this motivates arguments in favour of a margin of appreciation. States will and do respect interpretations of the Convention that appear to be both respectful of the signatory states' views and reasonable, but continue to advance their own instantiations before the Court; they do not simply resign themselves to the Court's judgments.

[58] For criticisms of the theory, see J Finnis, 'On Reason and Authority in *Law's Empire*' (1987) 6 Law and Philosophy 357, 370–5. From 375: 'A case is hard, in the sense which interests lawyers, when there is more than one right, i.e, not wrong, answer.'

5. Current state practice as an external factor affecting the margin of appreciation in practice

Current state practice operates in the deliberations of the Tribunals as an external factor, since the practice of the contracting states does not directly bear on the substance of the dispute. Instead, it operates as a reason to strengthen or heighten scrutiny of the arguments of the state. If there is a clear trend in the behaviour of other states against the respondent state's argument, then there is very little reason to accord strength to the views of the state. Likewise, if all states appear to agree with the respondent state, then there is reason to give greater weight to its arguments. As discussed in section 4 of this chapter, however, the nature of human rights treaties means that the intention of the states alone cannot be determinative of the matter. Instead, where current state practice shows the states grappling with their approaches to the human rights standard and producing a similar outcome, this becomes a factor for the Tribunals to consider. Similarly, if there is no consensus from state to state about how to implement the human rights standard, then this indicates that the states collectively do not consider there to be a single standard required by international law: ordinarily, such an *opinio juris* would go hand in hand with state practice. This gives strong cause for the Tribunals to give a margin of appreciation to the respondent state, since it appears that there ought to be discretion to states given in the implementation of that standard.

The role of current state practice has proven to be a significant factor in assessing the strength of reasons for a margin of appreciation. Consensus has affected the margin of appreciation in three main ways. First, there are cases in which, as a result of a lack of consensus, the Tribunals give greater deference to the state. Secondly, the Tribunals might heighten their scrutiny because there is a common trend amongst states that favours the applicant's case. Thirdly, state practice might clearly favour the state's position, and thus strengthen deference to the state. Case law exemplifying these different types of deference across the Tribunals is assessed in the following sections.

a. Lack of consensus increases deference

i. *European Court of Human Rights (ECtHR)*

The clearest reliance by the Tribunals on consensus as a factor for the margin of appreciation is seen in the ECtHR. The foundational case of *Handyside v UK*[59] employs the 'consensus' factor as an explanation for deferring to the national party's reasoning. After explaining that the Convention machinery of protection is subsidiary to national systems safeguarding of human rights, especially with regard to Article 10(2) ECHR (whether restrictions on freedom of speech were 'necessary in a democratic society . . . for the protection of . . . morals'), the judgment states that:

[59] *Handyside v UK* No. 5493/72 (1976) (ECtHR).

In particular, it is not possible to find in the domestic law of the various Contracting States a uniform European conception of morals. The view taken by their respective laws of the requirements of morals varies from time to time and from place to place, especially in our era which is characterised by a rapid and far-reaching evolution of opinions on the subject.[60]

The Court goes on to say that '*[c]onsequently*, Article 10(2) leaves to the Contracting States a margin of appreciation'.[61] The subsequent paragraph in the judgment shows the Court deciding that reasons in favour of deference strengthened in this case by the lack of consensus on morality need nevertheless to be weighed against other relevant factors. The national margin of appreciation respects sovereign freedom to define human rights issues, especially where there is no consensus, but this deference is limited by the supervision of the ECtHR.[62]

The ECtHR has explained that where there are diverse legal approaches to a particular moral question, then this can indicate that there is no international standard possible. In *Vo v France*,[63] in which a coil-removal procedure was negligently conducted on a pregnant woman leading to a loss of the foetus, the case involved the question of whether there was a right to life of the unborn child so as to require criminal action against the doctor. Noting the diversity of views in the state, the ECtHR cited the following opinion of the Commission with approval: 'It is not only legally difficult to seek harmonization of national laws at Community level, but because of lack of consensus, it would be inappropriate to impose one exclusive moral code.'[64] Given the lack of European consensus,[65] the Court was 'convinced that it is neither desirable, nor even possible as matters stand, to answer in the abstract the question whether the unborn child is a person for the purposes of Article 2 of the Convention', and thus found the matter to be within France's margin of appreciation.[66] The formulation that such a finding would not even be possible reveals the strength of the impact of consensus on the reasoning of the ECtHR.[67]

The following series of cases show both the way in which deference to the state is increased where there is a lack of consensus, but also that this lack of consensus will not always be determinative. In *Cossey*,[68] the ECtHR found that a transsexual's rights were not violated by the UK's policy not to alter the birth certificate to read female instead of male (the Article 8 ECHR claim), nor to alter its marriage laws to

[60] Ibid, [48].   [61] Ibid (emphasis added).

[62] 'The domestic margin of appreciation thus goes hand in hand with a European supervision': ibid, [49].

[63] *Vo v France* No. 53924/00 (2004) (ECtHR (GC)).

[64] Ibid, [82].   [65] Ibid, [84].   [66] Ibid, [85].

[67] For another example of deference on the basis of the lack of consensus, see *Evans v UK* No. 6339/05 (2007) (ECtHR (GC)), [77] ('Where, however, there is no consensus within the Member States of the Council of Europe, either as to the relative importance of the interest at stake or as to the best means of protecting it, particularly where the case raises sensitive moral or ethical issues, the margin will be wider'), and [79] and [81]–[82] regarding the lack of European consensus as to when gamete providers' consent becomes irrevocable. See also *Pye (Oxford) Ltd v UK* No. 44302/02 (ECtHR (GC)), [71]–[72] and [74] (the way in which contracting states regulate laws on adverse possession varies, widening the margin of appreciation).

[68] *Cossey v UK* No. 10843/84 (1990) (ECtHR).

enable the applicant to marry a man notwithstanding this fact (the Article 12 claim). The ECtHR held that, on both counts, these were still, 'having regard to the existence of little common ground between the Contracting States, an area in which they enjoy a wide margin of appreciation'. The Court did acknowledge that some states had made changes to their laws,[69] but this was far from forming a new consensus, and consequently 'it cannot at present be said that a departure from the Court's earlier decision[70] is warranted in order to ensure that the interpretation . . . on the point at issue remains in line with present day conditions'.[71]

In the later case of *Sheffield and Horsham v UK*,[72] which involved the same issue, the ECtHR affirmed its approach in *Cossey*, but mentioned that the UK should have reviewed its legislation and urged it to do so before further cases arose. This hinted towards the idea that, notwithstanding the lack of consensus in the applicant's favour, there might be cause to find against the UK on the basis that it had not properly considered whether current societal conditions required the prohibition of altering birth certificates.[73] The issue was raised again in the case of *Christine Goodwin v UK*,[74] which involved a post-operative transsexual applicant (male to female) claiming a number of grievances, such as harassment at work and embarrassment when undertaking insurance policies, as a result of being unable to change the details on her birth certificate. Referring to its previous findings on this question, the ECtHR said that whilst there was no doctrine of precedent, it was preferable to maintain consistency. However, the Court was also minded to consider 'the changing conditions within the respondent State and within Contracting States generally and respond, for example, to any evolving convergence as to the standards to be achieved'.[75] The Court recalled the finding in *Sheffield and Horsham* that there was an emerging consensus within Europe to provide legal recognition following gender reassignment,[76] but that the consensus was not clear enough for the case to fall outside of the state's margin of appreciation. Liberty, a third-party intervener, provided additional information in *Christine Goodwin* to show that, whilst the situation in Europe had not changed since the case of *Sheffield and Horsham*, there was continuing evidence of a global trend towards the legal recognition of transsexuals, in particular citing cases from Canada, South Africa, Israel, Australia, New Zealand, and all except two US states. The ECtHR took this evidence into account, not placing emphasis on European consensus (which it recognized had not really changed), but being influenced by the growing international trend towards legal recognition of gender reassignment, particularly the approaches taken in Australia and New Zealand.[77]

---

[69] See ibid, [40], for Article 8, and [46] for Article 12.
[70] Referring to *Rees v UK* No. 9532/81 (1986) (ECtHR).
[71] *Cossey v UK* (n68) [40]. This refers to Article 8; see [46] for Article 12.
[72] *Sheffield and Horsham v UK* No. 22885/93, 23390/94 (1998) (ECtHR).
[73] Ibid, [60].   [74] *Christine Goodwin v UK* No. 28957/95 (ECtHR (GC)).
[75] Ibid, [74].   [76] Ibid, [84], citing *Sheffield and Horsham v UK* (n72) [35].
[77] *Christine Goodwin v UK* (n74) [84]–[85].

At first glance, it appears as if the Grand Chamber is limiting the margin of appreciation of the UK on the basis of actions by non-signatory states. Consensus as a factor for deference is indicative of the appropriate interpretation of a text between signatory states only, and this is the normal practice in the ECtHR: see *Bayatyan v Armenia*,[78] for example, which made reference to a wide variety of international instruments and decisions, but appeared to be influenced only by the practice of Council of Europe states when considering how much deference to give to the state.[79]

It is arguable that international trends ought to affect the European Convention if they are indicative of the emergence of a customary international norm. But this cannot be the case in *Christine Goodwin v UK*: the handful of states discussed can hardly be representative of the international community of states. Instead, they share in common the fact that they are liberal democracies.

It appears, instead, that the emphasis of the reasoning by the Grand Chamber in *Christine Goodwin* was not in fact based on consensus. Indeed, the Court explicitly said that there was no evidence of a European consensus,[80] and instead placed emphasis on the clear and uncontested 'growing international trend', not any international consensus. The basis of the reasoning consequently appears to be that the international trend undermined the rationale of the UK's argument that there would be systematic difficulties in changing the system to assess gender other than at the time of birth, especially since Australia and New Zealand's legal systems were so similar to that of UK, leading the Court to find instead that the impact on the applicant was unacceptably severe.

These cases show that whilst the lack of consensus is a factor that the Tribunals use to strengthen deference to states, this deference is not determinative and other factors may instead result in a finding against the state.[81] As with all second-order

---

[78] *Bayatyan v Armenia* No. 23459/03 (2011) (ECtHR (GC)).

[79] Ibid, [123], which expressly mentions the impact on the margin of appreciation that a near consensus amongst member states brings: it means that Armenia 'enjoys only a limited margin of appreciation and must advance convincing and compelling reasons to justify any interference'.

[80] Ibid, [85]: 'the lack of such a common approach among forty-three Contracting States with widely diverse legal systems and traditions is hardly surprising.'

[81] Another example can be seen in the case of *Dickson v UK* No. 44362/04 (2007) (ECtHR (GC)), in which the ECtHR found the UK in violation of Article 8 ECHR (private and family life) for its refusal to allow a prisoner and his wife to access artificial insemination treatment—notwithstanding the Court's recognition of a wide margin of appreciation where there is no European consensus, it would not be all-embracing where the government did not take sufficient steps to assess the individualized impact on the applicants: ibid, [78]–[79], [82] and [85]. See also *T v UK* No. 24724/94 (1999) (ECtHR (GC)), in which the Court assessed the compatibility of the trial of the accused in the Bulger case, in which a young boy was violently murdered. The trial attracted widespread public attention, and the accused complained that they had suffered violations of Articles 3 and 6(1) because of their young age and the fact that the trial was so public, accusatory, and used adult and formal procedures, etc. In Lord Reed's concurring opinion, he emphasized the state's margin of appreciation on the Article 6 matters, on the basis that 'there is a wide variation in the ways in which different member States organise their systems of criminal justice so as to protect the interests of the individual child and the wider public interest'. Nevertheless, he went on to agree with the majority that there was a violation of Article 6 in the particular circumstances of the case because, despite the efforts of the judge to ameliorate the trial conditions to make them suitable for an 11-year-old, the formality of the proceedings and the imposing glare of the media rendered the trial unfair.

reasoning, it is one of the factors to be considered along with all other relevant factors in the case.

ii. United Nations Human Rights Committee (UN HRC)

In the context of the UN HRC, the case of *Larrañaga v Philippines*[82] involves consideration of similar reliance on the practice of other signatory states. In this case, in which a number of violations of the Covenant were found in a death row trial, Committee Member Ruth Wedgewood's dissenting opinion is critical of the approach of the majority and relies on state practice to support her argument.

In effect, Wedgewood argued that since so many states undertake similar practices to the Philippines, in which judges ask leading questions during a trial, there should not be a violation on these issues. In reaching this conclusion, Wedgewood was of the view that greater deference should have been shown to the Philippines on the basis of a lack of consensus amongst signatory states of the Covenant. The majority did not appear even to consider the issue, which is unfortunate.

iii. Inter-American Court of Human Rights (IACtHR)

In the case of *Castañeda Gutman v México*,[83] the IACtHR discussed the wide and varying approaches of states in the region to the arrangement of voting systems for a country's presidency. The Court gave examples from a variety of different states in a footnote,[84] and went on to argue that it was not possible to make a determination as to which types of electoral system—those that allowed independent candidacies or those that required a political party—were more or less restrictive than the others.[85]

Although not expressed in these terms, it was implicit in the reasoning of the Court that the level of diversity amongst the states was a factor that weighed in favour of allowing a margin of appreciation to the state in the organization of its electoral system.[86]

b. Current state practice in the applicant's favour heightens scrutiny

Where there is consensus by the contracting states in the applicant's favour against the respondent state, then this heightens the Tribunals' scrutiny of the state's arguments.

---

[82] *Larrañaga v Philippines* CCPR/C/87/D/1421/2005 (2006) (HRC).
[83] *Castañeda Gutman v México* Series C No. 184 (2008) (IACtHR).
[84] Ibid, [199], fn 66.   [85] Ibid, [200].
[86] See Chapter 4.6.a.i.

i. ECtHR

In the case of *Sørensen and Rasmussen v Denmark*,[87] the applicants complained about the 'closed shop' agreements connected with their recent employment, which required them to subscribe to only one choice of trade union, with the political views of which the applicants took issue. The agreements were lawful in Denmark, but breached the European Social Charter. Whilst the ECHR does not specify a negative freedom of association in Article 11, the ECtHR examined the changing consensus of contracting states, finding that:

[A] trend . . . has emerged in the Contracting Parties, namely that such agreements are not an essential means for securing the interests of trade unions and their members and that due weight must be given to the right of individuals to join a union of their own choosing without fear of prejudice to their livelihood. In fact, only a very limited number of Contracting States including Denmark and Iceland continue to permit the conclusion of closed-shop agreements.[88]

The Court went on to find, taking into account all relevant factors,[89] that the state's allowance of closed-shop agreements was not compatible with Article 11. One of the relevant factors in the case was clearly the lack of European consensus upholding closed-shop agreements, and indeed the emergence of an opposite consensus.[90]

ii. IACtHR

The same sort of deference is seen in the IACtHR. In *Claude-Reyes v Chile*,[91] the applicant requested information from the government about how it decided to grant concessions and contracts to foreign investment companies, which was refused. The IACtHR made clear reference to the consensus of signatory states as follows: '[I]t is important to emphasize that there is a regional consensus among the States that are members of the Organization of American States . . . about the importance of access to public information and the need to protect it'.[92]

The Court was clearly influenced by the consensus of the signatory states here and found that Chile had violated Article 13 of the American Convention on Human Rights (ACHR) (freedom of thought and expression—including the right to seek and receive information). In addition, the Court mentioned separately consensus amongst non-signatory states.[93] This reference to non-signatory states appears to highlight the fact that, globally, transparency and access to information are regarded as common requirements of the legitimacy of state conduct. The reference to such non-signatory values does not, though, appear to influence the IACtHR's reasoning in the same way as the regional consensus.

---

[87] *Sørensen and Rasmussen v Denmark* Nos 52562/99, 52620/99 (2005) (ECtHR (GC)).
[88] Ibid, [70].   [89] Ibid, [75]–[76].
[90] See also *Tănase v Moldova* No. 7/08 (2010) (ECtHR (GC)), [87]–[93] and [172].
[91] *Claude-Reyes v Chile* (n30).   [92] Ibid, [78].
[93] Ibid, [82]: 'The Court also finds it particularly relevant that, at the global level, many countries have adopted laws designed to protect and regulate the right to accede to State-held information.'

iii. UN HRC

The UN HRC similarly recognizes this form of deference. In the case of *Yoon and Choi v Republic of Korea*,[94] the HRC was asked to consider communications from two Jehovah's Witnesses, who were punished for their failure to undertake military service, despite their religious objections. The state here argued that its particular national security requirements prevented it from developing a conscientious objector exception to military service, and that it would damage national cohesion. Notwithstanding these factors, which would tend to strengthen deference, the Committee considered the approach of other nations, which had retained compulsory military service (since many have abandoned the practice):

> The Committee also notes, in relation to relevant State practice, that an increasing number of those States parties to the Covenant which have retained compulsory military service have introduced alternatives to compulsory military service, and considers that the State party has failed to show what special disadvantage would be involved for it if the rights of the authors under article 18 would be fully respected.[95]

This case is interesting because it showed the HRC appearing to heighten scrutiny on the basis that the current practice of contracting states favoured exceptions for compulsory military service for conscientious objection. It is apt to note that the decision was not unanimous,[96] and that, on matters of deference, it is not unusual to find differences of opinion. Committee Member Ruth Wedgewood submitted a separate opinion, arguing that whilst the practice was harsh and there had been growing international calls for exceptions to be made for conscientious objectors, this had not reached a level at which it could be said that the meaning of Article 18 of the International Covenant on Civil and Political Rights (ICCPR) had to be interpreted differently.[97] Nevertheless, even in the dissenting opinion, the argument is about the extent of consensus, not whether consensus has relevance to the decision at all.[98]

---

[94] *Yoon and Choi v Republic of Korea* CCPR/C/88/D/1321-1322/2004 (2007) (HRC).

[95] Ibid, [8.4].

[96] The reasoning has been unanimously accepted in later cases: see *Min-Kyu Jeong and others v Republic of Korea* CCPR/C/101/D/1642-1741/2007 (2011) (HRC).

[97] *Yoon and Choi v Republic of Korea* (n94), Ruth Wedgewood's dissenting opinion. The following extract shows her disagreement starkly:

> The practice of States parties may also be relevant, whether at the time the Covenant was concluded or even now. But we do not have any record information before us, most particularly, in regard to the number of parties to the Covenant that still rely upon military conscription without providing de jure for a right to conscientious objection.

[98] For another HRC case heightening scrutiny on the basis of state consensus, see *Roger Judge v Canada* (n18), in which the Committee, finding Canada in violation of Article 6 ICCPR (the right to life) for extraditing a convict to Pennsylvania to face the death penalty, was influenced to interpret Article 6(2) narrowly because of the 'broadening international consensus in favour of abolition of the death penalty, and in states which have retained the death penalty, a broadening consensus not to carry it out': ibid, [10.3].

iv. Summary

This section has shown that where there is an international consensus against the state, this provides grounds for heightened scrutiny of the state's conduct. It is, of course, possible for the Tribunals to find in the state's favour notwithstanding an ostensible consensus that goes against it. A fascinating example of this is seen in the case of *Odièvre v France*,[99] in which the ECtHR assessed France's wide policy of maternal anonymity when a child sought to trace his or her mother's identity, but was unable to do so without his or her mother's consent. The Court accepted that the consensus of European states was largely against the French approach,[100] but found also that this consensus was not uniform: there were some states that did not impose a duty on natural parents to disclose their identities, and thus the majority of the Court on this basis found that there was some margin of appreciation. In this context, the majority found in favour of France, notwithstanding that the French approach was an isolated minority within Europe. This is borne out more clearly by the dissenting judgment, which notes in greater detail that no country in Europe has quite the same protection for mothers as France, and that those few countries that do allow discreet births have very different levels of protection for mothers compared with the child's right to know.[101] The clear differences in approach to consensus here show the Court arguing about the nub of the argument. The fact that the majority found some diversity appears to be used by the Court to bolster its position. The dissenting opinion exposes the logic of the majority, and argues for the opposite approach. This is a good example of transparent second-order reasoning.

The majority could have explained their reasons more boldly. One way in which they might have done this would be by accepting that there appeared to be a growing consensus against the approach taken by France. They could then have explained that nevertheless, on the basis of the wide and deep debate within France about how to resolve these societal issues and its connection with such matters as an attempt to reduce the number of abortions (and thus deference on the basis of democratic legitimacy), the French state was justified in its approach.

---

[99] *Odièvre v France* No. 42326/98 (2003) (ECtHR (GC)).

[100] Ibid, [47]:

> The Court observes that most of the Contracting States do not have legislation that is comparable to that applicable in France, at least as regards the child's permanent inability to establish parental ties with the natural mother if she continues to keep her identity secret from the child she has brought into the world.

[101] Ibid, [12]–[14]; at [16], the dissenting opinion of Judges Wildhaber, Sir Nicholas Bratza, Bonello, Loucaides, Cabral Barreto, Tulkens, and Pellonpää includes the following:

> [T]he majority have stood the argument concerning the European consensus on its head and rendered it meaningless. Instead of permitting the rights guaranteed by the Convention to evolve, taking accepted practice in the vast majority of countries as the starting-point, a consensual interpretation by reference to the virtually isolated practice of one country (see paragraph 47 of the judgment) is used to justify a restriction on those rights.

As the Grand Chamber put it in *SH v Austria*[102] was another case in which the Court found an emerging European consensus in favour of the applicant (allowing in vitro fertilization (IVF) treatment involving donors), but nevertheless such consensus did not decisively narrow the margin of appreciation to the state.

Whilst there is, of course, scope for other cases that do not narrow the margin of appreciation definitively against the state where international consensus is also against them, it is not likely to be a common occurrence.[103] Instead, it is more likely that there will be heightened scrutiny, and greater numbers of findings of violations against the respondent state.

c. Current state practice in the state's favour increases deference

There are a number of cases in which the consensus of states affirms the approach taken by the respondent state.

i. ECtHR

In *Pretto v Italy*,[104] the ECtHR, rather than adopting a literal interpretation of the phrase 'public pronouncement' in Article 6 ECHR, instead drew on the fact that 'many Member States of the Council of Europe have a long-standing tradition of recourse to other means, besides reading out aloud, for making public the decisions of all or some of their courts'[105] to decide that other means may on occasion be compatible with the Convention, such as deposit in a registry accessible to the public. Here, it is clear that the consensus favours Italy, and the Court does not find a violation of Article 6.[106]

---

[102]   *SH and others v Austria* No. 57813/00 (2011) (ECtHR (GC)), [96]. It should be noted that the handling of the 'consensus' factor was not without controversy in this case. The separate opinion of Judge De Gaetano regarded such a factor as a distraction that 'deflects attention' from the issue of whether a 'particular act or omission or limitation enhances or detracts from human dignity': ibid, [4]. The dissenting opinion of Judges Tulkens, Hirvelä, Lazarova Trajkovska, and Tsortsoria was vehemently opposed to the fact that the Grand Chamber recognized a consensus, but did not give it the weight that these judges felt that it should have. However, the judges went further than this and suggested that because the consensus was not determinative, this had led to legal uncertainty: see ibid, [6]–[8]. This complaint is overstated. There are certainly other cases in which there has been evidence of an emerging or extant consensus that has not been 'determinative' and therefore such a situation is not 'unprecedented' (see [8]) as the dissenting opinion states. It is noteworthy, though, that these judges make reference to one of the Court's tasks being to harmonize rights across Europe. For further discussion on this point, see Chapter 3.3.

[103]   The partly dissenting opinion in *A, B and C v Ireland* No. 25579/05 (2010) (ECtHR (GC)), [6] (emphasis added), in a context in which the majority found a consensus existed against the state in relation to laws allowing abortion: 'We believe that this will be one of the *rare times* in the Court's case-law that Strasbourg considers that such consensus does not narrow the broad margin of appreciation of the State concerned.'

[104]   *Pretto v Italy* No. 7984/77 (1983) (ECtHR).

[105]   Ibid, [26].

[106]   An assessment of state practice similarly supported the approach of the respondent state in *Palomo Sánchez and others v Spain* No. 28955/06 (2011) (ECtHR (GC)). The Grand Chamber stated, at [75], that the homogeneity of European legal systems, as to the broad discretion that employers were granted to determine accusations against an employee, was a relevant factor to consider.

In *Maaouia v France*,[107] the ECtHR decided that Article 6 ECHR did not even apply to the case on the basis that the contracting states, on a proper interpretation, never intended that it should. The case involved a Tunisian man, married to a Frenchwoman, who after being convicted of criminal offences was subject to a deportation order and an exclusion order. He was able to get his deportation order quashed, but it took him four years to get the exclusion order rescinded, and he claimed that this was an unreasonable time contrary to Article 6. In finding that Article 6 did not apply, the Court drew on the intention and understanding of the states. The majority based its reasoning on two main matters: first, that the Commission had never found expulsion orders or the like to be a 'civil right or obligation' or a criminal matter, and thus within the scope of Article 6(1); and secondly, that the states, in implementing Article 1, Protocol 7, ECHR (which granted procedural guarantees to lawfully resident aliens subject to an exclusion order), implied that Article 6(1) guarantees did not apply in this sort of case. The majority thus, on the latter ground, had reason to defer to France on the basis of a consensus in its favour. Nevertheless, this was controversial and the dissenting judges (Judge Loucaides, joined by Judge Traja) disputed both grounds of reasoning. They disputed the first on the basis that, without scrutiny of the rationale of the Commission, relying on their finding was unconvincing and that instead the meaning of 'civil' obligations ought to be construed widely as 'non-criminal'. On the second, they disputed the rationale that the adoption of Article 7, Protocol 7, could have any meaning for the interpretation of Article 6(1), because: (i) protocols exist to add to Convention rights, not to restrict or abolish them; (ii) the Article gives additional administrative procedural guarantees to those being expelled, and does not affect judicial guarantees; and (iii) the explanatory report saying that the Article does not disturb the Commission's interpretation of Article 6 as excluding cases such as this cannot amount to an endorsement of that interpretation or prevent the Court's development of the jurisprudence. In the view of the dissenting judges, then, there was no evidence of a consensus on which to defer to France. Instead, the Court ought to have interpreted the convention broadly in favour of the applicant, perhaps assisted by the fact that judicial guarantees come within the expertise of the Court.[108] The case interestingly shows the majority basing their reasoning on the consensus of the states on the meaning of Article 6(1) to the extent of finding that the Article was not even applicable to the facts of the case.

ii. UN HRC

In the UN HRC, there are a number of cases in which the Committee gives a margin of appreciation to the respondent state on the basis of a clear consensus among signatory states. In *Joslin v New Zealand*,[109] the communicant sought recognition of gay marriage under the Covenant. The HRC, finding for the state, found the following support: 'The universal consensus of State practice supports

---

[107] *Maaouia v France* No. 39652/98 (2000) (ECtHR (GC)).
[108] Chapter 6.5.   [109] *Joslin v New Zealand* CCPR/C/75/D/902/1999 (2002) (HRC).

this view: no States parties provide for homosexual marriage; nor has any State understood the Covenant to so require and accordingly entered a reservation.'[110]

Similarly, in *Love v Australia*,[111] the HRC found that there had been no violation of Article 26 ICCPR (equal treatment) where an air pilot was compulsorily retired at the age of 60. In making this finding, 'the Committee [took] into account the widespread national and international practice, at the time of the author's dismissals, of imposing a mandatory retirement age of 60'.[112]

iii. Summary

The practice of the Tribunals shows that a margin of appreciation is given to the state where there is a clear international consensus affirming the approach of the state. This margin of appreciation is, again, not determinative of the matter and can be overridden. In the case of *Kyprianou v Cyprus*,[113] the ECtHR assessed the practice of contempt of court in Cyprus, where a frustrated lawyer who accused the judges of passing romantic notes to each other was found in contempt. A number of states, including the UK, were alarmed at the lack of deference shown by the ECtHR to the widespread practice of contempt of court and its equivalent in civil law jurisdictions. Finding against the state, the ECtHR made it clear that it was not intending to review the law of contempt generally,[114] but that in this case, because the judges were personally insulted, there was a risk of bias to the applicant. Notwithstanding the practice of contempt of court in which the sitting judges are able to make a determination, in this particular case there was a risk of bias, and thus the margin of appreciation generally accorded to the state on the basis of consensus did not result in a finding in favour of the state.

Across the Tribunals, but most clearly in the ECtHR, international consensus affects the margin of appreciation as follows: (a) it strengthens deference to states where the consensus is inconclusive; (b) it heightens scrutiny where current state practice opposes the argument of the respondent state; and (c) it strengthens deference where the consensus supports the respondent state. In each of these situations, the margin of appreciation is not determinative, and there are examples of cases that show the Tribunals taking into account consensus, but reaching a decision based on the strength of other factors in the case. This provides further evidence for the argument that the margin of appreciation is not a sort of 'justiciability in disguise', but a form of second-order reasoning that is one factor among many for consideration by the Tribunals in their exercise of judgment.

---

[110] Ibid, [4.3].
[111] *Love v Australia* CCPR/C/77/D/983/2001 (2003) (HRC).
[112] Ibid, [8.3].
[113] *Kyprianou v Cyprus* No. 73797/01 (2005) (ECtHR (GC)).
[114] Ibid, [125].

d. Current state practice is not calculated with precision

The use of current practice by the ECtHR has attracted concern about the way in which consensus is calculated. Howard Yourow has expressed this concern in the following terms: 'Especially vexing in any attempt to uncover the further meaning of the consensus factor is the consistently unsubstantiated nature of the Court's pronouncements.'[115] Laurence Helfer has similarly complained that the ECtHR has failed to establish a coherent methodology for its consensus inquiry.[116] What these writers seem to assert is that there should be some sort of uniform method to determine the effect of state practice: for example, where 85 per cent of member states share the same approach, then a new Convention standard for or against the state has developed, or if more than 60 per cent of states share an approach, this gives additional weight for or against the state, and if there is anywhere between 0 per cent and 60 per cent consistency, the lack of uniformity signifies that there is no convention standard at all and a lack of jurisdiction for the Court to decide the question, or non-applicability of the right in issue. The argument in favour of some sort of more scientific methodology is that, without it, the states might begin to ignore the Court's ad hoc and unprincipled decisions.[117]

But, for three main reasons, it is not desirable for the Tribunals to calculate the current practice of states with precision and the concerns about ambiguity are overstated. First, on the suggested approach to consensus, the Tribunals take the practice of states into account in their decision-making as only one factor amongst a number in assessing whether or not there has been a violation of the international human rights treaty. Given the multitude of relevant considerations that might occur in different cases, the amount of information about state consensus will rightly vary with its relative importance to the case. It is partly because of the varying roles of current state practice in the reasoning of the Tribunals from case to case that a uniform methodology is undesirable. For the Tribunals to prescribe a formulaic role to state practice in their reasoning would be for them to misrepresent that consensus is merely one factor amongst numerous other reasons, all of which are relevant in resolving the dispute.

A second and related reason why it is undesirable for there to be a precise approach to the assessment of state practice is that it is not possible to determine with certainty what is or is not a required level of consensus amongst states. When there is not unanimity amongst states, what level of consensus is appropriate for a legal norm to have emerged? Some issues are not even regulated by some states, or do not affect them (for example the rights of Roma communities where such communities do not exist). In such situations, should the Tribunals look only at

---

[115] HC Yourow, *The Margin of Appreciation Doctrine in the Dynamics of European Human Rights Jurisprudence* (DPhil, University of Michigan 1995; Kluwer Law International, The Hague 1996) 195.
[116] L Helfer, 'Consensus, Coherence and the European Convention on Human Rights' (1993) 26 Cornell Intl LJ 133, 135 and 138–41.
[117] Ibid, 141.

affected states or ought such situations to change the relevant numbers of states needed for an appropriate consensus? Given the huge diversity of case scenarios and issues, it is better to leave to the judgment and discretion of the Tribunals what criteria are needed for an appropriate consensus from case to case.

Thirdly, the desirability of the Tribunals having discretion when assessing the appropriateness of consensus from case to case also reflects the balancing of apologism and utopianism in their reasoning.[118] Limiting the amount of information given in the judgments about the methodology for reaching consensus provides the Tribunals with a mechanism for balancing what might otherwise appear to be apologist or utopian reasoning. Finding some sort of trend amongst states that goes against the respondent state might make a controversial decision appear more palatable. Similarly, finding a lack of consensus or practice favouring the state might make a decision that appears overly conservative or apologist appear prudent.

Having argued as a general matter that the Tribunals are likely to explain their reliance on consensus without a formulaic rigidity, there are nevertheless good reasons in the interests of transparency for the Tribunals to explain, wherever possible, the grounds for their reasoning on consensus and the role that it plays in their decision-making. It is important therefore for the Tribunals not simply to state the existence or lack of existence of a common trend, but to explain with as much clarity as they can the evidence upon which such a judgment is made. There is evidence of such specificity in some of the foregoing cases, for example in *Cossey*,[119] in which the ECtHR referred to the diversity of opinions in the Parliamentary Assembly of the Council of Europe. There are many cases, though, that simply assert that there either is or is not a consensus, and even though there ought not be a formulaic method for assessing consensus, the Tribunals should give information in the interests of transparency.

Empirical studies revealing the uniformity of approaches to particular human rights problems can furnish information that will assist the Tribunals. Such comparative research based on national and international cases, some of which involve 'transnational judicial conversations',[120] could be submitted by the parties to the dispute,[121] or by third parties (such as the reports by Liberty in the cases of *Sheffield and Horsham*[122] and *Christine Goodwin*[123]). Alternatively, the Tribunals themselves can conduct research. The Grand Chamber of the ECtHR now has a research division that enables it to ask for in-house

---

[118] See section 2 of this chapter.

[119] *Cossey v UK* (n68) [40].

[120] C McCrudden, 'A Common Law of Human Rights? Transnational Judicial Conversations on Constitutional Rights' (2000) 20 (4) OJLS 499, especially fn112 and fn113.

[121] See *Stubbings v UK* No. 22083/93 (1996) (ECtHR), [54]: 'It appears from the material available to the Court that there is no uniformity amongst the member States of the Council of Europe with regard either to the length of civil limitation periods or the date from which such periods are reckoned.' This implies that the Court was relying on the information provided by the parties.

[122] *Sheffield and Horsham v UK* (n72).

[123] *Christine Goodwin v UK* (n74).

information on comparative and international law information on the cases before it.[124] This is an important and useful development that should lead to greater transparency.

When consensus is in a state of flux and international norms are developing, the Tribunals can either speed this process up or wait for the states to develop their approaches. Again, this is not often discussed as a matter of precision, but in more general terms. For example, in the case of *Chapman v UK*,[125] the ECtHR assessed the rights of gypsies to settle in an area in which land was subject to development restrictions on environmental grounds. The applicant argued that there was an international trend to uphold the rights of gypsies. The ECtHR said, however, that 'the Court is not persuaded that the consensus is sufficiently concrete for it to derive any guidance as to the conduct or standards which Contracting States consider desirable in any particular situation'.[126] The consensus in the case was not yet solid enough and the Court explained why. There was an international treaty discussing the rights of gypsies, but it simply 'sets out general principles and goals' and the states were 'unable to agree on means of implementation'.[127] Whilst this is not a scientific explanation, it explains with sufficient clarity the reasoning of the Court, and provides guidance to states about what sort of factors will affect how consensus operates as a factor for deference, whilst leaving sufficient discretion to the Tribunals.

This section has concluded the chapter's discussion of current state practice as an external factor for a margin of appreciation. The section expounded the relevant case law from the Tribunals and revealed three different ways in which this factor operates in practice. The section concluded with an analysis of the way in which trends amongst state practice are determined, and argued that it was not desirable for consensus to be calculated precisely. The chapter as a whole has argued that the current practice of states operates as an external factor for a margin of appreciation because the Treaties are emanations of the intention of states, the VCLT requires the practice of states to be considered by the Tribunals when interpreting the Treaties, and, in a context of vague human rights standards, state practices in implementing human rights standards have weight in determining what those standards require. The nature of international human rights treaties necessitates that this is simply a matter of deference and should not be determinative of the matter. The Tribunals must consider all other relevant matters to ensure that individuals are receiving the appropriate protection.

The next section considers the place of the Tribunals in the international legal system in four other contexts to explore the impact that these different contexts have on claims for deference by respondent states.

---

[124] DJ Harris, M O'Boyle, C Warbrick, and E Bates, *Harris, O'Boyle & Warbrick: Law of the European Convention on Human Rights* (2nd edn, OUP, Oxford 2009) 10.
[125] *Chapman v UK* No. 27238/95 (2001) (ECtHR (GC)).
[126] Ibid, [94].   [127] Ibid.

6. Deference to international norms, institutions, and organizations

Thus far, the chapter has observed that the role of the Tribunals involves holding a complex number of matters in tension, including the importance of deference to state sovereignty, developing norms towards moral truth, and being aware of the epistemological problems surrounding the discovery of moral truth, each of which relates to the legitimacy of tribunal norm-making. In a number of cases, the Tribunals must also hold in tension their role in relation to other international institutions and organizations. Are there reasons to defer to other international institutions and organizations? How would this deference interrelate with or affect requirements to give a margin of appreciation to the views of the state?

International law scholarship concerned with the 'fragmentation' of international law notes the widespread differing tribunals and systems dealing with a multifarious number of issues. Christopher Greenwood has argued that such talk of 'fragmentation' is misplaced where the systems are not themselves breaking up from a unified system, but have developed piecemeal over time.[128] He commented that 'diversity is a fact of life in international law', and is nothing to be concerned about in relation to international law's future. One of the reasons not to be concerned, Greenwood argued, was that tribunals are sensitive to their overlapping competencies. This claim is supported in the following sections in relation to the main interactions that the Tribunals have with other international institutions and organizations, including each other, as well as with customary international law.

Whilst numerous international institutions and organizations interact with the ECtHR, IACtHR, and UN HRC, the main ones are: (a) each other, for example the ECtHR referring to communications of the UN HRC, or the IACtHR referring to judgments of the ECtHR; (b) the institutions of the European Community (EC) as they interact with the ECtHR; and (c) the United Nations Security Council (UNSC) impacting the Tribunals. In addition, (d) customary international norms affect the interpretative exercise undertaken by the Tribunals. Decisions of the Tribunals have referred to such diverse international bodies as NATO,[129] the European Space Agency (ESA),[130] the United Nations High Commissioner for Refugees, or UN Refugee Agency (UNHCR),[131] the European Social Charter,[132] the International Criminal Tribunal for the former Yugoslavia (ICTY),[133] the International Civil Aviation Organization (ICAO),[134] and many others. It is not possible to assess in detail the reasons for or against deference to each one of these diverse bodies. Due consideration would need to be given to each

---

[128]   C Greenwood, 'The Unity and Diversity of International Law', 33rd Annual FA Mann Lecture (Lincoln's Inn, London 4 November 2009).

[129]   *Banković v Belgium* (n17).

[130]   *Waite and Kennedy v Germany* No. 26083/94 (1999) (ECtHR (GC)).

[131]   *Saadi v UK* (n18).

[132]   *Sørensen and Rasmussen v Denmark* (n87).

[133]   *Caesar v Trinidad and Tobago* Series C No. 123 (2005) (IACtHR).

[134]   *Love v Australia* (n111) [4.12].

of their functions and the sovereignty transferred to each by states parties. Instead, the purpose of this section is to assess deference to international organizations and international law where it most commonly impacts the reasoning of the Tribunals, and consequently to provide examples with which other international organizations can be compared by analogy.

a. Decisions of other international human rights tribunals

The Tribunals are autonomous, and are not required to harmonize their approaches to the protection of human rights. Indeed, the states of one region may purposefully choose to include protections that are excluded from other regions, for example the explicit protection of the unborn child in the ACHR,[135] which is left out of the ECHR and the ICCPR. Nevertheless, decisions of the other human rights tribunals are frequently used in the arguments of lawyers, and are also referred to in the Tribunals' decisions. The decisions are not binding, but are regarded as persuasive. What impact do the decisions of other human rights tribunals have and what, if any, should their role be? There is a strong possibility that judges unwittingly rely on the reasoning of the other tribunals when deliberating, without making their reliance on such materials clear in their reasoning. It is not possible to trace these undercurrent influences and so the examination of the materials that follows assesses only where such reliance is made expressly.

Other human rights tribunals' reasoning has been used to shed light on the interpretation of treaty provisions with which the tribunal itself has not had to deal before, helping to fill a temporary gap in the Tribunals' own jurisprudence.

i. ECtHR

This can be seen in the case of *Saadi v UK*,[136] in which the ECtHR was asked for the first time to interpret the meaning of the limitation of the right to liberty in Article 5(1)(f) ECHR. The case involved a person's arrest to prevent unauthorized entry into the country or for deportation and extradition purposes. Among the many international materials that the ECtHR considered were the relevant communications of the UN HRC.[137] In particular, the ECtHR referred to the idea that arbitrariness was more than merely non-compliance with domestic law,[138] a finding that the ECtHR affirmed in its own judgment without referencing the HRC decision again.[139] The bulk of the reasoning of the ECtHR was by analogy with

---

[135] Article 4 ACHR (protection of the right to life 'in general from the moment of conception'). See P Alston, 'The Unborn Child and Abortion under the Draft Convention on the Rights of the Child' (1990) 12 HRQ 156, 175–7.

[136] *Saadi v UK* (n18).

[137] Ibid, [31], referring to *A v Australia* (n35), *C v Australia* CCPR/C/76/D/900/1999 (2002) (HRC), and *Celepi v Sweden* CCPR/C/51/D/456/1991 (1994) (HRC).

[138] From *A v Australia* (n35).

[139] *Saadi v UK* (n18) [67].

other ECHR jurisprudence on the meaning of arbitrariness in other contexts.[140] Nevertheless, the fact that the communications of the HRC were cited and then a similar approach was taken shows that the HRC views appeared to have had some influence. As with other factors in favour of giving a margin of appreciation, reference to this factor will not be determinative. In fact, different textual approaches by the institutions can justify quite different approaches, for example in the case of *A and others v UK*,[141] in which the Grand Chamber, whilst noting that UN HRC has observed that derogations from the ICCPR must be of 'an exceptional and temporary nature',[142] found that the ECtHR's case law had not to date required the emergency to be temporary, nor would it be, notwithstanding the HRC's different approach.[143]

The ECtHR has also referred to the jurisprudence of the IACtHR. In *Sergey Zolotukhin v Russia*,[144] the applicant was punished twice for taking his girlfriend into a restricted military compound, raising issues related to Article 4, Protocol 7, ECHR (right not to be tried or punished twice). In considering how best to interpret this right, the Grand Chamber referred to other international materials, including Article 8(4) ACHR and its interpretation by the IACtHR.[145] The IACtHR compared the ACHR text to that which prevents being tried again for '*the same cause*' rather than '*the same crime*' in the wording of the ICCPR. Interestingly, the Grand Chamber discusses the reasoning of the IACtHR,[146] and rather than adopting a narrow reading of Article 4, Protocol 7, on the basis that the text refers to '*an offence*', as the IACtHR's reasoning might have been understood, the Grand Chamber instead decided that Article 4 would have a broad reading. As a result, and despite its narrower text, the Grand Chamber ensured that this right would provide the same level of protection as that provided by the ACHR.

In *Šilih v Slovenia*,[147] the Grand Chamber referred to decisions of both the HRC and the IACtHR. The case involved the obligations of the state to investigate medical negligence in a case in which the applicant's son, who suffered from severe allergies, died in hospital. The Grand Chamber referred extensively, inter alia, to the HRC and IACtHR.[148] These references were expressly relied upon in this case by the Grand Chamber to argue that the state's duty to carry out an effective investigation under Article 2 ECHR had developed into a distinct duty.[149]

---

[140] Ibid, [68]–[74].
[141] *A and others v UK* No. 3455/05 (2009) (EctHR (GC)), [178].
[142] Ibid, [109], noting General Comment No. 29 on Article 4 ICCPR (24 July 2001).
[143] Ibid, [178].
[144] *Sergey Zolotukhin v Russia* No. 14939/03 (2009) (ECtHR (GC)).
[145] Ibid, [39]–[40], referring to *Loayza-Tamayo v Peru* Series C No. 33 (1997) (IACtHR),[66].
[146] *Sergey Zolotukhin v Russia* (n144) [79].
[147] *Šilih v Slovenia* No. 71463/01 (2009) (ECtHR(GC)).
[148] Ibid, [111]–[118].
[149] Ibid, [159].

ii. IACtHR

The IACtHR occasionally expressly relies on ECtHR jurisprudence. This can be seen in the case of *Loayza-Tamayo v Peru*,[150] which involved the mistreatment of a female university professor detained on the basis of a connection with a terrorist organization. She denied all connections to the organization, and alleged horrendous treatment while in detention. In discussing violations of Article 5 ACHR (right to humane treatment), the IACtHR explained that the right contained several gradations ranging from humiliation to torture, and in explaining this further relied exclusively on decisions of the ECtHR.[151]

iii. UN HRC

There is also evidence of careful consideration of ECtHR judgments by the UN HRC, for example *Kindler v Canada*,[152] in which the issues were addressed directly as follows: 'In this context the Committee has had careful regard to the judgment given by the European Court of Human Rights in the *Soering* case.'[153] The Committee went on to reason carefully on the basis of *Soering v UK*,[154] explaining how the case was 'distinguishable' from the facts of *Kindler*.

Interestingly, there was much discussion of ECtHR case law by the parties in *Singh v France*,[155] but no discussion of these cases by the Committee. In that case, the Committee was asked for its views on the requirement for a Sikh man to appear bareheaded on an identity photograph for residency purposes, and the concomitant loss of residency status and access to other social benefits that require residency should he refuse to do so. Although the Committee included discussion of the relevant ECtHR case law in the course of its communication, such discussion did not form part of the Committee's 'consideration of the merits'. This is unfortunate. It would have been helpful to see how the Committee's approach either was influenced by the European cases to which it had been

---

[150] *Loayza-Tamayo v Peru* (n145).

[151] Ibid, [57], citing *Ireland v UK* (n21) [167], and *Ribitsch v Austria* No. 18896/91 (1995) (ECtHR), [36] and [38]. For another example, see the reference by the IACtHR in *Genie-Lacayo v Nicaragua* Series C No. 30 (1997) (IACtHR), [77] (emphasis added), to the ECHR jurisprudence on trials within a reasonable time (Article 6 ECHR) to interpret the Article 8 ACHR right to a fair trial within a reasonable time:

> Article 8(1) of the Convention also refers to reasonable time. This is not an easy concept to define. In defining it, *one may invoke the points raised of the European Court of Human Rights* in various decisions in which this concept was analyzed, this article of the American Convention *being equivalent in principle* to Article 6 of the European Convention for the Protection of Human Rights and Fundamental Freedoms.

See also *Lopez-Mendoza v Venezuela* Series C No. 233 (2011) (IACtHR), [199].

[152] *Kindler v Canada* CCPR/C/48/D/470/1991 (1993) (HRC).

[153] Ibid, [15.3].

[154] *Soering v UK* (n33).

[155] *Singh v France* CCPR/C/102/D/1876/2009 (2011) (HRC), [3.5], [4.2], [5.1]–[5.2], and [6.6].

referred, or how these cases were distinguished or considered to be unpersuasive by the Committee.[156]

iv. Summary

It is difficult to see exactly how the Tribunals relied on each other's decisions. It could be that they were seeing those decisions as providing helpful guidance about how to interpret the same or very similarly worded provisions of the respective Treaties. Alternatively, it could be that there is a desire to respect the findings of the other human rights Tribunals, and where there is no previous decision of its own on which to rely, the reference to another tribunal is a helpful way of promoting consistent human rights protection. Possibly referring to the decisions of the other Tribunals is a way of boosting their reputation and standing. Alternatively, it is a way for a tribunal to legitimize its own decision. This sort of reliance on the decisions of the other Tribunals can be used as a judicial 'distancing device', to use Raz's terminology, when making what appear to be novel developments, to show that the developments are being made independently of the personal tastes of the judges.[157] However, this sort of reasoning may not be regarded as legitimate because states could complain that conceptions of human rights in one region cannot appropriately be thrust on nations from another region.

Is reference to the decisions of other international human rights tribunals justified and, if so, on what basis? Ought such references lead to deference to the other tribunal, or to narrow the margin of appreciation to the state? These questions have not furnished much discussion amongst commentators. Where states have acceded to more than one international human rights treaty system, there is the possibility of conflicting interpretations of similar provisions. This possibility provides some grounds for deference to the other Tribunals—it can avoid unnecessary conflict between the various provisions. This sort of argument does not provide grounds for deference by the IACtHR to the ECtHR, however, because no state is a member of both of these treaties.

Whilst it is feasible for the Tribunals to have inconsistent human rights requirements, it is undesirable for such conflicts to exist where the very same or a similar fact scenario exists. This raises the unwelcome position of a state being in violation of one or other of its international human rights obligations where two inconsistent decisions are given by different Tribunals. For this reason, the concept of international litispendence exists, but even in such cases the Tribunals have been slow to deny access to individuals, although such multiple access has sometimes led to ostensibly inconsistent outcomes. In *Folgerø v Norway*,[158] a case with nearly

---

[156] For a case that does, to a greater extent, reveal the impact of ECtHR decisions on the Committee's reasoning, see *Denis Yevdokimov and Artiom Rezanov v Russian Federation* CCPR/C/101/D/1410/2005 (2011) (HRC), [7.5], which refers to *Hirst v UK (No. 2)* No. 74025/01 (2005) (ECtHR (GC)), [71].

[157] J Raz, 'On the Authority and Interpretation of Constitutions: Some Preliminaries' in L Alexander (ed) *Constitutionalism: Philosophical Foundations* (CUP, Cambridge 1998) 152, 190.

[158] *Folgerø v Norway* No. 15472/02 (2007) (ECtHR (GC)).

identical facts had been decided by the UN HRC, but the ECtHR nevertheless went on to consider the case. The dissenting judgment decided that it was a case of international litispendence and should have been declared inadmissible by the ECtHR on that basis. Although the Tribunals reached different outcomes, they were not particularly in conflict—the HRC found that there had not been a violation of the Covenant, whereas the ECtHR found by nine to eight that the provision for parents for their children not to be taught in line with Christian values fell foul of ECHR standards—a result that implies there was a higher standard required under the ECHR than was required by the ICCPR. This is an acceptable outcome because there is likely to be greater convergence amongst contracting states of the ECHR than the Optional Protocol of the ICCPR. The case nevertheless highlights the possibility of conflicting standards between different human rights systems. The desirability of avoiding this provides some grounds for deference to the decisions of the other international human rights tribunals.

b. The European Court of Justice (ECJ) and the European Court of Human Rights (ECtHR)

Is there any role for deference by the ECtHR to the European Court of Justice (ECJ) or the other institutions of the European Union (EU)? The answer to this is complex, and cannot be dealt with comprehensively here. Rather, the sorts of considerations that will provide a clearer answer are outlined. The role of the EU institutions is to harmonize the systems of compliance between member states on matters within the EU's competence. Traditionally, this has been for the purpose of economic integration, and whilst this remains a core aim of the Union, there is an increasing harmonization of practices within member states relating to such diverse matters as the regulation of employment rights and certain matters relating to immigration. The expanding reach of EU legal regulation impacts the understanding of member states' protection of fundamental rights. The interplay between the EU's fundamental rights jurisprudence and the ECtHR is not entirely clear. The purposes, whilst overlapping, are distinct. The EU's aim is to ensure compliance of fundamental values within its own jurisdiction, which is more limited than the deeper (that is, affecting more areas of contracting states' behaviour) and more widespread (that is, affecting greater numbers of states) impact of the ECHR. There can therefore be legitimately different standards in EU and in ECHR jurisprudence. Where there are incompatible standards, this can cause difficulty and undesirable inter-institutional tension. Comity between these organs provides grounds for mutual deference in the interpretation of fundamental human rights norms. This is particularly the case in the spheres of their particular expertise: the ECtHR for the interpretation of human rights norms; the EU for matters relating to the integration of common interests of its member states, which on occasion impacts human rights norms. Furthermore, the EU has received authorization from numerous member states, which can be said to have consented to its findings and transferred sovereignty to it.[159] In this context, there may be additional grounds to defer to EU institutions on the basis that its determinations can be reflective of the consensus and obligations of a large number of contracting states.

A case that shows the ECtHR paying attention to the purposes of the EU institutions in making its determination is *Matthews v UK*,[160] in which the ECtHR assessed the fact that the UK had not made provision for citizens in Gibraltar (which was neither part of the UK nor of the EU, but was subject to them both) to vote in European Parliament elections. The majority found that Article 3, Protocol 1, ECHR was violated because of the complete banning of the applicant from voting. The dissenting judgment focused on the fact that the European Parliament could not rightly be described as a legislature within the EU system,[161] and that the UK anyway would not have been able to grant voting rights within Gibraltar other than by amendment of the multilateral treaty.[162] The dissenting judges made the following telling comment, as an example that deference to EU institutions can affect the reasoning of the Court: '[T]he view has throughout weighed heavily with us that a particular restraint should be required of the Court when it is invited, as it is here, to pronounce on acts of the European Community or consequent to its requirements.'[163]

Deference by the ECtHR to the ECJ can be seen in the case of *Kress v France*,[164] in which the ECtHR assessed the role of the government commissioner in the French *Cour de Cassation*. The government commissioner was allowed to give an opinion to the *Cour de Cassation*, whereas the applicant was unable see the opinion in advance or respond to it in submissions. The government commissioner was able to attend the deliberations of the *Cour de Cassation*, but was unable to vote. The French government, as well as explaining the importance of the role to the heritage of the French judicial system and highlighting its respected pedigree, including its support by the French legal community, also argued that particular emphasis should be placed on the fact that the EC had borrowed the role in its Advocate General, and thus the ECtHR should be cautious in holding the role to be incompatible with fair trial rights (Article 6 ECHR). On the point about the government commissioner's submissions, the ECtHR found that parties were able to ask in advance for the general tenor of his opinion and, crucially, to respond to his submissions in a written memorandum. The ECtHR on the whole tended to view the role with suspicion, but nevertheless found this aspect not to be in violation of the ECHR. As well as deference to the state, there also appears to have been deference to the ECJ's use of the Advocate General. This is most clearly seen in the finding of a violation of the general commissioner's role in the deliberations of the *Cour de Cassation*. Despite the clear praise of this aspect of

---

[159] Sarooshi (n14) ch 6.II.1.
[160] *Matthews v UK* No. 24833/94 (1999) (ECtHR (GC)).
[161] Ibid, [6]–[8], dissenting opinion of Judges Sir John Freeland and Jungwiert.
[162] Ibid, [9], Judges Sir John Freeland and Jungwiert.
[163] Ibid, [2], Judges Sir John Freeland and Jungwiert.
[164] *Kress v France* No. 39594/98 (2001) (ECtHR (GC)).

the role by France and defence of the presence in deliberations,[165] the ECtHR was affirmed in its decision that this violated Article 6(1) by the fact that the Advocate General of the ECJ is not present in its deliberations. Whilst there are thus similarities of the ECJ's Advocate General with the French government commissioner, the arguments in favour of having the Advocate General present during deliberations were not adopted in the context of the ECJ, and this appears to have influenced the ECtHR.[166]

There are occasions on which the ECtHR seems to place too much emphasis on the EU institutions. This is seen in the case of *Pellegrin v France*,[167] in which the ECtHR decided the criterion that determines whether or not civil servants can enjoy protection under Article 6(1) ECHR for employment matters. The ECtHR decided that the criterion would be 'functional'[168]—that is, whether or not the employment flowed from the state's exercise of public powers, rather than just being administrative. This is a controversial finding because if the same job were done privately, ECHR procedural guarantees would apply. The ECtHR relied on the approach of the ECJ in this decision.[169] However, it seems strange that the ECtHR sought to harmonize the approach of the ECHR and the EU in this case. It need not be inconsistent for Article 6(1) rights to be applicable to all government workers, but for EU freedom of movement rights to be excluded from a limited class of government employees.

There is clear evidence that the ECtHR does, on occasion, defer to the EU institutions. This topic warrants further study. The aspects of deference mentioned can sometimes act as additional second-order reasons to follow the reasoning of the respondent state, and at other times can act as reasons to limit the margin of appreciation given to the state.

c. Resolutions of the United Nations Security Council (UNSC)

Another fascinating and emerging issue is how and whether the Tribunals should defer to UNSC Resolutions. This has similarly not been an area that has furnished a great deal of jurisprudence or commentary to date, but the recent cases involving UNSC Resolutions have generated significant interest. One of the first matters to consider is whether UNSC Resolutions should be matters for deference or obedience? In Article 25 of the UN Charter, states agree to accept and carry out decisions of the UNSC, and Article 103 provides that 'In the event of a conflict between the obligations of the Members of the United Nations under the present Charter and

---

[165] Ibid, [77]–[78].
[166] Ibid, [86]: 'The Court is confirmed in this approach by the fact that at the Court of Justice of the European Communities the Advocate General, whose role is closely modelled on that of the Government Commissioner, does not attend the deliberations.' In affirmation of this reasoning, see *Martinie v France* No. 58675/00 (2006) (ECtHR (GC)), [53]–[55]. For a similar case, see *Meftah v France* No. 32911/96 (2002) (ECtHR (GC)), [45]–[46] and [51]–[52].
[167] *Pellegrin v France* No. 28541/95 (1999) (ECtHR (GC)).
[168] Ibid, [64].
[169] Ibid, [66], referring to its citations of the judgments of the ECJ using the 'functional criterion' at [37]–[41].

their obligations under any other international agreement, their obligations under the present Charter shall prevail'. States then are bound to follow the decisions of the UNSC.

Whilst themselves not subject to the UNSC, and thus not required as a matter of authority to abide by the decisions of the UNSC, if the Tribunals' decisions result in a conflict with a UNSC Resolution, states appear likely to abide by their UNSC obligations and not the decision, based on Article 103 of the UN Charter. When such cases come before the Tribunals, there is a choice: to be deferential to the UNSC, or to make decisions intentionally knowing that this will cause a conflict, with the strong risk that their own decisions will thus not be followed.

i. ECtHR

In two decisions that have raised this matter in the ECtHR, both have found in favour of the state following the UNSC Resolution.[170] In *Bosphorus Airways v Ireland*,[171] the ECtHR assessed the impounding of a plane owned by the Turkish applicant company and leased to the Yugoslav national airline. Ireland held the plane as a result of a European Regulation implementing a UNSC Resolution designed to prevent the funding of the conflict in the Balkans. The case is an important decision about deference, because the ECtHR rejected the applicant's claim under Article 1, Protocol 1, ECHR on the basis that the plane was impounded while implementing Ireland's obligations under the European Regulation, and the EU took into account the same standards of protection as the ECHR (indeed, the ECJ refers to the ECHR as its own benchmark).[172] Thus where there is recognition of human rights standards to the same level of the ECHR, there will be a deferential presumption in favour of the international organization, but a presumption that can be overridden.[173]

Although the international obligations involved in *Bosphorus Airways* were EC Regulations, interpreted by the ECJ, they were implementing UNSC Resolutions governed by the UNSC Sanctions Committee. On this occasion, it appears that the Court was put at ease by the fact that the EU institutions took into account human

---

[170] Compare the recent approach of the ECJ, which ruled in C-402/05 *Kadi v Council* [2008] 3 CMLR 41 (ECJ) that following the relevant UNSC Resolution was incompatible with EU obligations. This is a controversial decision based on the horizontality of the Community legal order with the international legal order. It will be fascinating to see whether this case impacts the approach of the ECtHR.

[171] *Bosphorus Airways v Ireland* No. 45036/98 (2005) (ECtHR (GC)).

[172] Ibid, [77]–[81].

[173] Ibid, [156]:

> If such equivalent protection is considered to be provided by the organisation, the presumption will be that a State has not departed from the requirements of the Convention when it does no more than implement legal obligations flowing from its membership of the organisation. However, any such presumption can be rebutted if, in the circumstances of a particular case, it is considered that the protection of Convention rights was manifestly deficient. In such cases, the interest of international cooperation would be outweighed by the Convention's role as a 'constitutional instrument of European public order' in the field of human rights.

See *Loizidou v Turkey (Preliminary Objections)* (n17) [75].

rights considerations.[174] What happens where it is difficult to see whether the UNSC's reasoning is proportionate? It is arguable that difficulties with transparency in the UNSC Sanctions Committee give reason to heighten scrutiny of its interpretations of the resolution.[175]

In the case of *Behrami v France*,[176] French military involvement in the UNSC Resolution 1244 authorized mission in Kosovo (the Kosovo Force, or KFOR) was under scrutiny for death and injury resulting from a mine. The applicants argued that:

[T]he substantive and procedural protection of fundamental rights provided by KFOR was in any event not 'equivalent' to that under the Convention within the meaning of the Court's *Bosphorus* judgment, with the consequence that the presumption of Convention compliance on the part of the respondent States was rebutted.[177]

This gave the Court the opportunity to scrutinize French compliance with ECHR standards when implementing a UNSC Resolution. The Court emphasized the important role of the UNSC in the maintenance of implementing peace and security.[178] This deferential position to the UNSC seems to have played a role in the ECtHR finding that the French involvement could not be separated from KFOR involvement, and that KFOR's actions were directly attributable to the UN,[179] which is not within the jurisdiction *ratione personae* of the Convention, and thus the case was inadmissible. Such a finding might be regarded as a missed opportunity to scrutinize the decisions of the UNSC. But instead it seems to be a prudential recognition by the ECtHR of its role in the international legal system.

There appears to be grounds for deference to the UNSC, but there may be occasions on which, in the implementation of a UNSC Resolution, a state is clearly falling foul of its human rights obligations, either procedurally or substantively. In such situations, the ECtHR will have to tread a careful path in deciding how much to defer, and when to make a finding of a violation. Whilst such a finding may result in non-compliance by the state of the ECtHR decision, it may also provoke useful consideration by the UNSC about how to implement human rights safeguards in its operations. It will consequently be wise for the ECtHR to make such a finding cautiously and in a clear-cut case, in which the reasons to overcome the grounds for deference to the UNSC will be clearest.

---

[174] Ibid, [54], for the following extract from the relevant ECJ judgment:

As compared with an objective of general interest so fundamental for the international community, which consists in putting an end to the state of war in the region and to the massive violations of human rights and humanitarian international law in the Republic of Bosnia-Herzegovina, the impounding of the aircraft in question, which is owned by an undertaking based in or operating from the [former Republic of Yugoslavia], cannot be regarded as inappropriate or disproportionate.

[175] D Hovell, 'The Deliberative Deficit: Transparency, Access to Information and UN Sanctions' in JM Farrall and K Rubenstein (eds) *Sanctions, Accountability and Governance in a Globalised World* (CUP, Cambridge 2009).

[176] *Behrami v France* No. 71412/01 (2007) (ECtHR (GC)).

[177] Ibid, [150].

[178] Ibid, [148].

[179] Ibid, [151].

ii. UN HRC

The UN HRC has considered a case involving deference to the UNSC and expressly discussed giving a margin of appreciation to states when implementing UNSC Resolutions. In *Nabil Sayadi and Patricia Vinck v Belgium*,[180] the state party placed the names of the authors on the sanctions list, which prevented them from being able, inter alia, to enjoy the right to free movement (Article 12 ICCPR). Whilst the right to free movement can be restricted, any limitations must be proportionate (see General Comment 27). It later transpired that the authorities requested the authors' names to be removed from the sanctions lists. Nevertheless, the HRC found violations of the Covenant, including Article 12. The HRC considered the fact that the state was implementing a UNSC Resolution and stated that, 'whatever the argument', it was competent to assess the national measures taken to implement it, and 'to consider to what extent the obligations imposed on the State party by the Security Council resolutions may justify the infringement of the right to liberty of movement, which is protected by article 12 of the Covenant'.[181] The HRC went on to reject Belgium's argument that it was required to disclose the names of the authors on the basis of the practice of other states, which had not disclosed the names of employees of other branches of the charity.[182]

As with many cases in which issues of deference are relevant, there were various differing views, represented by concurring and dissenting separate opinion in *Nabil Sayadi and Patricia Vinck v Belgium*, both on admissibility and the merits. Ms Ruth Wedgewood's dissent was most deferential to the UNSC.[183] Mr Ivan Shearer, dissenting, emphasized that the state should have a margin of appreciation when giving effect to binding decisions of the UNSC, noting that it was not Belgium that ordered the listing of the authors' names, but the Security Council. The concurring opinions of Mr Yuji Iwasawa showed greater deference to the UNSC by explaining in further detail the basis for the Committee's approach, in particular noting that it may be that UNSC Resolutions justify restrictions of the Covenant, but referring to

---

[180] *Nabil Sayadi and Patricia Vinck v Belgium* CCPR/C/94/D/1472/2006 (2008) (HRC).
[181] Ibid, [10.6].
[182] Ibid, [10.7].
[183] Ibid. Indeed, her opinion goes beyond deference, arguing that the matter is outside the jurisdiction of the Committee (emphasis in original):

> Article 48 (2) of the United Nations Charter provides that Security Council decisions '*shall be carried out* by the Members of the United Nations *directly* and through their action in the appropriate international agencies of which they are members' (emphasis added). Article 25 likewise provides that 'The Members of the United Nations *agree to accept and carry out the decisions* of the Security Council in accordance with the present Charter' (emphasis added). And ultimately, Article 103 provides that 'In the event of a conflict between the obligations of the Members of the United Nations under the present Charter and their obligations under any other international agreement, their obligations under the present Charter shall prevail'.
>
> The Committee is not entitled to use the hollow form of a pleading against a State to rewrite those provisions. As the Committee acknowledges, it has no appellate jurisdiction to review decisions of the Security Council. Neither can it penalize a State for complying with those decisions. It would be inconsistent with the constitutional structure of the United Nations Charter, and its own responsibilities under the Covenant.

the point that, on the facts of that case, the state could have acted differently while continuing to comply with the requirements of the UNSC Resolution by not disclosing the authors' names, as other states had also done (again making reference to the practice of other states). The concurring opinion of Sir Nigel Rodley explained that the opinion left to others the risk of a conflict between the HRC and the UNSC, and decided that there was indeed a violation. Sir Nigel suggested that the factor of state practice had been decisive, but nevertheless opined robustly that the UNSC ought to prepare procedures to ensure compliance with human rights standards.

In *Nabil Sayadi and Patricia Vinck v Belgium*,[184] then, the HRC was of the view that Belgium had violated the ICCPR in its implementation of the UNSC Resolution. Was it wise to take this approach? On careful analysis, it appears that this may have been an appropriate case to make such a finding. Rather than directly scrutinize the UNSC Resolution, the Committee instead noted the approach that other states had taken to their discretion regarding whether or not to list individual names, and thereby only indirectly reviewed the actions of the UNSC. The states' discretion was founded on the fact that the Resolution required the 'main persons connected' with the charity for which the authors worked to be disclosed. It was arguably within the state's discretion to determine which persons fell into this category and in this respect to consider whether or not the effects of the UNSC Resolution should apply to those persons. This discretion would, on this view, operate within the framework of the state's international human rights obligations. The view that the HRC came to was therefore cautiously critical of the UNSC, by finding that it was the exercise of the state's discretion that violated international human rights law.

d. Other international law norms

There are at least three additional ways in which international law norms affect the second-order reasoning of tribunals. They have relevance because the Treaties 'cannot be interpreted and applied in a vacuum'[185]—a statement that accords with Article 31(3)(c) VCLT, which provides that 'any relevant rules of international law applicable in the relations between the parties' shall be taken into account along with the context.

First, customary international norms affect the interpretation of the Treaties. If such a norm predates the treaty, the tribunal enquires whether or not the treaty was intended to implement or modify the prior standard, and whether or not the tribunal has the scope to interpret the treaty so as to modify it. The best example of this is seen in cases that assess the impact of general laws of immunity on the application of the ECHR. In *McElhinney v Ireland*,[186] the ECtHR assessed the immunity claimed in the Irish courts. The applicant claims to have been waved

---

[184] Ibid.
[185] *Loizidou v Turkey* No. 15318/89 (1996) (ECtHR (GC)).
[186] *McElhinney v Ireland* No. 31253/96 (2001) (ECtHR (GC)).

over the border from Northern Ireland, but then was pursued by Northern Irish soldiers and attacked with weapons. The applicant sued the soldiers in the Irish courts, but there was a claim of immunity. The ECtHR found that immunity did not breach Article 6(1) ECHR. In reaching this conclusion, the Court found that immunity based on following the rules of public international law was a legitimate aim[187] and proportionate, notwithstanding the arguments that standards had changed for personal injury.[188] The ECtHR found that these reasons based on international law kept the action of the state within the margin of appreciation, implying that supportive customary international law norms provide external reasons to defer to that standard. This conclusion is supported by the fact that the dissenting judgment of Judges Caflisch, Cabral Barreto, and Vajić argued for a different approach to the law of immunity.[189] The approach taken in this case by the majority has been followed in subsequent cases.[190] However, where the claim for immunity is demonstrated to be wrong as a matter of international law, the ECtHR has found a violation of Article 6(1) ECHR: see *Cudak v Lithuania*[191] and *Sabeh El Leil v France*.[192]

A second additional way in which international norms affect the second-order reasoning of the Tribunals is the role of other treaty norms. The type of treaty involved will have an impact here. If it is a multilateral treaty representative of international consensus, this is very likely to provide reasons for deference to that standard.[193] However, the same cannot be said of a treaty between a small number of states. In *Slivenko v Latvia*,[194] the ECtHR explained that whilst it was not primarily its task to interpret a bilateral treaty[195] regarding the return of Russian armed forces and their families following independence, it would not thereby be hampered in its task of determining whether Latvia's treatment of the applicant was compatible with the ECHR.[196] The Court found that the treaty system itself in this case allowed exceptions for hardship, corresponding to the proportionality

---

[187] Ibid, [35].

[188] Ibid, [38], where it was also found that such changes were 'by no means universal'.

[189] Ibid, dissenting opinion of Judges Caflisch, Cabral Barreto, and Vajić. The separate opinion drew on the International Law Commission's Commentary on its Draft Articles on Jurisdictional Immunities of States and Their Property, Article 12, which concerned personal injury and damage to property. The dissenting judges argued that whilst the Draft Articles met with problems and were not adopted, none of the difficulty related to Article 12: 'This must mean that there were no significant challenges against the approach followed by the ILC. The foregoing considerations lead to the conclusion that Article 12 reflects the law as it is at present and that it squarely covers the case at hand.'

[190] For example, *Al-Adsani v UK* No. 35763/97 (2001) (ECtHR (GC)) and *Fogarty v UK* No. 37112/97 (2001) (ECtHR (GC)). For a well-argued criticism of this approach, see Orakhelashvili (n28) 551–66.

[191] *Cudak v Lithuania* No. 15869/02 (2010) (ECtHR (GC)), [59], [67], and [74].

[192] *Sabeh El Leil v France* No. 34869/05 (2011) (ECtHR (GC)), [57]–[68].

[193] See discussion of the Torture Convention in Orakhelashvili (n28) 553–5.

[194] *Slivenko v Latvia* No. 48321/99 (2003) (ECtHR (GC)).

[195] Ibid, [105].

[196] Ibid, [120]: '[T]he Court reiterates that the treaty cannot serve as a valid basis for depriving the Court of its power to review whether there was an interference with the applicants' rights and freedoms under the Convention, and, if so, whether such interference was justified.'

assessment under the Convention, which, applied on the facts, led to a finding of a violation of Article 8.[197]

Thirdly, *jus cogens* and *erga omnes* obligations can impact the way in which the Tribunals defer to states on human rights definitions. Where an international obligation *erga omnes* or *jus cogens* relates to the way in which a state has dealt with a matter, then there may be reasons to defer to the state. Where other obligations are not in issue, there may be fewer grounds for deference to the state. This latter position appears to be the approach taken in the dissenting judgment of Judge Loucaides in *McElhinney v Ireland*: '[O]ne should be reluctant to accept restrictions on Convention rights derived from principles of international law such as those establishing immunities which are not even part of the *jus cogens* norms.'[198]

In the case of *Caesar v Trinidad and Tobago*,[199] in which a man found guilty of attempted rape was given a corporal punishment as well as a prison sentence, the IACtHR undertook a thorough review of human rights tribunals, domestic practice, and other international law developments to find that there was a 'growing trend towards recognition, at international and domestic levels, of the impermissible character of corporal punishment'.[200] The IACtHR consequently decided that:

a State Party to the American Convention, in compliance with its obligations arising from Articles 1(1), 5(1) and 5(2) of that instrument, is under an obligation *erga omnes* to abstain from imposing corporal punishment, as well as to prevent its administration.[201]

It appears as if the IACtHR sought to justify the lack of deference to the state on the basis of a countervailing obligation *erga omnes*.

Mere compatibility with *erga omnes* or *jus cogens* norms may not be worthy of deference, since they may be the lowest common denominator whereas the Treaties protect higher standards. Where state action appears to be contrary to such a norm, there are strong grounds for heightened scrutiny.[202]

7. Conclusion

This chapter has looked at the Tribunals' assessment of their role in the international legal order. The extent of a common trend amongst the practice of

---

[197] Again, this reasoning appears to have affected the second-order reasoning of the Court: ibid, [128] ('the Court considers that the Latvian authorities overstepped the margin of appreciation enjoyed by the Contracting Parties in such a matter'). See further *Waite and Kennedy v Germany* (n130) [67]–[68].

[198] *McElhinney v Ireland* (n186).   [199] *Caesar v Trinidad and Tobago* (n133).

[200] Ibid, [70].   [201] Ibid.

[202] This view is reflected in the opinion of Judge Loucaides in his dissenting opinion in *Al-Adsani v UK* (n190):

Indeed, once it is accepted that the prohibition of torture is a *jus cogens* rule of international law prevailing over State immunity rules, no such immunity can be invoked in respect of any judicial proceedings whose object is the attribution of legal responsibility to any person for any act of torture.

contracting states as to the interpretation and implementation of their obligations under the Treaties is an important factor affecting the margin of appreciation. Its importance reflects the nature of the international treaty systems as emanations of international law made by sovereign states. Whilst it is inaccurate to suggest that the treaty systems are akin to municipal constitutional orders where the Tribunals are given discretion to strike out state action like a national supreme court overturning legislation, the Tribunals have an important role to play in developing or crystallizing international human rights standards,[203] and ought not display the same level of deference to states as in traditional spheres of international law.[204] Where the Tribunals draw the line results in a demarcation of state sovereignty in human rights.

The Tribunals undergo a careful balancing act when deferring to state practice. In doing so, they are cognizant both of the apologist tendencies of international norms that reflect the intention of states and of the utopian tendencies of international law, particularly in the field of international human rights, to constrain state action. Contracting states have voluntarily entered the Treaties. These Treaties require interpretation and the states have submitted to the jurisdiction of the Tribunals, to which they have given a measure of authority to act as arbiters in the international contestation of sovereignty in the sphere of human rights. But states expect such decision-making to be respectful of their role in primarily protecting human rights, warranting deference on the basis of the current practice of states.

When states know better what the requirements of human rights standards are within their jurisdiction, they have greater expertise about what the international standard should be. It is to the matter of deference on the basis of such expertise that the next chapter turns.

---

[203] See *Loizidou v Turkey (Preliminary Objections)* (n17) [84], which refers to the Convention as a 'law-making treaty'.

[204] See *Ivcher-Bronstein v Peru* Series C No. 54 (1999) (IACtHR), [48] (emphasis added):

In effect, international settlement of human rights cases...cannot be compared to the peaceful settlement of international disputes involving purely interstate litigation...since, as is widely accepted, the contexts are fundamentally different, *States cannot expect to have the same amount of discretion in the former as they have traditionally had in the latter.*

But see [51] for how, in this case, the intention of the states remained an important consideration.

6

Expertise and Competence

1. Introduction

One of the key factors affecting reasons for a margin of appreciation to the state is the respective level of expertise or competence[1] that the state or government authority has when compared with the Tribunals. What is deference to the expertise of others? Is such deference appropriate for the Tribunals? In what contexts do the Tribunals give a margin of appreciation to states on the basis of greater expertise or competence? Such questions are addressed in this chapter.

Deference to the views of another on the basis of expertise is fairly common in a variety of contexts. We defer to the opinions of our doctor or lawyer. Deference on the basis of expertise is also a common feature of legal practice, particularly deference to lower tribunals' findings of fact in municipal systems. When a case has reached an appellate court that has jurisdiction over law and fact, the court will accord weight to the findings of fact of the lower court by reason of its closer examination of the evidence, although in these circumstances it is odd to use the terminology of 'expertise' of a lower court. Similarly, in the domestic context, deference is granted on the basis of the expertise of executive bodies or technical agencies in public law.

In practice, deference to expertise sometimes operates as an exclusionary second-order reason. This happens when we take the word of the expert at face value and decide no longer to deliberate on the first-order reasons. If this were always the case, deference to expertise by a tribunal would be evidence that deference to expertise operates like a doctrine of non-justiciability.

Some commentators argue that it is not possible for a court to assess evidence or arguments that draw upon expertise because the nature of expertise means that judges are not competent to scrutinize such matters. This view is discussed below, and rejected, relying on the arguments of Déirde Dwyer.[2] On the contrary, arguments and opinions of experts are reviewable by decision-makers in many contexts. The relative intensity of scrutiny depends on the role of the expert vis-à-vis the decision-maker, and the relative competence. For example, if one goes to a garage to

---

[1] In some cases, it is more apt to refer to expertise; in other contexts, it makes better sense to refer to deference to superior competence, or the fact that the state is 'better placed' to make the decision. The sense of competence here refers to skill or ability rather than its legal sense of sphere of authority.

[2] DM Dwyer, *The Judicial Assessment of Expert Evidence* (CUP, Cambridge 2008).

find out how to fix one's car, one could take the mechanic's word as the final answer, and is likely to do so if one is unfamiliar with the workings of a car. Alternatively, one might take into account the mechanic's advice and nevertheless proceed to conduct one's own research before making up one's mind. The level of deference accorded to a more experienced mechanic is likely to be greater, and will also differ depending on the extent of one's own expertise.

Expertise or the superior competence of the state is an external factor for deference. On the whole, deference on such grounds is regarded as less controversial than the reasons for deference discussed in Chapters 4 and 5. A significant proportion of this chapter assesses how expertise affects human rights decision-making in practice, and in what types of case the Tribunals defer or heighten scrutiny on the basis of expertise.

2. Epistemology, expertise, and judicial responsibility

The practical reasoning involved in legal decision-making requires tribunals to come to a final determination in a case. Knowledge more generally does not have the same strictures, and consequently communities of scholars throughout the ages have revised opinions on practically every subject. If a court makes a decision upon a matter, then it does so on the basis of evidence rather than knowledge. And yet the court must reach a decision even if there is not sufficient evidence to justify what could ordinarily be declared as the 'true' state of affairs. Epistemology in law, then, is about justified belief rather than the ascertainment of knowledge.[3]

A corollary of the fact that practical reasoning in law is based on justified belief might be that when the court bases its view on an expert opinion, it is in effect adopting the expert's approach to the problem rather than exercising its judicial function. When the Tribunals defer to state expertise, does this involve them abdicating responsibility to decide the case? It might be said, for example, that if the Tribunals defer to a state's perspective about what action is necessitated by national security concerns, this is an abdication of their judicial responsibility.

Socio-legal studies of expert evidence have on occasion differentiated strongly between expert and legal knowledge. Such accounts could support the position that relying on expert evidence is akin to judicial abdication of responsibility. Dwyer discusses these socio-legal studies as involving a 'dichotomy between the legal and expert view(s) of the world',[4] and in particular critiques what she calls 'strong epistemological constructivism'.[5] This view maintains that different bodies of knowledge are distinct and thus cannot be assessed by non-experts. Dwyer argues convincingly that whilst this approach offers useful insights to evidence theory, it is flawed both philosophically and empirically: philosophically because, for law to be involved in stabilizing normative expectations in society, it must interact with other disciplines; and empirically because (i) law does in fact interact with other

---

[3] See Dwyer (n2) 70–2.   [4] Ibid, 368.   [5] Ibid, ch 2.5.3.

disciplines, (ii) some practitioners have professional experience in multiple fields, and (iii) over time normative generalizations influence other systems.

It is not the case, then, that expert evidence can ever absolve the judge of his or her responsibility to make a determination in a matter because knowledge cannot be segmented into exclusive zones. Judges are well acquainted with assessing evidence and are required to do so as an ordinary part of their judicial practice. Furthermore, judges are required to consider the entirety of the evidence before them, which involves considerations that go beyond the sphere of competence of the expert. Finally, the role of the court within the system requires that it is the court that makes the relevant determination—this function cannot be delegated to experts.

In the context of international human rights law, it is the Tribunals that are required to determine the dispute. The Tribunals must consider the wider ramifications of their decision—they cannot simply adopt the position of local decision-makers without scrutiny. Deference to the expertise of the state cannot absolve the Tribunals of their responsibility to scrutinize and assess such evidence, making their own determination. This understanding of the role of the Tribunals is reflected well by the civilian maxim, commonly referred to in the context of expert evidence in Italy, *iudex peritus peritorum* ('the judge is the expert of the experts').

Since regarding reliance on expert evidence as a judicial abdication of responsibility misconstrues its nature, how then does such evidence influence the decision-making process? Experts are able to offer assistance of probative value to the Tribunals. As discussed above, the fundamental approach to assessing the evidence of experts is the same as for other types of evidence, and thus the Tribunals are 'epistemically competent'[6] to assess it. However, this does not mean that the Tribunals ignore expertise. Rather, following Dwyer, the Tribunals have 'limited epistemic competence',[7] since whilst they are competent to assess the 'syntactical similarities between expert and non-expert reasoning [they] do not allow us to extend the competence to differences in the semantic content of the knowledge applied by experts and non-experts'.[8]

The limited epistemic competence of the Tribunals leads to deference. The Tribunals assess arguments before them and weight is given in this assessment to the state's expertise. A number of factors affect the weight to be accorded to state expertise, such as the level of experience of the state entity, the comparative expertise between the tribunal and expertise, the subject matter itself, and whether the judges share any specialist understanding of the issues.

The following section moves on from these general matters relating to expertise to their application in practice in the various Tribunals. How does the case law of the Tribunals exemplify deference to expertise or superior competence? As a matter of doctrine, which types of expertise or competence strengthen reasons for deference and which seem to reduce them?

---

[6] Ibid, 131.   [7] Ibid, 368.   [8] Ibid, 131.

3. Expertise as a factor for the margin of appreciation in practice

Each of the jurisdictions assessed in this book has produced decisions that show the impact that expertise has on the Tribunals' reasoning processes. The Tribunals sometimes regard the states or their decision-making authorities as having particular expertise and for this reason will strengthen grounds for a margin of appreciation to the state. On other occasions, the Tribunals regard themselves as having expertise on matters, either to an equivalent level as or greater level than state authorities, and consequently there is less reason to defer to states on this basis.

a. European Court of Human Rights (ECtHR)

In the ECtHR, the way in which expertise affects the margin of appreciation to the state is readily identifiable in the case of *DN v Switzerland*.[9] In this case, the ECtHR was required to determine whether the state's incarceration of a woman with schizophrenia was lawful. The ECtHR concluded that the psychiatrist who sat as judge rapporteur on the Administrative Appeals Commission had, before the hearing, formed an opinion that the patient should not be released. The patient consequently had legitimate fears that the expert judge's preconceived opinion meant that he was not acting impartially, which was reinforced because he was the sole psychiatric expert and the only person who had interviewed her, and yet he was involved in making the final determination in the case. The ECtHR found that Article 5(4) of the European Convention on Human Rights (ECHR) had been breached on this basis. In this sort of case, the ECtHR would ordinarily defer to the expertise of the national authorities,[10] on the basis that the medical experts are closer and more attuned to the situation that an international tribunal of non-experts who have not been able to examine the patient. Here, though, the ECtHR is suspicious of the way in which expertise is used in the case, and examines the appropriate use and weight to be accorded to expertise in the making of its decisions. The following extract exemplifies this well:

Experts are only called upon to assist a court with pertinent advice derived from their specialized knowledge without having adjudicative functions. It is up to the particular court and its judges to assess such expert advice together with all other relevant information and evidence.[11]

In this case, the problem was that the decision relating to the applicant's liberty appeared to be marred because one of the judges called upon to exercise an impartial assessment of the expertise was the author of the expert evidence. The appearance of bias within legal decision-making is not something that falls more

---

[9] *DN v Switzerland* No. 27154/95 (2001) (ECtHR (GC)).
[10] See section 4.c of this chapter.   [11] *DN v Switzerland* (n9) [53].

into the expertise of the state than the ECtHR.[12] Thus the level of expertise about the decision itself was outweighed in this instance by the fact that the decision became procedurally marred in a way that the ECtHR was competent to assess without deference.

In the case of *Papachelas v Greece*,[13] the ECtHR is seen to give deference to the state on the issue of its assessment of the land valuation for the purposes of paying compensation for its expropriation. The Greek authorities had valued the land at 52,000 drachmas per square metre, and the applicants used the average of two expert reports to show that the amount should more likely have been 100,000 drachmas, and made reference also to an expert report by the Association of Sworn Valuers, which valued it at 53,621 drachmas. The ECtHR referred to the margin of appreciation and found that 'the price paid to the applicants bore a reasonable relation to the value of the expropriated land'.[14] This decision shows that the ECtHR did not refuse to look at the basis for the valuation notwithstanding that matters of an economic nature normally involve a 'wide' margin of appreciation to the state.[15] Indeed, it explicitly took into account the expert report of the Association of Sworn Valuers when making the decision and scrutinized the substantive decision of the Greek authorities. However, the level of scrutiny was thin in this case (as was the depth of reasoning), and the Court explicitly defers to the state on the value of the decision. In such a case as this in which the Court does not regard itself as having expertise, it did not seek to assess the relative value of all of the expert reports, and instead deferred to the superior ability of the local courts to make such an evaluation.

When a case implies that a wider margin of appreciation to the state is warranted based on expertise, it is nevertheless not determinative of the matter. Instead, it is just one factor to be weighed along with the other second-order and first-order reasons. This is exemplified well in Europe by the case of *K and T v Finland*,[16] in which the parents of children taken into care complained that assessments of the mother's mental health were rudimentary based on her history of psychotic illness rather than her current state of health. This case split the Court. The majority decided, amongst other matters, that the state violated Article 8 ECHR with respect to the emergency care order of the infant child, not because such an order per se violates Article 8, but because the manner of its implementation was so extreme, leading to the removal of the infant from the mother immediately following birth before the mother had even been able to breastfeed the child for the first time. It is common for the Tribunals to defer to states on what is in the best interests of the child on care matters.[17] Notwithstanding this deference to the state, all other

---

[12] Indeed, this is a matter in which the Tribunals tend to regard themselves as having expertise and is thus a reason for heightened scrutiny: see section 5.a of this chapter.

[13] *Papachelas v Greece* No. 31423/96 (1999) (ECtHR (GC)).

[14] Ibid, [49].

[15] See section 4.f of this chapter.

[16] *K and T v Finland* No. 25702/94 (2001) (ECtHR (GC)).

[17] See section 4.b of this chapter.

reasons were assessed, leading to a finding that the action of the authorities was disproportionate.[18]

In some cases, there are very few grounds for a margin of appreciation to the expertise of the state notwithstanding that the state is better placed to deal with some issues than the Tribunals. This is likely to be the case where the state has not been cooperative, or where there is a case of systematic and widespread violations of human rights, or where the inadequacy of the national protection is not regarded as worthy of deference on the basis of 'expertise' or otherwise. This heightened scrutiny can be seen in the case of *Freedom and Democracy Party (ÖZDEP) v Turkey*,[19] which involved the dissolution of a political party on the basis of concerns about the 'territorial integrity of the State and the unity of the nation'. Whilst the protection of national security normally gives rise to deference,[20] such deference was not warranted here, because the reasoning of the state was based on an unacceptable 'assessment of the relevant facts'.[21] Although reasons for heightened scrutiny existed in this case because of the ECtHR's concern to protect democracy and democratic rights,[22] it is also clear that very little deference was accorded to the expertise of the state in assessing the requirements of territorial integrity, notwithstanding that it is ordinary in such circumstances to show deference.

b. Inter-American Court of Human Rights (IACtHR)

The IACtHR has given a margin of appreciation to expertise in a number of contexts. It has not explained in clear terms that it is attaching weight to the state's expertise, but there is evidence from the case law that this aptly describes what happens in practice. In the case of *Palamara-Iribarne v Chile*,[23] the IACtHR showed deference to local expertise, but in this case it was not to the government. Here, the naval court martial reversed a trial court's judgment acquitting the complainant for contempt and convicted him for publishing a book entitled *Ética y Servicios de Inteligencia* (*'Ethics and Intelligence Services'*). The Naval Prosecutor claimed that the author used his experience in the navy to write the book, making him guilty of contempt. The evidence sought by the naval prosecutor, however, made clear that the information in the book 'may be obtained from open sources'.[24] The IACtHR leaned on this expert advice in finding that there had not been any breach of confidentiality, going on to decide that the case involved a violation of Article 13 of the American Convention on Human Rights (ACHR) (freedom of expression). Along with the protection of such democratic rights, this

---

[18] This decision was controversial. Judge Palm (joined by Jörundsson) argued that the Court overstepped its supervisory role in finding a violation in the case of the infant, and should have been more deferential.

[19] *Freedom and Democracy Party (ÖZDEP) v Turkey* No. 23885/94 (1999) (ECtHR (GC)), [38].

[20] See section 4.a of this chapter.

[21] *Freedom and Democracy Party (ÖZDEP) v Turkey* (n19) [39].

[22] See section 6.a of this chapter.

[23] *Palamara-Iribarne v Chile* Series C No. 135 (2005) (IACtHR).

[24] Ibid, [75].

case shows the Court attaching weight to the naval experts, and assessing the implications for the case in that light.

Salvador-Chiriboga v Ecuador[25] exemplifies how the IACtHR might show deference to relevant state expertise. The case involved expropriation of property of the complainants to be annexed to the metropolitan park of the city of Quito, without paying compensation. On a claim that there had been unequal treatment (because an adjacent property had been allowed to develop), the state argued[26] that, for 'technical reasons', the expropriation of this piece of land was necessary, whereas others would be excluded. The IACtHR in this case found that there was 'not enough evidence'[27] to decide whether or not there had been a violation of Article 24 (the right to equal protection), in a context (the use of land) that ordinarily involves deference to the state.[28] It is difficult to see how the IACtHR would have responded if the state had provided more reasons. This raises a question about where the burden of proof lies. Ordinarily, if there is a difference of treatment, it should be justified objectively. Does the reference to expertise ('technical reasons') in this case mean that the prima facie appearance of a difference in treatment is to be regarded as justified? If so, this looks more like abdicating judicial responsibility. The IACtHR in this case might in effect be saying: 'There is not enough evidence to counter the claim of the state that this prima facie unequal treatment was necessary for technical reasons.' An alternative assessment might be that because there is normally deference to the expertise of the state on the use of property, the burden of proof rests on the complainant to show that the state used unequal treatment. This alternative analysis appears unconvincing since such evidence is likely only to be in the control of the state. It seems that here the IACtHR ought to have demanded greater reasoning from the state before according such deference.

In other cases, the IACtHR shows that it does not rely on expertise to abdicate its judicial responsibility. This is aptly seen in the case of *Las Palmeras v Colombia*,[29] in which the Court assessed expert evidence that it had itself requested. The issue in that case related to the cause of death where there had been killings that the national courts had attributed to the state. The Commission sought internationl condemnation in addition to the national courts' findings. However, the IACtHR did not find that there was a violation of the right to life, largely on the basis that there was insufficient evidence upon which to base that finding. In reaching this conclusion, the IACtHR had to assess expert evidence. The evidence expressed strong conclusions, but without stating the grounds on which those conclusions rested. The following extract shows that expertise does not lead to the IACtHR abandoning reasoned decision-making:

> 46. An analysis of Mr Fernández' assertion shows that his remarks are not based on any reasoned logic, and therefore lack any evidentiary value.

---

[25] *Salvador-Chiriboga v Ecuador* Judgment of 6 May 2008, Series C No. 179 (IACtHR).
[26] Ibid, [127].   [27] Ibid, [129].   [28] See Chapter 8.3.d.
[29] *Las Palmeras v Colombia* Series C No. 90 (2001) (IACtHR).

47. The Court has carefully examined the statements and arguments given by the parties and the evidence they offered. It has evaluated them mindful of the time and place wherein they occurred. It has concluded that the evidence produced during these proceedings has not been sufficient for the Court to find that Hernán Lizcano Jacanamejoy was executed by State forces in violation of Article 4 of the American Convention.

c. United Nations Human Rights Committee (UN HRC)

The UN HRC likewise gives a margin of appreciation to expertise. The case of *EB v New Zealand*[30] is an example of a case in which on one issue the HRC defers to the state and on another issue the HRC heightens scrutiny based on its superior relative competence. The case involved a divorced father who was denied access to his children, following an accusation from the mother that he had sexually abused the children. Whilst the police investigations did not conclude that an offence had been committed, the family court decided that it was in the best interests of the children to prevent the father from having access. The first issue in the case related to whether the father's rights under Article 17 (interference with privacy and family) and Article 23 (family) of the International Covenant on Civil and Political Rights (ICCPR) had been violated. The following excerpt from the decision shows how the HRC relies on the state's assessment of the situation:

The Committee notes that the trial judge in the Family Court proceeded to a full and balanced evaluation of the situation, on the basis of testimony of the parties and expert advice, and that, while acknowledging the far reaching nature of the decision to deny the author's application for access, the trial judge decided that it was in the children's best interest to do so. In the particular circumstances of the case, the Committee cannot conclude that the trial judge's decision violated the author's rights.[31]

The fact that the trial court's reasoning was full and balanced, took into account expert advice, and was a judgment based on all of the evidence of what was in the best interests of the children led the HRC to give a margin of appreciation to its decision. This clearly did not amount to an abdication of judicial responsibility because the judgment is critically assessed ('a full and balanced evaluation of the situation'). The HRC did not, however, give details of its assessment, which is regrettable. On the second issue as to whether there had been undue delay in resolving these matters contrary to Article 14, the HRC was less deferential, regarding itself, it appears, as well able to assess whether or not this matter of procedure was compliant with the ICCPR. The Committee, finding a breach of Article 14, explained that:

In particular, the State party has not shown the necessity of police investigations of the extended period of time that occurred in this case in respect of allegations which, while

---

[30] *EB v New Zealand* CCPR/C/89/D/1368/2005 (2007) (HRC).   [31] Ibid, [9.5].

certainly serious, were not legally complex and which at the factual level involved assessment of oral testimony of a very limited number of persons.[32]

The HRC, similarly to the other tribunals, will not simply defer because the subject matter falls within the sphere of competence in which the Tribunals would ordinarily extend deference to states as a matter of expertise. The case of *Weismann and Perdomo v Uruguay*[33] exemplifies this caution well, whereby the HRC did not defer to the state when it sought to justify the ill-treatment of the husband and wife communicants in its 'prompt security measures'. Instead, the HRC stated that 'the Covenant (Art 4) does not allow national measures derogating from any of its provisions except in strictly defined circumstances, and the Government has not made any submissions of fact or law to justify such derogation'.[34] This is a categorical indication that mere reference to a justification that might give grounds for deference will not be accepted on face value, not even on the basis of national security. The HRC expects more reasoned justification, which was entirely lacking in this case, leading to numerous findings of violations of the ICCPR.[35]

4. Types of expertise where there are commonly stronger grounds for a margin of appreciation

The types of expertise to which the Tribunals have extended a margin of appreciation to the state include cases that involve: (a) national security; (b) child protection; (c) healthcare decisions; (d) educational needs; (e) police and civil servants' organization; and (f) economic matters. This book is not the place to provide a comprehensive assessment of the case law relating to these areas. Rather the aim of this section is to exemplify and assess the way in which the Tribunals have employed the margin of appreciation to the state on the basis of their expertise.

Some matters on this list overlap with considerations that were discussed when considering the impact of democratic legitimacy on the margin of appreciation. Mindful of the overlap, the task of this chapter is to focus solely on the aspects of the decisions that relate to expertise and how the Tribunals lean on the expertise of the state in reaching their own decisions.

a. National security

The right of states to defend themselves is given paramount importance in international relations. National security, as a core governmental concern, often requires the implementation of state policies and action that limit the freedoms protected by human rights laws. Whilst these decisions can be made after careful deliberation by

---

[32] Ibid, [9.4], and see also [9.3].
[33] *Weismann and Perdomo v Uruguay* CCPR/C/9/D/8/1977 (1980) (HRC).
[34] Ibid, [15].
[35] Articles 7 (torture), 9 (liberty), 10 (persons deprived of liberty to be treated humanely), 14 (fair trial), and 19 (free speech).

the national authorities of local requirements, there is also scope for governmental caution to go too far in the protection of national security. The task of the international judge involves giving deference to the state where the state has expertise, and yet ensuring that the decision is guided by that expertise and not by fear.

i. ECtHR

This careful use of the margin of appreciation based on the state's expertise can be seen in the European context in one of the earlier cases in the ECtHR, *Ireland v UK*.[36] In this case, the Court assessed the interrogation techniques used in Northern Ireland against Irish Republican Army (IRA) terrorist suspects in the late 1960s and early 1970s. The UK government did not contest that these techniques violated Article 3 ECHR and gave an undertaking not to use such techniques. The Court nevertheless went on to discuss the matters and find violations of the ECHR. In the course of the decision, Ireland sought to exclude some evidence of UK government officials given to the Commission in the absence of the parties and without cross-examination. Immediately following discussion of the margin of appreciation given to states,[37] the ECtHR went on to explain that the ECtHR would have regard to this evidence as a type 'which, being evidence coming from senior British officials, falls into a similar category to the respective statements made by the representatives of the two Governments to the Commission and the Court'.[38] The implication here is that such evidence normally gives rise to deference, but that 'it was obtained under conditions which reduce its weight'.[39] In this respect, whilst deference to states' expertise will be given, it will by no means be untempered.

One context in which deference to expertise is given is assessing the validity of derogations under Article 15 ECHR. In *Brannigan and McBride v UK*,[40] the Court assessed the UK's derogation. In discussing the role of the margin of appreciation in this assessment, the ECtHR stated that:

[I]t falls to each Contracting State, with its responsibility for 'the life of [its] nation', to determine whether that life is threatened by a 'public emergency' and, if so, how far it is necessary to go in attempting to overcome the emergency. By reason of their direct and continuous contact with the pressing needs of the moment, the national authorities are in principle in a better position than the international judge to decide both on the presence of such an emergency and on the nature and scope of derogations necessary to avert it. Accordingly, in this matter a wide margin of appreciation should be left to the national authorities.[41]

---

[36] *Ireland v UK* No. 5310/71 (1978) (ECtHR).   [37] Ibid, [207].
[38] Ibid, [210].   [39] Ibid, [210].
[40] *Brannigan and McBride v UK* No. 14553/89; 14554/89 (1993) (ECtHR).   [41] Ibid, [43].

This oft-cited extract[42] shows that the ECtHR regards the state has having expertise worthy of deference in determining whether or not national security requires a derogation. In response to calls by Amnesty for 'strict scrutiny',[43] the ECtHR explained again that any margin of appreciation is 'accompanied by European supervision', involving consideration of the following first-order matters: 'the nature of the rights affected by the derogation, the circumstances leading to, and the duration of, the emergency situation.'[44] The derogation in this case arose because the practice of extended detention was found by the ECtHR in a previous case to be in violation of Article 5 ECHR,[45] and yet the UK felt that the extended detentions were a necessary measure. The ECtHR took all of these factors into account and yet placed particular emphasis on the expertise of the state, finding that 'where the judiciary is small and vulnerable to terrorist attacks, public confidence in the independence of the judiciary is understandably a matter to which the Government attach great importance'.[46] The Court found in the case that the margin of appreciation given to states had not been exceeded.

A margin of appreciation to the expertise of the state in situations involving national security concerns arises also in the context of provisions other than Article 15 ECHR. One example is Article 8,[47] in relation to which, in *Klass v Germany*,[48] the Court accepted that a margin of appreciation would be given to the way in which the state responded to the threat of terrorism when conducting surveillance over postal and telecommunications.[49] The discretion given to states is, however, scrutinized: 'The Court must be satisfied that, whatever system of surveillance is adopted, there exist adequate and effective guarantees against abuse.'[50] Another example is Article 5. In the case of *Fox, Campbell and Hartley v UK*,[51] again in the context of Northern Ireland, the applicants were arrested for suspicion of terrorist activity and detained without charge for between 30 and 45 hours. The applicants argued that the police had no 'reasonable' suspicion that they had been involved in terrorist activity. The Court accepted that there would be deference to the state in this assessment as follows:

Certainly Article 5 § 1 (c) of the Convention should not be applied in such a manner as to put disproportionate difficulties in the way of the police authorities of the Contracting States in taking effective measures to counter organised terrorism . . .[52]

---

[42] For example, *A and others v UK* No. 3455/05 (2009) (ECtHR (GC)), [173]–[174]. It should be noted too that the expertise does not belong to the executive or legislature alone, but also to the courts as they assess the role of these bodies: see ibid, [180] and [184].

[43] *Brannigan and McBride v UK* (n40) [42].

[44] Ibid, [43].

[45] *Brogan v UK* No. 11209/84 (1988) (ECtHR).

[46] *Brannigan and McBride v UK* (n40) [59].

[47] For example, *Leander v Sweden* No. 9248/81 (1987) (ECtHR), especially [59].

[48] *Klass v Germany* No. 5029/71 (1978) (ECtHR).

[49] Ibid, [48]–[50].

[50] Ibid, [50].

[51] *Fox, Campbell and Hartley v UK* No. 12244/86 (1990) (ECtHR).

[52] Ibid, [34], and see also [32]:

As the Government pointed out, in view of the difficulties inherent in the investigation and prosecution of terrorist-type offences in Northern Ireland, the 'reasonableness' of the suspicion justifying such arrests cannot always be judged according to the same standards as are applied in dealing with conventional crime.

However, notwithstanding this deference, the ECtHR went on to show, appropriately, that such expertise alone would not be determinative: the state would need to show evidence to the ECtHR to satisfy it that there was reasonable suspicion for holding the applicant, especially because, in this case, the law required a less stringent test of 'honest suspicion'. The government did not provide such information and thus the ECtHR found that Article 5(1) had been violated. The three dissenting judges were more deferential, finding that the police 'must have had some basis in information received by them' for their 'genuine suspicion', and, along with the prior records of the offenders, were satisfied that there were 'reasonable grounds for suspicion' as required by Article 5(1). Whilst the dissent may have been right on this occasion, the problem with their approach is that it leaves too much to trust. Whilst it is appropriate for the ECtHR to defer to the state here, such deference ought not be blind,[53] and the police ought to have given enough information to the ECtHR to show objective grounds for their suspicion without jeopardizing their sources.

ii. IACtHR

Similarly, in the IACtHR, there are indications that a margin of appreciation to the state's expertise on national security issues is given, although there are fewer examples of the nuances found in the ECHR jurisprudence.[54] In the case of *Castillo-Petruzzi v Peru*,[55] the Court considered whether the actions of the state were consistent with the ACHR in the context of an emergency in the early 1990s in Peru that involved widespread acts of terrorism. The IACtHR declared that a state 'has the right and the duty to guarantee its own security',[56] although it must exercise the right and duty within limits that it is the Court's duty to safeguard. The case involved extended detention without judicial supervision. The state argued that the laws authorizing such action implicitly suspended the ACHR guarantees, but the IACtHR decided that suspension of guarantees must be carefully limited and specified with precision.[57] In this case, the detentions for fifteen days, extendable for a further period of fifteen days, were contrary to Article 7(5) ACHR (liberty)).

In *Durand and Ugarte v Peru*,[58] the armed forces were called in to quell a prison riot. The IACtHR reiterated its view that 'undoubtedly, the state has the right and duty to guarantee its own security'.[59] Under different circumstances, the IACtHR might have given deference to the state's view of what was necessary to keep control

---

[53] See further *Murray v UK* No. 14310/88 (1994) (ECtHR (GC)), [58]:

[The challenge of investigating terrorist offences] does not mean, however, that the investigating authorities have carte blanche under Article 5 to arrest suspects for questioning, free from effective control by the domestic courts or by the Convention supervisory institutions, whenever they choose to assert that terrorism is involved.

[54] Although see the foregoing discussion of *Palamara-Iribarne v Chile* (n23), which shows some nuance in the context of national security.

[55] *Castillo-Petruzzi v Peru* Series C No. 52 (1999) (IACtHR).

[56] Ibid, [89].   [57] Ibid, [109].

[58] *Durand and Ugarte v Peru* Series C No. 68 (2000) (IACtHR).   [59] Ibid, [37].

in the prisons, and prevent an escape that led to wider insecurity. However, in this case, in which the force used by the forces was clearly excessive, the Court took the opportunity to emphasize its role in limiting any state discretion:

[D]espite the seriousness of certain actions by inmates and their responsibility for some felonies, it is not admissible that power can be exerted in such a limitless way or that the State can use any proceedings to reach its objectives, without respecting law and morality. No State activity can be grounded on disregarding human dignity.[60]

In a more recent case, the IACtHR has shown that it will defer to state explanations about the level of force used. In the case of *Zambrano-Vélez v Ecuador*,[61] during a large-scale drugs operation, the applicants' home was broken into and they were killed. The state sought to rely on the suspension of the ACHR (Article 27) and to argue that there was no violation of the right to life (Article 4) on the basis that the attacks were in self-defence. On the Article 27 point, the Court took a similar approach to that taken by the ECHR, both representing deference to the state's expertise (the first sentence of the below extract) and taking care not to allow this to become an abdication of judicial responsibility (the second sentence of the extract):

It is the obligation of the State to determine the reasons and motives that lead the domestic authorities to declare a state of emergency and it is up to these authorities to exercise appropriate and effective control over this situation and to ensure that the suspension decreed is limited 'to the extent and for the period of time strictly required by the exigencies of the situation', in accordance with the Convention. States do not enjoy an unlimited discretion; it is up to the Inter-American system's organs to exercise this control in a subsidiary and complementary manner, within the framework of their respective competences . . .[62]

On the Article 4 point, the state sought deference on the basis of thin evidence that the killings were a result of self-defence. Here, it is pertinent that the right to life requires certain special procedures to be undertaken that lead to additional reduction of deference.[63] The IACtHR explained its criteria for assessing a state's use of force (exceptionality, necessity, proportionality, and humanity), which included some leeway for states to justify their actions. In the context of state expertise, the Commission and the victims argued that there was no evidence given by the state that the alleged victims were bearing arms at the time of the killings. The IACtHR noted that the state 'asserted' that the deaths 'irrefutably . . . [took place in the context of] self-defence',[64] whereas the victims and other witness accounts were very different, implicating the officials.[65] The evidence of the witnesses, however, was not given the same weight as that of the state; furthermore, it was given by family members of victims and so was less reliable.[66] This is an indication that state evidence may give rise to grounds for deference. However, the IACtHR found a

---

[60] Ibid. [61] *Zambrano-Vélez v Ecuador* Series C No. 166 (2007) (IACtHR).
[62] Ibid, [47]. [63] See Chapter 8.3.a.
[64] *Zambrano-Vélez v Ecuador* (n61) [99] (brackets in original), quoting the state's answer to the application.
[65] Ibid, [106]. [66] Ibid, [107].

violation of Article 4(1) on the basis that there was no evidence to demonstrate that the force was 'necessary and proportional'.[67] Had such evidence been given, it appears that it may have resulted in some deference.[68]

iii. UN HRC

In the HRC, there is also a margin of appreciation to the national security expertise of states. Such deference does not lead to the judicial abdication of responsibility.[69] In the case of *Celepli v Sweden*,[70] the Committee showed deference to the national security expertise of the state. A Turkish national was given leave to remain in Sweden (not as a refugee under the 1951 UN Convention relating to the Status of Refugees) and received an expulsion order as a result of alleged terrorist activities. He was not expelled for fear of persecution upon his return to Turkey, and instead was allowed to live in a restricted area in Sweden, without permission to leave that area, despite not having been convicted of any charge. Finding in the state's favour, the HRC relied on the state's rationale of upholding national security. Indeed, in this case, the HRC seemed to rely too much on this, mentioning merely that the state 'invoked' reasons of national security.[71] However, it is difficult to tell, given the paucity of reasoning in the decision, the extent to which the HRC deferred on this basis. It is possible that this was only one factor alongside a careful scrutiny of the state's reasons. Indeed, the fact that the HRC went on to mention that the state lifted the restrictions implies that there was some concern over the measures, and perhaps their limited time span kept the HRC from finding a violation. This is somewhat speculative given the lack of clear reasoning. The important point to note is that the national security expertise of the state was clearly a factor that affected the HRC.

The state's expertise in national security does not lead the HRC to overlook the nature of a state's response to perceived threats. In *Jeong-Eun Lee v Republic of Korea*,[72] the HRC was not convinced by the state's assertion that the communicant was a national security threat so as to justify his conviction for membership in a student organization, Hanchongnyeon, contrary to the freedom of association (Article 22 ICCPR). The HRC explained that '[the state] has not specified the precise nature of the threat allegedly posed by the author's becoming a member of Hanchongnyeon'.[73] Whilst therefore the HRC does respect and give deference to the state's national security expertise, it will not do so blindly, and will expect a level of justification. The state's evidence, although expert, will only be one consideration that the HRC scrutinizes when reaching its decision.

---

[67] Ibid, [108].

[68] A violation of Article 4 was also found due to the lack of an effective investigation by the state into the killings.

[69] See discussion in text of *Weismann and Perdomo v Uruguay* (n33).

[70] *Celepi v Sweden* CCPR/C/51/D/456/1991 (1994) (HRC).

[71] Ibid, [9.2].

[72] *Jeong-Eun Lee v Republic of Korea* CCPR/C/84/D/1119/2002 (2005) (HRC).

[73] Ibid, [7.3].

iv. Summary

The foregoing case analysis from the Tribunals shows that, in its various expressions, the margin of appreciation to state expertise in assessing national security needs is a second-order reason only, to be weighed along with other factors, and is not a cause of the abdication of judicial responsibility. Nor is the margin of appreciation here simply a case of the Tribunals pragmatically deferring to ensure their own credibility with states. The case law instead shows that the Tribunals are unafraid of finding violations in cases that purport to involve states' protection of their national security.

b. Child protection

Another area in which the state is given a margin of appreciation by the Tribunals as a result of their superior expertise is the assessment of child protection. As a generality, the state is far closer to the people concerned, and if officials have met with and understand the issues over time, they are better placed to make an assessment of what is in the best interests of the child than the Tribunals. As with national security, the Tribunals do not regard this expertise as determinative, but instead assess all of the evidence available to them, seeing the expertise of the state as one factor to consider amongst many.

i. ECtHR

In the fascinating case of *Elsholz v Germany*,[74] the ECtHR was split as to whether to find violations of Articles 8 (privacy) and 6 (the right to a fair hearing) ECHR. The case involved the German courts' refusal to order an expert witness to assess whether the applicant's former partner (the mother of his son) turned the son against him. The German courts had found that it was in the best interests of the child not to grant him custody, based on the son's stated preference. The German courts did not assess the applicant's evidence that the mother had turned the son against the applicant because he had blamed her when the son broke his arm. Had an expert been appointed, it would have been possible, in the applicant's submission, to show that the son had been a victim of parental alienation syndrome (PAS). The ECtHR made clear that 'it must be borne in mind that the national authorities have the benefit of direct contact with all the persons concerned'.[75] Given that the German courts did not take measures to find out whether the child had been adversely influenced, the ECtHR found that their reasoning was no longer safe, and was a violation of Articles 8 and 6. The dissenting judgment found that the margin

---

[74] *Elsholz v Germany* No. 25735/94 (2000) (ECtHR (GC)).

[75] Ibid, [48]. See also [49], which explains that the margin of appreciation, although wide in care cases as a result of the state's expertise, is nevertheless limited when looking at the restriction of access, which rigidly restricts the parents' right to a family life (Article 8). See also *Neulinger and Shuruk v Switzerland* No. 41615/07 (2010) (ECtHR (GC)), [138].

of appreciation was wide enough to cover this case, since the German courts were best placed to assess 'the strained relationship between the parents'.[76]

It should be noted here, though, that some of the rationale of the dissenting judgment in *Elsholz* was based on a concern that it would lead to too many applications on the basis that the parents disliked the assessment by their national courts of the relationships. This concern seems overstated, however, because the reasoning of the majority was largely connected with the refusal of the local courts to assess the need for expert evidence, a procedural defect in the case. The focus on procedural propriety in child protection cases[77] evidences a broader margin of appreciation in this context.

ii. IACtHR and UN HRC

The IACtHR appears to affirm the approach of the ECtHR in this area,[78] but there have not yet been any cases directly related to child protection issues brought in the San José Court.

The UN HRC shows deference to the state on the basis of its expertise in child protection cases. This can be seen in the case of *EB v New Zealand*,[79] discussed in section 3.c of this chapter. Such deference can also be seen in the separate concurring opinion of Committee Members Ruth Wedgewood and Sir Nigel Rodley in *X v Spain*,[80] which affirmed that, 'In its general practice, the Committee has deferred to the reasoned decisions of national courts as to the evaluation of evidence presented at trial'. However, the opinion went on to discuss the facts of the case, which involved the exclusion of video evidence with leading questions and repeated suggested answers in a child rape case, and stated that whilst the Committee deferred to this decision, there were grounds for caution in the exercise of this deference on the basis that children have a 'moral and legal right to protection against physical and sexual abuse'.[81] In effect, the opinion affirmed that any margin of appreciation given to the state in assessing the best interests of the child are not determinative, and that the Committee was entitled to ensure compliance with the ICCPR.

In *Hendriks v the Netherlands*,[82] the HRC appears to have gone too far, however, by in effect abdicating its responsibility. The case involved a German father who sought relief under Article 23 ICCPR (family life) because the Dutch courts refused him access to his son and, based on the mother's vehement opposition to access,

---

[76] Ibid, dissenting judgment of Judge Baka, joined by Judges Palm, Hedigan, and Levits.

[77] *W v UK* No. 9749/82 (1987) (ECtHR), [64] and [67], for not including the parents in the process of adoption of their child, who was at the time in foster care, and *Hokkanen v Finland* No. 19823/92 (1994) (ECtHR), [55], for not supplying relevant or sufficient reasons for the state action.

[78] *Juridical Condition and Human Rights of the Child* Advisory Opinion OC-17/02 Series A No. 17 (2002) (IACtHR), in particular [74]. See also the importance that the Court places on the discretion of state officials in cases of juvenile justice: ibid, [120], especially fn 218.

[79] *EB v New Zealand* (n30).

[80] *X v Spain* CCPR/C/93/D/1456/2006 (2008) (HRC).

[81] Ibid.

[82] *Hendriks v the Netherlands* CCPR/C/33/D/201/1985 (1988) (HRC).

deemed denial of access to be in the child's best interests. The HRC in the case decided that '[t]he unilateral opposition of one of the parents, cannot, in the opinion of the Committee, be considered an exceptional circumstance' sufficient to justify interference with Article 23.[83] However, it went on to decide that 'it was the [domestic] court's appreciation in light of all the circumstances' to deny access,[84] and thus that 'the Committee cannot conclude that the State party has violated article 23'.[85] This is tantamount to a denial of responsibility by the Committee. The dissenting opinion of Mr Amos Wako here provides the better approach. He correctly explains that it is prudent not to act as a 'fourth instance' court, but that this is not what would be happening here, since the HRC had declared the case admissible, thus subjecting the domestic court's decision to the jurisdiction and scrutiny of the HRC.[86] As Mr Wako says:

The Committee should therefore have applied [the] criteria [established by the Committee] to the facts of the Hendriks case, so as to determine whether a violation of the articles of the Covenant had occurred. The Committee, however, makes a finding of no violation on the ground that the discretion of the local courts should not be questioned.[87]

The majority's decision is a rare example of where the HRC mistook reasons for deference to be a form of exclusionary reasoning tantamount to non-justiciability.

In a more recent child protection case, *Juan Asensi Martínez v Paraguay*,[88] the HRC has reassuringly not continued this approach. In this case, the Paraguayan authorities had denied the author's custody rights over his daughters, which had been granted by the Spanish authorities. The Paraguayan authorities had noted that this would be in 'the child[ren]'s best interests' and to have moved them back to their father would have placed them at 'psychological risk'. It appears as if there is an implicit, but unstated, assumption by the HRC that if the Paraguayan authorities had properly explained these concepts and applied them, there would be a margin of appreciation given to their approach. Instead, the HRC noted that 'the judgments do not explain what either court understands by "best interests" and "psychological risk" or what evidence was considered in reaching the conclusion that there was in fact such a risk'.[89] On this basis, and for a number of other factors, any margin of appreciation that there might have been given to the Paraguayan authorities did not prevent the Committee from finding violations of Articles 23 and 24 ICCPR.

---

[83] Ibid, [10.4].   [84] Ibid, [10.5].

[85] Ibid, [11]. See the separate opinion also of Messrs Vojin Dimitrijevic and Omar El Shafei, Mrs Rosalyn Higgins, and Mr Adam Zielinski at [4]: 'It is not for us to insist that the courts were wrong, in their assessment of the best interests of the child.'

[86] Ibid, [3] and [4], separate opinion of Mr Amos Wako.

[87] Ibid, [4], separate opinion of Mr Amos Wako.

[88] *Juan Asensi Martínez v Paraguay* CCPR/C/95/D/1407/2005 (2009) (HRC).

[89] Ibid, [7.3].

c. Health care

Another area in which state entities possess greater expertise than the Tribunals, warranting deference, is in the assessment of the provision of health care and medical treatment.

i. ECtHR

In the case of *DN v Switzerland*,[90] in which the ECtHR assessed the applicant's psychiatric detention, the dissenting opinion placed emphasis on the medical nature of the expertise, as well as the fact that two other medical experts had examined the applicant.

ii. IACtHR

The IACtHR approach to medical expertise can be seen in the case of *Albán Cornejo v Ecuador*.[91] In this case, a girl with meningitis and in hospital was injected with morphine, which led to her death. The state was found liable for inadequately investigating her death and for failing to seek extradition of a doctor who had fled the country as a result. A state medical body found that the death could not be attributed clearly to medical malpractice. The Court noted that this decision was not binding on it, but would carry weight.[92] In Sergio García-Ramírez's separate opinion, he stated that the decisions of such medical experts 'will have remarkable bearing on the definition and exercise of the rights'[93] and obligations of health-care providers.

iii. UN HRC

The UN HRC similarly places value on medical expertise, finding a violation by the state in *Jansen-Gielen v The Netherlands*.[94] The national court refused to append a psychiatric report of the applicant to her case file in her appeal of a decision to declare her 80 per cent disabled and incapable of work. Her argument was that her traditional Roman Catholic beliefs caused a conflict in her role as a teacher, which made her ill for over a year, but she was not disabled. The declaration of disability prevented her from getting another job. The Committee placed emphasis on the lack of clarity on procedural rules of disclosure, but also on the importance of the medical expertise, appearing to give rise to implicit deference.[95]

---

[90] *DN v Switzerland* (n9), discussed in section 3.a of this chapter.
[91] *Albán Cornejo v Ecuador* Series C No. 171 (2007) (IACtHR).
[92] Ibid, [74]–[78].   [93] Ibid, [22], separate opinion of Sergio García-Ramírez.
[94] *Jansen-Gielen v The Netherlands* CCPR/C/71/D/846/1999 (2001) (HRC).
[95] See especially the separate, concurring, opinion of David Kretzmer and Martin Scheinin, ibid: '[T]he State party has offered no explanation why, given the centrality of the report to the author's case, the court did not take measures to allow consideration of the report by the other party rather than simply ignoring it.'

As ever, any margin of appreciation given to the competent state authorities by the HRC will not be determinative. This is aptly shown in the case of *Ernest Sigman Pillai and others v Canada*.[96] The HRC was asked to consider the immigration authorities' decision to deport the author to Sri Lanka, on the basis that they had failed adequately to consider his account of alleged torture because of a diagnosis of post-traumatic stress disorder (PTSD). The Committee regarded this omission, along with other factors, as relevant, and thus stated:

Notwithstanding the deference given to the immigration authorities to appreciate the evidence before them, the Committee considers that further analysis should have been carried out in this case. The Committee therefore considers that the removal order issued against the authors would constitute a violation of article 7 of the Covenant if it were enforced.[97]

d. Education

i. ECtHR

On matters of educational policy, too, there are grounds for the Tribunals to defer to the local expertise of the state, as can be seen in the case of *Leyla Şahin v Turkey*.[98] This case involved compatibility of the banning of the wearing of head-scarves in the University of Istanbul with the ECHR. Whilst this case was about freedom of religion, the Court made note of the special deference to be given to the state 'when it comes to regulating the wearing of religious symbols in educational institutions',[99] because it is more in touch with the context to be able to judge accurately whether such a restriction is needed.

ii. UN HRC

A similar approach can be seen in the HRC case of *Lindgren v Sweden*.[100] The communicants were parents whose children attended private schools. They complained that they were being discriminated against because they were not granted subsidies by the state for textbooks, tuition, school meals, and transport, whereas some other private schools in other municipalities benefited from such subsidies. The state argued that it delegated this decision making to the municipalities, which were best able to judge local educational needs. The HRC explained that such delegation nevertheless required objective and reasonable criteria, but in this case the Committee declared itself unable to conclude that the schools' denials of subsidies were incompatible with Article 26 ICCPR (equality and non-discrimination). This seemingly shifts the burden to the communicant to show that the differential treatment was illegitimate from the state having to explain it, and signifies deference to the expertise of officials involved in local educational decisions.

[96] *Ernest Sigman Pillai et al v Canada* CCPR/C/101/D/1763/2008 (2011) (HRC).
[97] Ibid, [11.4].
[98] *Leyla Şahin v Turkey* No. 44774/98 (2005) (ECtHR (GC)).
[99] Ibid, [109].
[100] *Lindgren v Sweden* CCPR/C/40/D/299/1988 (1990) (HRC).

e. Policing and civil service

There will also be a margin of appreciation to the state on the basis of how to organize its local police forces and other aspects of civil service. The member state is best placed to know what form a particular agency will take, or indeed whether or not a particular agency is needed at all in the context of the particular social and historical conditions within each state. There is no uniformly required approach to government, and it is not for human rights law to circumscribe either the method or functioning of government agencies. The Tribunals will instead, in a relevant case, ensure that such agencies that do exist comply with international human rights obligations.

i. ECtHR

An example of this can be seen in the case of *Rekvényi v Hungary*.[101] In this case, a new constitutional provision was brought in prohibiting police involvement in politics. The applicant complained that it lacked clarity about what activities were included, and whilst this was later clarified to allow his activities in the trade union, he complained that the intervening period violated his rights to free speech (Article 10 ECHR), association (Article 11), and non-discrimination (Article 14). In finding no violation, the ECtHR explained that the special margin of appreciation for the state in determining the duties and obligations of civil servants[102] applied to police officers.[103]

f. Economic matters

The margin of appreciation granted to the state on the basis of being best able to assess local economic matters (including the use of property) often overlaps with grounds for a margin of appreciation on the basis of democratic legitimacy, because economic matters involve policy considerations. In this chapter, the matter of expertise alone is considered. Even Dworkin, who does not seem to support the concept of judicial deference on the basis of democratic legitimacy, appears to accept that deference on the basis of economic expertise may be appropriate.[104] This section sets out some examples of cases that reveal that the expertise of the state is one external factor, alongside democratic legitimacy, which the Tribunals assess in these sorts of cases.

---

[101] *Rekvényi v Hungary* No. 25390/94 (1999) (ECtHR (GC)).

[102] Established in the case of *Vogt v Germany* No. 17851/91 (1995) (ECtHR (GC)), [53], in which a teacher's dismissal for her political activities was found to be disproportionate, notwithstanding the special margin of appreciation for the duties and obligations of civil servants specified.

[103] *Rekvényi v Hungary* (n101) [43].

[104] R Dworkin, *Law's Empire* (Hart, Oxford 1998) 398.

i. ECtHR

In *Papachelas v Greece*,[105] the ECtHR deferred to the local courts' assessment of the land valuation experts concerning the value of land that would make way for a new road. Likewise, in the case of *Stec v UK*,[106] the ECtHR found that pension policy warranted deference on the basis of the state's expertise: 'The Court considers that such questions of administrative economy and coherence are generally matters falling within the margin of appreciation.'[107]

However, just because there are grounds for a broader margin of appreciation to the state in respect of economic policies, this does not, as ever, mean that the state has *carte blanche* to implement any policy regardless of its impact on individuals. This is exemplified well by the case of *Andrejeva v Latvia*,[108] in which the applicant was not granted a pension for her employment in Latvia on the basis that she was not a Latvian citizen, but only a permanent resident. The Grand Chamber stated that:

being mindful of the broad margin of appreciation enjoyed by the State in the field of social security, the arguments submitted by the Government are not sufficient to satisfy the Court that there was a 'reasonable relationship of proportionality' in the instant case that rendered the impugned difference of treatment compatible with the requirements of Article 14 of the Convention.[109]

The result reached by the Grand Chamber is reminiscent of the *Chassagnou*[110] decision in which the ECtHR in effect found the restriction to be manifestly without a reasonable foundation, but used more polite reasoning to reach this conclusion.[111]

ii. IACtHR

The same sort of approach to expertise in the sphere of economic matters is seen in the IACtHR in the case *Salvador-Chiriboga v Ecuador*,[112] which appears to favour the state's reference to 'technical reasons' in the assessment of land use, rather than requires clear justification for differential treatment between the grant of rights to develop the adjacent property to the applicants, whose property was expropriated.[113]

---

[105] *Papachelas v Greece* (n13), discussed in section 3.a of this chapter.

[106] *Stec v UK* No. 65731/01 (2006) (ECtHR (GC)).

[107] Ibid, [57]. See also *Chapman v UK* No. 27238/95 (2001) (ECtHR (GC)), [92], in which the ECtHR explained why planning authorities were better placed to respond to how land should be utilized, in this case in the context of provision of land for gypsies to live on:

[The Court] cannot visit each site to assess the impact of a particular proposal on a particular area in terms of beauty, traffic conditions, sewerage and water facilities, educational facilities, medical facilities, employment opportunities and so on. Because planning inspectors visit the site, hear the arguments on all sides and allow the examination of witnesses, they are better placed than the Court to weigh the arguments.

[108] *Andrejeva v Latvia* No. 55707/00 (2009) (ECtHR (GC)).

[109] Ibid, [89].

[110] *Chassagnou v France* Nos 25088/94, 28331/95, 28443/95 (1999) (ECtHR (GC)).

[111] See discussion in Chapter 4.4.a in relation to *Chassagnou v France* (ibid).

[112] *Salvador-Chiriboga v Ecuador* (n25), discussed in section 3.b of this chapter.

[113] This approach is affirmed in *Abrill-Alosilla et al v Peru* Series C No. 223 (2011) (IACtHR), [82].

iii. UN HRC

The UN HRC similarly shows deference to states' expertise in economic matters. In the case of *Kitok v Sweden*,[114] the HRC, having explained that '[t]he regulation of an economic activity is normally a matter for the State alone',[115] decided that the state regulation of reindeer husbandry by the indigenous Sami people was compatible with cultural rights (Article 27 ICCPR). Although the reasoning in the case was somewhat thin, the measures of the state were regarded as reasonable and consistent with Article 27, and it appears that there was some deference to the state's economic approach, especially since there were other cultural activities for the applicant to continue practising.

Further, in the case of *Fernando Machado Bartolomeu v Portugal*,[116] the standard of review that the Committee employed to assess whether the taxation regime at issue was discriminatory was low. The tax was on croupiers' tips. It applied only to croupiers' tips, not to waiters' or those of other service staff—even those working in the casino industry. On this basis, the communicant complained that the practice was discriminatory. The state party argued that there were legitimate differences, given the size of the sums involved and how they were distributed in the croupier profession was different. Noting the arguments for a unique and specific tax regime for croupiers, the Committee stated that it was:

not in a position to conclude that this taxation regime is unreasonable in the light of such considerations as the size of tips, how they are distributed, the fact they are closely related to the employment contract and the fact that they are not granted on a personal basis.[117]

This decision shows that the HRC will consider all of the first-order reasons, but will apply a less exacting standard of review, what was called a 'reasonableness' standard in *Fernando Machado Bartolomeu v Portugal*,[118] in the arena of the economy and taxation on the basis that the legislature is best placed to make such assessments.

In the case of *Erlingur Sveinn Haraldsson and Örn Snævar Sveinsson v Iceland*,[119] the HRC considered the way in which Iceland had historically regulated its fishing industry by distributing harvesting rights to a fixed number of fishermen, who could then trade licences for quota shares. The authors complained that this was a discriminatory practice. The Committee found that there was a violation of Article 26 ICCPR. However, the separate dissenting opinions of Sir Nigel Rodley[120] and

---

[114] *Kitok v Sweden* CCPR/C/33/D/197/1985 (1988) (HRC).

[115] Ibid, [9.2].

[116] *Fernando Machado Bartolomeu v Portugal* CCPR/C/100/D/1783/2008 (2010) (HRC).

[117] Ibid, [8.4].   [118] Ibid.

[119] *Erlingur Sveinn Haraldsson and Örn Snævar Sveinsson v Iceland* CCPR/C/91/D/1306/2004 (2007) (HRC).

[120] Ibid, dissenting opinion of Sir Nigel Rodley (emphasis added):

The State party has drawn attention to evidence supporting its contention that its ITQ system was the most economically effective (see para. 8.8) and, as such, reasonable and

Ms Ruth Wedgewood[121] argue that the HRC is required to give deference to the state on economic matters.

5. Heightened scrutiny where the Tribunals have expertise

In some situations, rather than regarding the state as having greater expertise, the Tribunals regard themselves as having sufficient knowledge and competence to assess for themselves the compatibility of state action with human rights standards. In these situations, the Tribunals heighten their scrutiny of state action.

The types of situation in which the Tribunals heighten scrutiny of the state are those involving: (a) legal procedures; (b) the length of time it takes to resolve a complaint or be granted legal redress; and (c) methods of legal interpretation. These factors, in relation to which the Tribunals have particular experience, do not give grounds for the Tribunals simply to act as a final appellate, or 'fourth-instance', court. By this 'fourth instance' doctrine,[122] Tribunals commonly state that it is not their function to act as a final appellate court in the interpretation of domestic law; rather, their role is to apply the applicable international human rights law. The aim of this section is to expound and to assess critically the ways in which the Tribunals have heightened scrutiny on the basis of their own expertise relating to such matters, which is quite different from the Tribunals acting as a final appellate court.

In some respects, these issues overlap with the nature of the right and case, and the importance attached to fair trial rights.[123] However, the significance of this section is to demonstrate that the Tribunals place greater weight on their own expertise in making decisions about legal procedure and the length of trials, rather than deferring to the approach of the states.

a. Legal procedures

Judges in the Tribunals have had distinguished careers, many of them in the judiciary of their respective states (some at the highest levels);[124] many also are experienced legal practitioners or academics. There is a wealth of experience among these judges that enables them to know how legal procedures work in a variety of contexts, and to be able to assess where legal procedures are deficient. It is

proportionate. These are practical arguments that the authors fail adequately to engage with in the reply (see para. 9.8). It was essential that they confront this issue, especially in the light of the difficulties for a *nonexpert international body itself to master the issues at stake and the deference to the State party's argument that is consequently required.*

[121] Ibid, dissenting opinion of Ms Ruth Wedgwood: '[T]he Human Rights Committee has a distinctly limited scope of review in economic regulatory matters pleaded under article 26.'

[122] See, e.g., *Hendriks v the Netherlands* CCPR/C/33/D/201/1985 (1988) (HRC), [3], separate opinion of Mr Amos Wako.

[123] See Chapter 8.3.b.

[124] For example, Peer Lorenzen, section president of the ECtHR, was previously a justice of the Supreme Court of Denmark, and Justice Bhagwati, member of the HRC, was previously chief justice of the Supreme Court of India.

unsurprising therefore that, in cases involving scrutiny of a state's legal processes, the Tribunals are less inclined to defer to the state. Whilst the Tribunals steer clear from directing the state how to organize their legal systems, they generally do not hold back from assessing whether those procedures comply with international standards.

i. ECtHR

The case of *Brumărescu v Romania*[125] exemplifies starkly how little deference can be given to states when there is a matter of legal procedure at issue in the case. Whilst acknowledging that '[i]t is not the Court's task to review the judgment [at issue] in the light of Romanian law or to consider whether or not the Supreme Court of Justice could itself determine the merits of the case', the ECtHR went on to find that the approach of the Supreme Court was defective. The case concerned property that had been owned by the applicant's parents, which was expropriated by the state. The applicant lived in one of the flats in the property, but it was later sold to a family living in one of the other flats. At first instance, the courts nullified that decision, ordering title of the property to the applicants. The state officials refused to implement the order, saying that compensation only would be given. The case went to the Supreme Court of Romania, which overruled the first-instance decision, saying that new legislation would be needed before the courts could correct the implementation of a legislative instrument. Finding that the Supreme Court's approach violated Article 6(1) ECHR and Article 1, Protocol 1, the ECtHR was quick to say that the approach of finding no jurisdiction in itself violated Article 6(1),[126] and the fact that there was no justification for the confiscation of the property in the public interest by the Supreme Court or other authorities led to a violation of Article 1, Protocol 1.[127]

In the case of *Rowe and Davis v UK*,[128] the ECtHR was asked to assess whether the non-disclosure by the prosecution that an informant was given a reward in a case involving a series of violent robberies and murders was compliant with Article 6(1) ECHR. Here, the ECtHR made clear that:

[I]t is not the role of this Court to decide whether or not such non-disclosure was strictly necessary since, as a general rule, it is for the national courts to assess the evidence before them. . . . Instead, the European Court's task is to ascertain whether the decision-making procedure applied in each case complied, as far as possible, with the requirements of adversarial proceedings and equality of arms and incorporated adequate safeguards to protect the interests of the accused.[129]

The ECtHR went on to examine the case closely, and decided that it was not sufficient that the Court of Appeal assessed the evidence on two occasions. It had

---

[125] *Brumărescu v Romania* No. 28342/95 (1999) (ECtHR (GC)).
[126] Ibid, [65].   [127] Ibid, [79]–[80].
[128] *Rowe and Davis v UK* No. 28901/95 (2000) (ECtHR (GC)).
[129] Ibid, [62].

not heard the original evidence and was not in the position of the trial judge to be able to assess properly the appropriateness of disclosure. The ECtHR thus determined that disclosure should have been decided by the trial judge in this case.[130] The ECtHR distinguished the facts from another case in which the defence had been given sufficient information to make detailed argument before the Court of Appeal as to the safety of the conviction. It is clear that the ECtHR is, on the whole,[131] far less deferential on matters relating to legal procedure than other matters of the organization of civil society. However, as ever, this does not mean that the Court always finds against the state in such cases.[132]

ii. IACtHR

Similarly, the IACtHR explains that whilst it allows for differences in legal proceedings, it will scrutinize rules of legal procedure. In the case of *Cantos v Argentina*,[133] a businessman claimed damages because the former governor of Santiago had promised him compensation for search and seizure operations that had affected his business. The Supreme Court ruled that since it was not a contractual arrangement, the time limit was only two years and had already expired. Further, the filing fees were 3 per cent, and since the case was worth nearly US$3 billion, the fees were exorbitant. The IACtHR found that the substantive decision itself was based on the law and not arbitrary, and thus did not presume to interfere with it. However, the disproportionately high filing fees were held to deny the applicant access to the Court. The IACtHR here stated that the right of access to a court is not absolute, and thus there should be some deference to the state.[134] The IACtHR went on to explain that the filing fees were excessive, and that such problems are 'compounded when, in order to force payment, the authorities attach the debtor's property or deny him the opportunity to do business'.[135]

iii. UN HRC

The HRC similarly is less deferential on the subject matter of legal procedures. In the case of *Robinson v Jamaica*,[136] the HRC found a violation of Article 14(3)(d) ICCPR (right to legal assistance where the interests of justice so require). The

---

[130] Ibid, [66].

[131] For example, the Court recognized the state's margin of appreciation in respect of organizing a jury system in *Taxquet v Belgium* No. 926/05 (2010) (ECtHR (GC)), [84], and in *Mangouras v Spain* No. 12050/04 (2010) (EctHR (GC)), [85], the Grand Chamber noted that the domestic courts were better placed than the ECtHR to assess matters relevant to security for bail, such as the accused's 'professional environment'.

[132] For example, *Kart v Turkey* No. 8917/05 (2009) (ECtHR (GC)), [79] *ff.*

[133] *Cantos v Argentina* Series C No. 97 (2002) (IACtHR).

[134] Ibid, [54], which cites the ECtHR decision of *Osman v UK* No.23452/94 (1998) (ECtHR (GC)), and in particular [147] at which it was decided that the right of access to a court is subject to a margin of appreciation.

[135] *Cantos v Argentina* (n133) [55]. See also *Barreto-Leiva v Venezuela* Series C No. 206 (2009) (IACtHR), [90].

[136] *Robinson v Jamaica* CCPR/C/35/D/223/1987 (1989) (HRC).

communicant was convicted of murder and sentenced to death (which was later commuted to life imprisonment). He initially had counsel representing him, but could not afford to retain counsel, and he refused legal aid. The HRC decided that capital cases required the state to provide legal representation, even if the communicant refused it.[137] This shows how the HRC regarded itself as having the requisite expertise and role of altering the standards, causing it to overturn the decision of the Privy Council.

In *Rameka v New Zealand*,[138] the HRC was asked by the state to defer to its approach to open sentencing or 'preventive detention'.[139] This practice involves sentencing dangerous offenders for a period of time to be assessed by reference to their expected dangerousness. The HRC, despite the request for deference, went on to scrutinize the procedure carefully, finding a violation of Article 9(4) ICCPR (the right to review legality of detention). The sentence was for 'at least 7.5 years', but only after ten years' imprisonment would the courts assess the dangerous of the offender—thus leaving two and a half years of unreviewable detention. The HRC showed deference to the state (finding that such forms of detention were within the discretion of states), but scrutinized carefully the particular practice on this occasion.[140]

The fact that a state is afforded deference for matters of legal procedure has led, on one occasion, to a startling chiding of the HRC by a cooperative state because the HRC was not being robust enough in guiding states as to the appropriate measures required to uphold Article 14 ICCPR. In the case of *Karttunen v Finland*,[141] there was potential bias in a bankruptcy action because two of the lay judges involved in the early proceedings had connections with the relevant bank.

---

[137] Ibid, [10.3].
[138] *Rameka v New Zealand* CCPR/C/79/D/1090/2002 (2003) (HRC).
[139] See ibid, [4.6]:

> The State party submits that it is within its discretion to resort to sentences such as preventive detention, while acknowledging the obligation that such sentences are carefully restricted and monitored, with appropriate review mechanisms in place to ensure that continued detention is justified and necessary.

[140] For similar combinations of deference to the state on procedure, but scrutiny of specific cases, see *Morael v France* CCPR/C/36/D/207/1986 (1989) (HRC), [9.4], where the Committee stated, in a case about the treatment of a former company manager in litigation following the company's bankruptcy, that 'It is not for the Committee . . . to pass judgement on the validity of the evidence of diligence produced by the author or to question the court's discretionary power to decide whether such evidence was sufficient to absolve him of any liability'. Nevertheless, the Committee went on to assess the evidence: in the same paragraph, after assessing the evidence, the Committee said, '[I]t is to be doubted that there was an increase in the amount charged to the author or that the principle of adversary proceedings and preclusion of *ex officio reformatio in pejus* were ignored'. See also *Kavanagh v Ireland* CCPR/C/71/D/819/1998 (HRC), [10.1], in which the Committee said, 'In the Committee's view, trial before courts other than the ordinary courts is not necessarily, per se, a violation of the entitlement to a fair hearing and the facts of the present case do not show that there has been such a violation', but went on to assess the use of a specialist criminal tribunal in the instant case, finding a violation of Article 26 (right to equal treatment and non-discrimination) because no demonstrable criteria were given as to why the special procedure was required or the ordinary courts were insufficient. See also *Larrañaga v Philippines* CCPR/C/87/D/1421/2005 (2006) (HRC), particularly Ruth Wedgewood's separate opinion. Finally, see also *MG v Germany* CCPR/C/93/D/1482/2006 (2008) (HRC).

[141] *Karttunen v Finland* CCPR/C/46/D/387/1989 (1992) (HRC).

The appeal courts took into account only one of the judges' connections. The state teed up the HRC to find a violation by saying that the appeal court's actions 'might be challenged'. It went on to criticize the HRC's jurisprudence on Article 14(1) (fair proceedings) for failing adequately to scrutinize the facts of cases:

The State party contends that while the Committee has repeatedly held that it is not in principle competent to evaluate the facts and evidence in a particular case, it should be its duty to clarify that the judicial proceedings as a whole were fair, including the way in which evidence was obtained.[142]

The HRC precisely did assess the proceedings as a whole, finding that oral proceedings before the Court of Appeal would have been necessary to prevent a violation of Article 14.[143] Whilst the state's argument here is not entirely fair in saying that the HRC fails to evaluate the proceedings as a whole,[144] it is a helpful case to show that states may agree that heightened scrutiny in this field may be appropriate, and that they may appreciate clear guidance.[145]

b. Reasonable time

The Tribunals do not defer much to the state in determining whether a case was so complex that it required a lengthy period of time. Indeed, often the Tribunals apply an objective standard, arguing that resource deficiency is not an excuse for unreasonably long judicial procedures,[146] recalling the Benthamite standard that justice delayed is justice denied.

i. ECtHR

This is clearly seen in the ECtHR case of *Bottazzi v Italy*,[147] in which the short judgment set out that Article 6(1) 'imposes on the Contracting States the duty to organise their judicial systems in such a way that their courts can meet the requirements of this provision',[148] and goes on to find that Italy is systematically in violation of this requirement in the present case, without any discernible deference to the state.[149]

ii. IACtHR

The IACtHR has followed the general approach of the ECtHR in these types of case, without much deference assessing 'a) the complexity of the case, b) the

---

[142] Ibid, [6.6].   [143] Ibid, [7.3].
[144] Although it is somewhat fair. See the discussion of *Morael v France* (n140), in which the HRC seems keen to oust its own scrutiny, and yet goes on to scrutinize the state's approach.
[145] The state party in this case appears to have been influenced by the jurisprudence of the ECtHR: ibid, [6.5].
[146] See, e.g., *Lubuto v Zambia* CCPR/C/55/D/390/1990 (1995) (HRC), [7.3].
[147] *Bottazzi v Italy* No. 34884/97 (1999) (ECtHR (GC)).
[148] Ibid, [22].   [149] Ibid, [23].

procedural activity of the interested party, and c) the conduct of the judicial authorities'.[150] The IACtHR will look at the domestic proceedings in detail, taking into account these considerations and deciding whether or not the length of time is compliant with the relevant international standards.[151]

iii. UN HRC

Likewise, in the HRC case of *EB v New Zealand*,[152] on the issue as to whether there had been undue delay contrary to Article 14 ICCPR, the HRC was not very deferential, regarding itself, it seems, as best able to determine the appropriateness of the length of the proceedings: '[The state party] has not shown the necessity of police investigations of the extended period of time that occurred in this case in respect of allegations which, while certainly serious, were not legally complex . . .'[153]

c. Legal interpretation

There are certain Articles in the Treaties that, as a prerequisite for testing the legitimacy of state action, require the action to be in accordance with the law or legality.[154] This necessarily entails the Tribunals making an assessment of the legality of national law on occasion, to see whether it complies with the notion of legality under the Treaties. Given the Tribunals' expertise in legal matters, there are reasons to heighten scrutiny of a state's notion of legality.

i. ECtHR

An example of the ECtHR taking a confident approach to legality can be seen in the case of *Amann v Switzerland*,[155] which involved assessing the legal procedures involved in authorizing evidence obtained through telecommunication 'tapping' surveillance technology. The law had been assessed by the ECtHR on a prior occasion and that case did not give rise to a violation of the ECHR. On this occasion, however, the particular conversation was not of an identified suspect, but was found 'fortuitously', a class of persons not regulated by the legislation.[156] Consequently, there had been a violation of Article 8 ECHR.

Another set of cases shows the Court having to be more careful. In the case of *Z v UK*,[157] the English law of the liability of public authorities in the tort of negligence

---

[150] *Suárez-Rosero v Ecuador* Series C No. 35 (1997) (IACtHR), [72].

[151] Ibid, [73]: '[A]fter comprehensive analysis of the proceeding against Mr. Suárez-Rosero in the domestic courts, the Court observes that that proceeding lasted more than 50 months. In the Court's view, this period far exceeds the reasonable time contemplated in the American Convention.'

[152] *EB v New Zealand* (n30), discussed in section 3.c of this chapter.

[153] Ibid, [9.4], and also [9.3].

[154] For example, Article 13 ICCPR: 'An alien lawfully in the territory of a State Party to the present Covenant may be expelled therefrom only in pursuance of a decision reached in accordance with law . . .'

[155] *Amann v Switzerland* No. 27798/95 (2000) (ECtHR (GC)).

[156] Ibid, [61].

[157] *Z v UK* No. 29392/95 (2001) (ECtHR (GC)).

was subject to the scrutiny of the Court. In a prior case,[158] the ECtHR had found that the English law of tort created a procedural immunity for the public authorities in denying a duty of care, in contravention of the Article 6 right of access to a court. In the case of *Z*, this position was modified. Whilst still scrutinizing in detail the judgments of the UK courts,[159] the ECtHR decided that 'in the light of the clarifications subsequently made by the domestic courts'[160] the inclusion of the 'fair, just and reasonable' criteria of the duty of care element of negligence was part of the substantive right of action and did not, after all, act as an immunity (in this case). The careful wording appears to be face-saving, whilst at the same time back-pedalling. Many regard the decision as a correction rather than a clarification. These cases show that the ECtHR should tread carefully in assessing the adequacy of legal provision within a domestic jurisdiction. The close scrutiny of the legal reasoning in such cases, though, appears to be an appropriate reflection of the Tribunals' legal expertise.

ii. IACtHR

A similar scrutiny of domestic 'legality' can be seen in the IACtHR. In the case of *Cesti-Hurtado v Peru*,[161] which involved the detention of a retired commander of the armed forces for setting up a military insurance company, the Court made clear that whilst it was for the Peruvian legal system to assess the legality of the detention under the laws of habeas corpus,[162] the state did not allow this assessment to progress, but diverted the case to the military tribunal. The state was thus too quick to deny the involvement of the civilian courts, notwithstanding that the commander was retired from the forces, in violation of Article 7(6) ACHR (habeas corpus rights) and Article 25 (the right to judicial protection).

iii. UN HRC

In the case of *Maroufidou v Sweden*,[163] the UN HRC also appeared to show less deference to the state in a case that involved determination of the 'legality' of state action. The case involved the expulsion of a Greek national for alleged involvement in a terrorist group. The HRC appeared to be quite deferential at the beginning of its reasoning,[164] but nevertheless went on to state in some detail the reasoning of

---

[158] *Osman v UK* (n134).

[159] In particular, the House of Lords' decisions of *X v Bedfordshire CC* [1995] 3 All ER 353 (HL) and *Barrett v London Borough of Enfield* [1999] 3 WLR 79 (HL).

[160] *Z v UK* (n157) [100].

[161] *Cesti-Hurtado v Peru* Series C No. 56 (1999) (IACtHR).

[162] Ibid, [130].

[163] *Maroufidou v Sweden* CCPR/C/12/D/58/1979 (1981) (HRC).

[164] Ibid, [10.1]:

> The Committee takes the view that the interpretation of domestic law is essentially a matter for the courts and authorities of the State party concerned. It is not within the powers or functions of the Committee to evaluate whether the competent authorities of the State party in question have interpreted and applied the domestic law correctly in the case before

the state and the communicant. The reasoning for the decision was thin, stating that, '[i]n the light of all written information made available to it by the individual and the explanations and observations of the State party concerned',[165] the domestic court's decision was in accordance with law. Whilst this appears to be quite deferential,[166] close attention is nevertheless paid to the rationale of the state as well as that of the communicant.

6. Conclusion: expertise and subsidiarity

It is hardly surprising that the Tribunals give a margin of appreciation to the expertise of the state when it is better placed to understand the details or factual considerations relevant to a case and best able to assess the needs of the affected parties. Deference on the basis of expertise is an outworking of the principle of subsidiarity inherent in the treaty protection of human rights. It is, in the first instance, for the state to protect human rights, often through a complex integration of social, medical, economic, and justice systems. Whilst it is the role of the state to implement and protect human rights, that role is held in tension with the state's ability and power to undermine human rights. For this reason, the Tribunals ought to defer to the state only in so far as their actions limiting human rights standards are based on carefully assessed expertise. On the whole, the case law shows that such deference does not prohibit an assessment of the evidence. Rather, the Tribunals weigh the state's arguments and evidence along with all of the other information available, and where appropriate assign weight to the state's expertise. It is for these reasons that there is a margin of appreciation, along with careful scrutiny, in such matters as national security, child protection, health care, education, the organization of police and civil servants, and in certain economic matters.

Such a margin of appreciation is not appropriate where the Tribunals have sufficient expertise to make an assessment of the state's arguments themselves. This is most clearly evident in cases that raise issues about the compliance of legal procedures with human rights, a notable example being the length of time that is taken for the procedures to be dealt with by the state. When a case involves ascertainment of whether state action could be deemed 'legal', similarly the Tribunals, as legal experts, are able to scrutinize such state arguments closely.

This chapter concludes assessment of the reasons for deference to the state. Each of Chapters 4–6 has provided a conceptual explanation for these reasons for deference, and doctrinal exposition of the details of these reasons for deference. The next two chapters assess the way in which these reasons for deference impact the first-order balance of reasons in the case, and thus ultimately how deference impacts the decision-making of the Tribunals.

---

 it under the Optional Protocol, unless it is established that they have not interpreted and
 applied it in good faith or that it is evident that there has been an abuse of power.
[165] Ibid, [10.2].
[166] Possibly as a result of the wording of Article 13 ICCPR.

PART III

THE STRUCTURE OF HUMAN RIGHTS ADJUDICATION: THE MARGIN OF APPRECIATION AND PROPORTIONALITY

Part Two of the book explored three factors for the margin of appreciation. It is often said that there are other factors affecting the margin of appreciation, such as the nature of the right or the type of case. Part Three explores how such 'factors' affect the margin of appreciation, and argues that they affect it differently from the other three factors. Rather than providing any justification for the margin of appreciation, the 'nature of the right' contains first-order considerations that must be weighed along with reasons for deference. In other words, the 'nature of the right' necessarily broadens or narrows the margin of appreciation by requiring stronger or weaker grounds for deference depending on the rights engaged or the type of case.

The factors for the margin of appreciation and all other factors in the case, such as the nature of the right, are weighed by the Tribunals as part of their decision-making process. This weighing process is often referred to as the 'proportionality assessment'. Discussions of proportionality in human rights rarely discuss how it interacts with the margin of appreciation doctrine. Chapter 7 proposes a new account of proportionality that considers how factors for a margin of appreciation interact with the other factors in a case, which is likely to be of primary interest to academics and students of international human rights law.

Chapter 8 discusses how the nature of the right impacts the margin of appreciation, and accordingly is likely to be of interest to those readers making and considering legal arguments for a margin of appreciation. The chapter explores how different rights or types of case may provide more or less scope for a margin of appreciation, and discusses a number of examples by way of illustration.

Accordingly, Part Three considers how the margin of appreciation fits with other factors to be considered by the Tribunals and suggests a structure for adjudication in human rights law.

7

Proportionality: Determining Rights

1. Introduction

Some accounts of proportionality[1] fail to provide accurate accounts of how decisions are made in human rights law. The descriptive exercise undertaken by these accounts focuses on debates amongst different theories of rights about how the proportionality assessment is best conceptualized under the commentator's preferred theory of rights. Whilst rights theories can more or less accurately accommodate the doctrine of proportionality, such discussions do not adequately reflect the nature of the legal proportionality test.

The key to providing an accurate portrayal of proportionality in international human rights law is an understanding of its relationship with the margin of appreciation. The approach to proportionality taken in this chapter attempts to explain the relationship between the margin of appreciation and proportionality, resulting in a structure of decision-making in human rights adjudication that is not only of theoretical interest, but also practical utility. It may be that different theories of rights or commentators' accounts of proportionality exist in part because of a difference in commitment to the role of the Tribunals and consequently to the margin of appreciation. For example, some commentators would probably prefer the Tribunals to decide rights without giving deference to the legislature's assessment of competing interests in defining rights.

The chapter begins, in section 2, with a brief exploration of the origins of proportionality, arguing that its role in human rights adjudication has developed significantly beyond its beginnings in ethical discourse to provide a legal doctrine for testing the legitimacy of state action and compliance with human rights obligations. Section 3 assesses approaches to proportionality, in particular those that rely on different theories of rights, arguing that these approaches can be vastly improved by connecting more concretely with the concept of the margin of appreciation as part of a more coherent theory of human rights adjudication. Section 4 sets out the approach to proportionality and the margin of appreciation espoused by the book, arguing that the Tribunals' jurisprudence in fact best reflects this approach to proportionality. The chapter concludes, in section 5, by setting out a structure of decision-making in human rights adjudication.

---

[1] Proportionality is sometimes referred to as a principle, and sometimes as a form of analysis or assessment. No major importance is attached to labelling in this book and a variety of different labels for proportionality are used interchangeably throughout this chapter.

2. The origins of proportionality

Today, proportionality is a common feature of decision-making in human rights contexts. It is a doctrine that seeks to police the justification of state interference with human rights, ensuring that the state places no greater limitation on rights than necessary.[2] The doctrine has become a familiar part of the reasoning process of the European Court of Human Rights (ECtHR), and is increasingly familiar in the context of the Inter-American Court of Human Rights (IACtHR) and United Nations Human Rights Committee (UN HRC).

The concept of proportionality did not begin as a legal concept, but rather its origins can be traced to ethical discourse, particularly the assessment of side effects.[3] The concept made the journey into national law, for example German constitutional law, before becoming a judicial doctrine in international human rights law.

In 1968, the ECtHR, in the seminal *Belgian Linguistics Case*,[4] introduced the concept of proportionality into the law of the European Convention on Human Rights (ECHR). Proportionality, like the margin of appreciation, was a judicial creation in Strasbourg. No mention is made of the concept in the ECHR itself. It is possible that national law conceptions, such as that of Germany, informed the introduction of the concept in the ECtHR. The doctrine is most prominently developed in the ECtHR jurisprudence, but can also be identified in the IACtHR and UN HRC human rights protection systems, playing an analogous role in the ECtHR.

In the IACtHR, the concept of proportionality and findings of state action as disproportionate featured in some of the early cases.[5] However, the principle was not set out in as clear a way as in the ECtHR until the 2002 case of *Cantos v Argentina*[6] (in which huge court fees, 3 per cent of a claim worth billions of dollars, were charged in a case in which the claim was held to be time-barred). The Court here referred to the proportionality assessment as follows:

---

[2] Whilst this is a common way of speaking about rights, it assumes that states interfere with rights and this interference requires justification. It is more accurate to say that assessing the legitimacy of state action helps to define the contours of the right. Hence the limitation clauses help to identify the proper bounds of state action rather than polices 'interferences' with 'rights'. This point is well made in GCN Webber, *The Negotiable Constitution: On the Limitation of Rights* (CUP, Cambridge 2009).

[3] M Luteran, *Some Issues Relating to Proportionality in Law and Ethics, with Special Reference to European Human Rights Law* (DPhil, Oxford University 2009). Whilst Luteran's thesis helpfully discusses the origin of proportionality discourse, it does not succeed in its argument 'for returning to some of the core principles of traditional action theory in human rights law'. Luteran argues that the central case of proportionality in ethics relates to assessing side effects, as the doctrine of double effect shows. Instead, it is clear that the legal proportionality test applies to state aims and means as well as side effects.

[4] *Belgian Linguistics Case* No. 1474/62 (1968) (ECtHR), [10], which states: 'Article 14 is likewise violated when it is clearly established that there is no reasonable relationship of proportionality between the means employed and the aim sought to be realized.'

[5] *Gangaram-Panday v Suriname* Series C No. 16 (21 January 1994) (IACtHR), [47]–[48].

[6] *Cantos v Argentina* Series C No. 97 (2002) (IACtHR).

This Court considers that while the right of access to a court is not an absolute and therefore may be subject to certain discretional limitations set by the State, the fact remains that the means used must be proportional to the aim sought. The right of access to a court of law cannot be denied because of filing fees.[7]

In the HRC, early cases seem to rely on the ideas inherent in the proportionality assessment, but do not always use its terminology.[8] A clearer use of the structure of proportionality reasoning came soon after, but it seems that the HRC is avoiding directly adopting the language of proportionality in a similar way—that it is 'speaking silently' the language of the margin of appreciation. In *Ballantyne v Canada*,[9] the HRC outlines the test for determining the scope of the rights to freedom of expression in a strikingly similar way to the proportionality structure under the ECHR:

Any restriction of the freedom of expression must cumulatively meet the following conditions: it must be provided for by law, it must address one of the aims enumerated in paragraph 3(a) and (b) of article 19, and must be necessary to achieve the legitimate purpose.[10]

The doctrine of proportionality in the Tribunals does not have any clear connection with the older concept of proportionality in ethics discourse. Instead, proportionality in international human rights law has developed as a legal principle in its own right that the Tribunals use to determine the limits of rights, sometimes simply as a matter of substance rather than by using the label 'proportionality'.

The doctrine of proportionality assesses both the means and the side effects of state action, and indeed on rare occasion the structure of proportionality reasoning applies even to the test within the limitation clause to assess the legitimacy of the state's aim. These different assessments are best shown by looking at three ECtHR cases. In *Dudgeon v UK*,[11] the ECtHR assessed the proportionality of the means used by the state to 'preserve public order and decency' in regulating homosexual conduct through the criminal law. In this case, no argument was made that the aim of such criminal legislation was not legitimate, but rather that the means employed were disproportionate to the aim. The majority of the ECtHR decided:

On the issue of proportionality, the Court considers that such justifications as there are for retaining the law in force unamended are outweighed by the detrimental effects which the very existence of the legislative provisions in question can have on the life of a person of homosexual orientation like the applicant.[12]

---

[7] Ibid, [54]. At the end of this extract, the original text refers to the ECtHR case of *Osman v UK* No.23452/94 (1998) (ECtHR (GC)), [147], [148], and [152], which references the margin of appreciation and proportionality, highlighting how closely connected the ECtHR and IACtHR conception of proportionality is.

[8] Examples of an early case that does not use the word 'proportionality', but which relies on the idea of it, is *Weinberger v Uruguay* CCPR/C/11/D/28/1978 (1980) (HRC),[14]–[15], and an early case that uses the term 'disproportionate' is *Suarez de Guerrero v Colombia* CCPR/C/15/D/45/1979 (1982) (HRC), [13.3].

[9] *Ballantyne v Canada* CCPR/C/47/D/385/1989 (1993) (HRC).

[10] Ibid, [11.4].

[11] *Dudgeon v UK* No. 7525/76 (1981) (ECtHR).

[12] Ibid, [60].

It can be seen here that proportionality of the means involved a judgment that the impact of this legislation led to an unjustifiable encroachment of the rights of the applicant and other homosexuals. It may be that a different law with an alternative rationale would not have breached Article 8 ECHR.

The same approach can be seen with respect to the side effects of state action as exemplified by the transsexual cases. In the seminal decision of *Christine Goodwin v UK*,[13] the ECtHR decided that the UK's decision refusing to allow the applicant to change her birth certificate and National Insurance number had certain negative side effects. The aim was to maintain historic integrity, the means was a refusal to allow a change to the birth certificate and National Insurance number, and the side effects on the applicant involved such matters as humiliation in taking out an insurance policy, employers being able to discover the applicant's previous gender, differences in the applicant's ability to claim bus passes and other benefits to which other women were entitled at the age of 60, but which the applicant would have to wait for the age of 65 to be able to claim, etc. The Court assessed the proportionality of the state's refusal to make the changes to its system in this case by using the terminology of 'fair balance'.[14] The decision in favour of the applicant results in a finding that the negative side effects for the applicant unacceptably infringe Article 8, and that therefore the state must allow changes in official documentation as a result of gender operations. The operation of the proportionality principle here in a case relating to side effects has a similar impact on the scope of Article 8.

More rarely, the proportionality assessment is used to assess the legitimacy of the state's aims. Normally, this will not happen, because the applicant will not argue that the aim itself is illegitimate. For example, if a highway is to be built over the applicant's land, the argument will not be about whether the state has a legitimate aim in building highways. The clearest example of a case in which a finding that there was no legitimate aim of the state was *Darby v Sweden*,[15] in which there was very little argument on the point since the state conceded that its actions in refusing non-residents exemption from the church tax were not justified by a legitimate aim. As a result of the concession, there was no need for consideration of the various first-order and second-order reasons for and against the state, nor reliance on a proportionality assessment. However, in the case of *Thlimmenos v Greece*,[16] the Grand Chamber of the ECtHR found that, as a result of disproportionality, the state's conduct lacked a legitimate aim. In that case, the state had jailed a Jehovah's Witness for refusing to join the army. As a result of his criminal record, the applicant was excluded from becoming an accountant. The applicant said that failure to differentiate between types of criminal record, such as crimes of conscience, resulted in a disproportionate exclusion and hence a failure to pursue a

---

[13] *Christine Goodwin v UK* No. 28957/95 (ECtHR (GC)).
[14] Ibid, [89]–[93].
[15] *Darby v Sweden* No. 11581/85 (1990) (ECtHR).
[16] *Thlimmenos v Greece* No. 34369/97 (2000) (ECtHR (GC)).

legitimate aim.[17] Thus the blanket exclusion of all those with criminal records from accountancy was, it was argued, not a legitimate aim.

It is seen that the legal proportionality test goes beyond the origins of proportionality in ethics discourse with its focus on assessing side effects. Indeed, the same structure of proportionality reasoning is employed in the assessment of the side effects, means, and even ends of state action. The reasons for deference discussed in Chapters 4–6 are relevant to assessing the state conduct. A proper account of proportionality in international human rights law will not only assess the first-order reasons, but also explain how second-order reasons are relevant to determining the content of rights.

Discussion of just these few ECtHR cases has shown that the proportionality assessment is represented in a variety of different ways, for example as a proportion between ends and means, and also as involving some sort of 'weighing' or balancing exercise. This highlights the major debate of the nature of proportionality in legal discourse to which we now turn.

3. Theories of rights: balancing, trumps, and human rights determinations

The doctrine of proportionality in human rights law has given rise to concern amongst some commentators, in particular from those who see the connection between balancing and proportionality as a potential threat to rights. The concern is that if rights can be overridden by other interests when placed in the balance, then human rights are themselves at risk.[18]

The major debate regarding the nature of the proportionality exercise has been whether it involves some sort of balancing exercise. In its crude form, the major positions are between whether the courts themselves select the standards or whether they apply a more objective measurement to determining the appropriate legal standard. Accounts on either side of the debate have omitted discussion of how second-order reasons are relevant to the determination of rights, and are consequently deficient.

The different approaches have found adherents amongst two main camps of rights theorist.[19] The first camp involves interest-based theorists of rights, such as Alexy, Raz, and Rivers. The second camp involves 'rights as trumps' theorists, such as Habermas, Dworkin, and Letsas. These different schools take a quite different theoretical approach to rights and consequently appear to produce a very different approach to proportionality. On closer inspection, however, the structure of the Tribunals' approach to proportionality is in fact compatible with a variety of these

---

[17] Ibid, [46]–[47].

[18] S Tsakyrakis, 'Proportionality: An Assault on Human Rights?' (2009) 7 (3) IJCL 468; Webber (n2).

[19] See, e.g., A McHarg, 'Reconciling Human Rights and the Public Interest: Conceptual Problems and Doctrinal Uncertainty in the Jurisprudence of the European Court of Human Rights' (1999) 62 MLR 671, especially 678–83.

approaches to rights. What instead is most significant is the approach of the courts to their own role and consequently the way in which the Tribunals take account of second-order reasons along with the first-order reasons in a case. Whilst interest-based theories of rights are preferable to trumps theories of rights and are more reflective of the approach of the Tribunals, a sound understanding of proportionality as a careful consideration of all first-order and second-order reasons in a case culminating in judgment can be shared by different theories of rights, with room for differences on how much weight is to be given to second-order reasons in the case depending on judicial philosophies of the role of tribunals and judges.

a. Interest-based theories

Some rights theories suggest that rights are based on interests, which may include people's interests in having rights.[20] Where there are competing interests, these need to be considered alongside each other, and can be set aside, for example, by stronger requirements of the common good. One of the most common ways of describing this process by interest theorists is to resort to the language of 'balancing'. In human rights law, the proportionality analysis employed by tribunals to assess competing interests has also used the terminology of balancing.

There are two main different possibilities at play when 'balancing' terminology is employed: (i) it may simply be a label or metaphor used to describe the process of determination of rights; and (ii) it may involve a structured process for determining rights. The latter is the view that appears to have been adopted by Alexy in some of his writings. In the section that follows, Alexy's thesis of proportionality as balancing, which can involve some rational balancing of competing interests, will be tested.

i. Balancing as a rational assessment of competing interests

Alexy's argument can be summarized as follows. Interests can be balanced against each other, whether they are rights or public interests, where they are principles that both require optimization. The way in which the principles are balanced is by comparing the intensity of the interference with each principle, bearing in mind the importance of each principle.

There are cases that imply that this is the way in which the Tribunals undertake the proportionality assessment. In *Hatton v UK*,[21] which assessed the policy of night flights at Heathrow, the ECtHR discussed whether the case should be analysed under Article 8(1) ECHR as a positive obligation or under Article 8(2) as an interference with a public authority, deciding that the applicable principles were similar. Having said this, the ECtHR explained that '[i]n both contexts regard

---

[20] J Raz, *The Morality of Freedom* (OUP, Oxford 1986) 186–92. See also J Finnis, *Natural Law and Natural Rights* (Clarendon Press, Oxford 1980) ch VIII.

[21] *Hatton v UK* No. 36022/97 (2003) (ECtHR (GC)).

must be had to the fair balance that has to be struck between the competing interests of the individual and of the community as a whole'.[22]

In *Evans v UK*[23] (whether to keep and have access to frozen fertilized eggs after the man had withdrawn his consent for their use), there was a dissenting judgment given by four judges (Türmen, Tsatsa-Nikolovska, Spielmann, and Ziemele). The majority found that the balance made by the UK was within the margin of appreciation, largely on the basis that it had been a difficult decision to prioritize the man's consent, or to protect the woman's ability to have her own biological children, and that deference should be given to the state because there was a lack of consensus among signatory states, and there had been rich democratic debate. However, the minority viewed the decision differently. In dissenting, they clearly use the language of balancing:

... Even though the majority accepts that a balance has to be struck between the conflicting Article 8 rights of the parties to the IVF treatment (paragraph [90]), no balance is possible in the circumstances of the present case since the decision upholding J's choice not to become a parent involves an absolute and final elimination of the applicant's decision. Rendering empty or meaningless a decision of one of the two parties cannot be considered as balancing the interests.[24]

The dissenting judgment here is clearly wrong that using the model of balancing can never result in the elimination of one of the interests being weighed in the scales—since a finding that the balance tilts in favour of either would result in a decision that eliminated the other's interest. However, the extract does show the Court (both the majority and dissenting judges) clearly using the language of balancing. Mere usage of the language of balancing does not mean that the ECtHR was actually adopting the approach to proportionality as balancing as outlined by Alexy. Indeed, the ECtHR was instead using the terminology as a heuristic metaphor to describe its reasoning process, as discussed further in section 3.a.iii of this chapter.

The fact that the language of balancing features in the decisions of international courts gives some credence to Alexy's explanation of proportionality.[25] However, Alexy's thesis is problematic for two main reasons: first, it assumes that it is possible to quantify both the level of interference with a principle and the importance of a principle; and secondly, it assumes that such principles are commensurable. Each of these problems will be presented briefly.

The problem of quantifying interferences with principles can be seen by assessing Alexy's examples.[26] Alexy argues that placing a health warning on tobacco products is a light interference with the freedom to pursue a profession, whereas a total ban on all tobacco products would be a serious interference. Another example is that awarding damages against a satirical magazine is a serious interference with free expression. If the magazine calls someone 'a born murderer', this is a moderate

---

[22] Ibid, [98].   [23] *Evans v UK* No. 6339/05 (2006) (ECtHR).
[24] Ibid, [7].   [25] Luteran (n3) ch 7 is a helpful analysis of Alexy's argument.
[26] R Alexy, *A Theory of Constitutional Rights* (OUP, Oxford 2002) 436–9.

interference, and possibly is a light interference (with the right to respect for personality), but calling a paraplegic person a 'cripple' is a serious breach of the right to respect for personality. However, to say that such conclusions as these are rationally obvious is questionable. There are circumstances in which an award of damages may in fact be less of a burden on a publisher than some other remedy, such as publishing a correction or apology. Also, the banning of publication of that particular article may not in fact be as draconian a measure as initially thought if, for example, the magazine is already in the third week of its monthly publication timetable. Thus it is not possible to predetermine that one type of interference with another right is more or less serious. Such a judgment would depend on the context and all relevant circumstances.

Whilst the comparison of banning the sale of tobacco products with the placing of a warning is obviously more serious as set out, it may, for example, be a less serious decision to ban all tobacco products sold without a filter, compared with the placing of an emotive warning that covers 90 per cent of the packaging of the product. Likewise, it may be that calling a paraplegic a 'cripple' is serious, but this may be less of an interference with his or her personality rights than, for example, slander or spitting at him or her.[27]

The same can be said of the importance of a principle in Alexy's theory of the law of balancing, which he calls proportionality.[28] He connects the severity of the interference with a principle with its importance.[29] Thus if we decide not to bring an accused with heart problems to trial for fear that the stress of the trial may kill him or her, then we place high importance on the right to life of the accused. Whilst this interferes with the rule of law principle, it shows the relative importance of each of these principles when considering the relative intensity of the interferences with them. Thus problems with arguments assessing the intensity of the interference apply also to determining the importance of a principle.

The problem of assuming that principles are commensurate is a major problem for Alexy. Many theorists have recognized the incommensurability of values and principles, and conclude that this leads to choices that have to be made.[30] Such choices can be trivial, such as whether one should eat an apple or a pear, or they can relate to one's entire life direction, for example whether to become a lawyer or a doctor. If all such matters were commensurable, then we would be guided to the right answers with mathematical precision. In the context of international human rights laws, the reality of incommensurables is pronounced, and yet the Tribunals are called upon to make a determination. Alexy argues that such commensuration can be made. But this implies that there are predetermined standards about how the different rights, principles, and values should be balanced. It is precisely the absence

---

[27] These latter examples are from Luteran (n3) 227.
[28] Alexy (n26) 102.
[29] Ibid, 441.
[30] See, e.g., Raz (n20) ch 13 and J Finnis, 'Commensuration and Public Reason' in R Chang (ed) *Incommensurability, Incomparability and Practical Reason* (Harv UP, Harvard 1997), especially 219–20.

of such predeterminations that leads to the Tribunals having to make a decision and resorting to the proportionality principle.

Balancing, then, offers the illusion of objective determination of the scope of human rights. However, it fails to deliver on this promise. The scope of human rights has to be determined by judges making choices and exercising judgment, not by mechanistic comparison of commensurable measurements that can be weighed in a balance.

There is another danger that commentators can fall into when discussing proportionality as balancing. The balancing terminology can give the impression that a decision is simply a matter of weighing the costs and benefits in reaching a decision. The danger of this ostensible commensurability is that it implies that certain fundamental values are amenable to be overridden. For example, Michael Fordham and Tom de la Mare articulate the narrow aspect of proportionality as involving the assessment of ends and means, but do so by using a cost–benefit analysis: 'So, if prevention of rape is a permissible aim (legitimacy), which can (suitability) and can only (necessity) be furthered by forced castration, the question is then one of overall cost and benefit (means/ends fit).'[31]

As Luteran aptly points out,[32] the cost–benefit analysis implies that if there were a conceivable situation in which forced castration would actually cause less harm than good overall, then this might become a proportionate response. Of course, the example was initially given to show that forced castration would not in fact be proportionate because the harms outweigh the goods, but it is conceivable that in some situations the opposite conclusion could be reached if a cost–benefit analysis were to be used. The cost–benefit analysis can produce a distorted representation of the reasoning process. Instead, assessing proportionality between ends and means involves judgment on the rectitude of state action by assessing all of the relevant reasons for and against that action. Involving incommensurables means that this is not some rational weighing process, but an exercise of choice about the importance of the relevant considerations taken together.[33]

ii. Proportion between ends and means

Proportionality as balancing is not the only way of articulating the nature of the legal proportionality test by commentators supportive of interest-based theories of rights. Luteran makes the case for avoiding the terminology of balancing in favour of the terminology of seeing proportionality as a proportion between means and ends, whilst adopting the interest-based theories of rights propounded by Raz and Finnis.[34] Luteran argues that the language of balancing should be abandoned, since it gives rise to a prevalent and unhelpful understanding of proportionality as

---

[31] M Fordham and T de la Mare, 'Identifying the Principles of Proportionality' in J Jowell and J Cooper (eds) *Understanding Human Rights Principles* (Hart, Oxford 2001) 28, fn 2.

[32] Luteran (n3) 186–7.

[33] See also M-B Dembour, *Who Believes in Human Rights? Reflections on the European Convention* (CUP, Cambridge 2006) 87–90.

[34] Luteran (n3) 260.

a cost–benefit analysis when instead the courts are assessing the proportion between ends and means of state action.

There is some support in the case law that the Tribunals adopt a conception of proportionality as proportion between ends and means, and not as balancing. In *Dudgeon v UK*,[35] the Court stated that:

Notwithstanding the margin of appreciation left to the national authorities, *it is for the Court to make the final evaluation* as to whether the reasons it has found to be relevant were sufficient in the circumstances, in particular *whether the interference complained of was proportionate to the social need claimed for it.*[36]

It cannot be maintained in these circumstances that there is a 'pressing social need' to make such acts criminal offences, there being no sufficient justification provided by the risk of harm to vulnerable sections of society requiring protection or by the effects on the public.[37]

Further, in the case of *Hirst v UK* [38] concerning prisoner voting rights, the ECtHR, finding that the blanket voting ban for prisoners was disproportionate, explained that '[t]he severe measure of disenfranchisement must not, however, be resorted to lightly and the principle of proportionality requires a discernible and sufficient link between the sanction and the conduct and circumstances of the individual concerned'.[39]

The above extracts show the ECtHR focusing on discussing the proportion between ends and means that involves choice and judgment based on the relevant criteria, and not some abstract balancing exercise. The same can also be seen in other cases. In *Jalloh v Germany*,[40] the police forcibly administered to the applicant drug trafficker an emetic to ensure that packages of drugs that had been swallowed were vomited up, leading to a narcotics conviction. The actions of the state were found to be in violation of Article 3 ECHR. The Court's reasoning was not in terms of balancing the various considerations, but assessing the means available to the state to retrieve the evidence.

The Court accepts that it was vital for the investigators to be able to determine the exact amount and quality of the drugs that were being offered for sale. However, it is not satisfied that the forcible administration of emetics was indispensable in the instant case to obtain the evidence. The prosecuting authorities could simply have waited for the drugs to pass through the applicant's system naturally.[41]

The Court's assessment of possible means available to the state, along with all other relevant criteria (such as side effects and other consequences of the state's action) in achieving its aims, shows that the reasoning process involves the exercise of judgment about what is required. The judgment exercised often involves a choice amongst competing incommensurable values, and consequently it is of the utmost importance that the courts express their reasoning transparently. Stavros Tsakyrakis helpfully points out that:

---

[35] *Dudgeon v UK* (n11).   [36] Ibid, [59] (emphasis added).   [37] Ibid, [60].
[38] *Hirst v UK (No. 2)* No. 74025/01 (2005) (ECtHR (GC)).   [39] Ibid, [71].
[40] *Jalloh v Germany* No. 54810/00 (2004) (ECtHR).   [41] Ibid, [77].

The problem with the rhetoric of balancing in the context of proportionality is that it obscures the moral considerations that are at the heart of human rights issues and thus deprives society of a moral discourse that is indispensable. It may be that our judges are worried about moral disagreement and that is why they try to bypass the moral arguments by masking their reasoning in neutral language. But the best way to resolve our disagreements is to spell them out and openly debate them.[42]

Luteran leans on this idea to justify a departure from the rhetoric of balancing in favour of the rhetoric of proportion between means and ends.[43] It is problematic that Luteran labels his theory as proportion between means and ends when the central case of his own re-articulation of proportionality is the assessment of side effects. The legal proportionality test in fact assesses all state actions, including aims, means, and side effects, and hence this new label is not accurate. However, the major factor militating against a change of terminology is that the language of balancing has become so embedded in the case law. It would be a radical upheaval to reject this language and could be justified only if there were no redeeming features of the label.

But the label of balancing can instead be used as a heuristic device to express the courts' action in undertaking the proportionality assessment, as is discussed in the next section. Whilst there are inherent dangers in the terminology of balancing, as already discussed in section 3.a.i, they are not fatal to the concept. The current possible problems with the terminology of balancing in judicial decision-making can be remedied without abandoning the label. Decisions can both be made transparently and without attempting to apply a mechanistic formula that inputs (in)commensurable values whilst maintaining the terminology of balancing.

iii. Balancing as a heuristic device

The foregoing sections have argued that expressing the proportionality assessment in terms of balancing ought not be considered as a mechanical structure of decision-making. Indeed, the comparison of intensity of different values and principles is inherently context-dependent. There is simply no set of scales for assessing the intensity of interference between different rights, nor are human rights sufficiently commensurable to operate a formulaic decision-making process. However, whilst the Tribunals have on occasion referred to other ways of articulating the proportionality principle, for example as proportion between ends and means, it is not desirable to abandon the commonly used language of balancing. As a matter of practice and also theory, the language of balancing can be employed as a rhetorical device to illustrate the judgments that the Tribunals are required to make.

The fact that, in the case law, the language of assessing proportion between ends and means is correlative with the language of balancing is well illustrated by *Cossey v UK*.[44] This was one of the cases under Article 8 ECHR involving transsexual

---

[42] Tsakyrakis (n18) 493.
[43] Luteran (n3) 296 and 305.
[44] *Cossey v UK* No. 10843/84 (1990) (ECtHR).

applicants, in which the applicant argued that Article 14 was relevant to the case at hand. The ECtHR said:

> The Court does not consider that this provision assists her. She appears to have relied on it not so much in order to challenge a difference of treatment between persons placed in analogous situations ... but rather as a means of introducing into her submissions the notion of proportionality between a measure or a restriction and the aim which it seeks to achieve. *Yet that notion is already encompassed within that of the fair balance that has to be struck* between the general interest of the community and the interests of the individual.[45]

That the discontent with the language of balancing can be regarded as redeemable from the possible dangers it presents can be seen by looking at the way in which Raz employs the concept of balancing in his theory of practical reasoning. Raz argues: 'Reasons have a dimension of strength. Some reasons are stronger or weightier than others. In cases of conflict the stronger reason overrides the weaker.'[46] Raz uses the language both of strength and weight heuristically to impart intelligibility to the difficult and abstract concept of acting on the balance of reasons. This is precisely what judges do when they use the language of balancing in their judgments.

Balancing for Raz is not about applying some objective mechanism to guide decision-making. Rather it is about determining which norm or reasons should guide the decision in a given case. And yet he uses the terminology of balancing because it helps to illustrate what is in fact a mysterious process that is immensely complex to pin down. Of course, the picture is extraordinarily limited. There may not be two sides to a set of scales; there may in fact be multiple potential outcomes to the decision-making process. However, in practical reasoning as also in law, the language of balancing is compatible with the usage of describing the process of decision-making. It is simply a metaphor and a heuristic device.

Julian Rivers, who translated the work of Alexy into English and largely supports it, nevertheless acknowledges that any such mention of cost–benefit analysis in proportionality is metaphorical.[47] He goes on to assert that whilst values are commensurable, such assessments can only be crude. This is an interesting position, taken it seems because he is committed to the language of commensurability in Alexy's theory. But he would do better, having acknowledged that the language can only ever be metaphorical, to remain less committed to a notion of commensurability of values since, as he rightly states, the test of balancing used by the courts 'asks whether the combination of certain levels of rights-enjoyment combined with the achievement of other interests is good or acceptable'.[48] This explanation of the decision-making process is very similar to Raz's use of 'selecting' the guiding norm.

---

[45] Ibid, [41] (emphasis added).
[46] J Raz, *Practical Reason and Norms* (OUP, Oxford 1999) 25.
[47] J Rivers, 'Proportionality and Variable Intensity of Review' (2006) 65 (1) CLJ 174, 201.
[48] Ibid, 200.

b. Rights as trumps (reason-blocking theories)

The foregoing discussion has shown that there are internal arguments amongst proportionality commentators sympathetic to interest-based theories of rights, particularly over the idea of proportionality as balancing. Proportionality as balancing in its strongest form (as propounded by Alexy) can be criticized, and an alternative understanding of balancing as a heuristic device can be employed, whilst remaining committed to interest-based accounts of rights. Commentators sympathetic to 'rights as trumps' approaches interpret the proportionality and balancing accounts quite differently.

George Letsas is committed to a Dworkinian account of rights,[49] and his account of proportionality and interpretation of the ECHR attempts to apply such a theory to this international context. Letsas rejects balancing as follows:

It is wrong to think that the limitation clauses of the ECHR open the door to an abstract balancing exercise between the various conflicting interests that are involved. The point of the limitation clauses is to invite the court to identify which principle justifies the right in question and to examine whether that principle applies to the applicant's case.[50]

According to Letsas, this entails that there is no margin of appreciation involved in deciding whether a religious minority can advertise on the radio,[51] and no balancing against the beliefs of the majority. Rather there is a simple application of the principle of the protection of free speech, which entails that it is unprincipled to protect political speech that shocks and offends, but to censor speech that offends religious sensibilities. He contends that protection of free speech does not extend to the classic example of falsely shouting 'Fire!' in a crowded theatre, since this creates a 'clear and present danger' to the life of others. Letsas does not say any more than this. Whilst one can agree with these somewhat uncontroversial examples, there is a problem with Letsas' methodology. How does he decide what is or is not contained within free speech? It seems that Letsas suggests relying on a particular understanding of rights.

For Letsas, proportionality as balancing, which he says is entailed by an interest theory of rights, contrasts with the rights as trumps, or 'reason-blocking', theories of rights approach.[52] Under this model, people have 'rights not to be deprived of a liberty or an opportunity on an inegalitarian basis',[53] and when the courts assess 'whether an interference with a right is "proportionate" [they are] screening governmental policies to filter out impermissible reasons'.[54] Impermissible reasons involve 'hostile external preferences'.[55] When these preferences are not present,

---

[49] R Dworkin, *Taking Rights Seriously* (Duckworth, London 1978) 197–8, 364.

[50] G Letsas, *A Theory of Interpretation of the European Convention on Human Rights* (OUP, Oxford 2007) 14.

[51] Ibid, referring to the case of *Murphy v Ireland* No. 44179/98 (2003) (ECtHR).

[52] Letsas (n50) 104. See also J Habermas, *Between Facts and Norms: Contributions to a Discourse Theory of Law and Democracy* (MIT Press, Cambridge, Mass 1998) 256.

[53] Letsas (n50) 104.   [54] Ibid.   [55] Ibid.

state action is proportionate; when they are, 'rights are activated and block enforcement of these policies'.[56]

The major difficulty with this argument is that no explanation is offered about how judges 'identify' what the relevant principles are that guide a decision; nor is there any adequate justification offered as to why tribunals are the appropriate entities to determine the content of rights, except for a very brief discussion[57] that reveals a general distrust of democratic institutions' abilities to determine the content of rights.

Steven Greer, an influential commentator on the ECHR system, attempts to steer a course between the alternative options presented by interest theories of balancing and the 'rights as trumps' alternative.[58] In setting forth his own approach, Greer favours the 'rights as trumps' approach, expressed through what he calls the 'priority to rights' principle,[59] but also incorporates aspects of the balancing model. He argues that the rights as trumps model cannot be adhered to completely because public interests are relevant to rights, but that when weighing the content of rights with other public interests concerns, the 'scales are loaded, but not conclusively, in favour of rights'.[60] Whilst it is difficult to categorize Greer as firmly in the camp of 'rights as trumps', it becomes apparent on closer analysis that this is where his account belongs. This is because, on the assessment of these rights, Greer regards the decision as being firmly for the courts to 'define' rights.[61] This is akin to the 'identification' of the relevant principles that make up the right articulated by Letsas. Greer states this as follows:

[T]he Court uses the doctrine of the margin of appreciation and the principle of proportionality to resolve conflicts between Convention rights when the task is more properly one of definition. While this may appear to be an overly subtle distinction it is, on the contrary, one with enormous juridical and political implications of the whole Convention system. The difference between 'defining' Convention rights to resolve conflicts between them, and 'balancing' them against each other according to the margin of appreciation doctrine and the principle of proportionality, is that under the former there is no real scope for discretion on the part of national non-judicial authorities.[62]

This theory is replete with difficulty. Greer states that there is no room for deference on the definition of rights, but that there is 'on the question of whether or not the disputed conduct is compatible with them thus defined'.[63] This presumes a difference between definition and deciding whether conduct is compatible with a right. However, as discussed elsewhere in this book,[64] deciding whether or not disputed conduct accords with a right inherently involves the state relying on

---

[56] Ibid.

[57] Ibid, 117 and 119. See discussion at Chapter 4.2 and 4.7.

[58] S Greer, *The European Convention on Human Rights: Achievements, Problems and Prospects* (CUP, Cambridge 2006) 203–13.

[59] One of Greer's 'primary constitutional principles'. See Chapter 3.3.a for criticism of these principles.

[60] Greer (n58) 210.   [61] Ibid, 212. Also 220, 225–7, 229, 259, and 266.

[62] Ibid, 220.   [63] Ibid, 212.   [64] See Chapter 3.3.a.

its own 'definition' of the right. The dispute is precisely about the contours of the relevant right both for the state and the Tribunals.

These difficulties become more apparent when Greer's examples are scrutinized. Discussing the content of freedom of expression, Greer makes a similar statement to that of Letsas noted above, but this time in the context of discussing *Otto-Preminger-Institut v Austria*:[65]

The scope of the freedom of expression in European democratic society can therefore be defined as including the freedom to criticize religious beliefs, but not to be abusive or gratuitously offensive towards those who hold them . . . . Whether this line has or has not been crossed is a question of fact to be decided by relevant national non-judicial public authorities subject to review by domestic courts and ultimately to the European Court of Human Rights at Strasbourg, according to an objective European standard with no reference to local demography. Only in this narrow sense, therefore, is there a margin of appreciation on the part of national non-judicial institutions.[66]

Rearticulating the crucial assessment as a 'question of fact' is a smokescreen that does not save Greer's theory that 'definition' is a task free of deference to the state. The decision, whichever way it goes, guides states and individuals in respect of the scope of the protection of those rights. It is by no means a mere question of fact, but rather a clear task of interpretation that results in new definitions of the scope of Article 10. To say that the margin of appreciation is 'narrow' in a case in which the entire issue rests upon whether or not the relevant 'line' is crossed is implausible.

Even more problematic for Greer's theory here is the incoherence to which this approach to proportionality leads. One of the examples that Greer gives when arguing that 'reconciling conflicts between Convention rights is quintessentially a judicial task, permitting no genuine margin of appreciation to national non-judicial institutions at all', is the right to life—'*especially* abortion'.[67] But only nine pages earlier in his chapter, Greer makes the following statement, which contradicts the aforementioned example:

Because, as the Court noted, the Convention does not clearly determine when the right to life is acquired, there is no fixed point in pregnancy when it could conclusively be said that the Convention's constitutional 'rights' principle comes into operation. . . . Therefore, so long as the abortion laws of any member state are the result of a genuine democratic debate, their content may vary from state to state and still be Convention-compliant.[68]

Greer approves of the majority's finding in *Vo v France*[69] that, as a result of a lack of consensus and the silence of the Convention, 'member states must be permitted a wide margin of appreciation in finding their own answers to the question'.[70] This contradiction is not surprising, and the conclusion reached is sensible. The example

---

[65] *Otto-Preminger-Institut v Austria* Series A No. 295-A (2004) (ECtHR).
[66] Greer (n58) 269.
[67] Ibid, 266 (emphasis added).
[68] Ibid, 257.
[69] *Vo v France* No. 53924/00 (2004) (ECtHR (GC)).
[70] Greer (n58) 256.

reveals how the argument that all definition of rights is to be conducted by the ECtHR is likely to lead to this type of incoherence.

The present section has looked at two ways of articulating what the Tribunals' approach to proportionality should be by commentators sympathetic to 'rights as trumps' theories. Both have been found wanting in different respects. Letsas' argument amounts to the idea that proportionality involves the identification of the relevant principles without any indication as to how this identification is to be done. This does not provide useful guidance to the courts. Greer falls into the same trap, arguing that the role of the courts is to 'define' rights. But again, no useful guidance is provided about how this definition is to take place.

The reluctance in Greer's theory to connect the margin of appreciation with proportionality in the definition of human rights by the courts is, it has been argued, problematic and leads to incoherence. The following section takes a different approach, setting out the argument that the margin of appreciation and proportionality work together to provide the courts with a useful structure of decision-making in international human rights law.

4. The margin of appreciation and proportionality in human rights adjudication

The foregoing sections have discussed both the approach of interest-based and 'rights as trumps' theories of rights to the proportionality assessment of courts used to delimit the scope of international human rights law obligations. Commentators who ascribe to both sets of these theories largely omit discussion of the relevance of second-order reasoning in their accounts of proportionality. Within these accounts, there is complex overlap between the conceptual accounts of rights, and the normative approach to the role of the Tribunals. If one were to separate out these arguments, it might be possible to maintain a commitment to one of the theories and yet take alternative approaches to the role of the Tribunals in determining rights and the relevance of arguments for deference. For example, it might be possible to maintain a commitment to the rights-as-trumps theory of rights, and yet argue that, in the context of international law, there is no general commitment to uniform conceptions of legal standards, that diversity is a reality of international relations, and thus that coherence within the international legal system will lead to an appropriate role for deference to states when making selections about what is required by international minimum standards of human rights protection.

For present purposes, it is sufficient to show that there is at least one account of rights that fits well with the account of deference set forth in this book, and which comports with the reality of decision-making in the Tribunals. The interest-based theory of rights and its application to proportionality as balancing (understood heuristically to illustrate the assessment of different reasons in the philosophy of practical reasoning) achieves just this. International human rights case law also better reflects an interest-based theory of rights, as conceded by Letsas.[71]

The way in which interest theories of rights are most clearly compatible with doctrines of deference in the determination of rights can be seen from John Finnis' discussion of the legal formulation of rights. Finnis argues[72] that human rights standards need to be considered in relation to other societal interests when specifying their legal content: 'Somebody must decide... about the many other problems... of reconciling human rights with each other and with other "conflicting" exercises of the same right and with public health, public order, and the like.'[73] Finnis aptly notes that:

[F]or most though not all of these coordination problems there are, in each case, two or more available, reasonable, and appropriate solutions, none of which, however, would amount to a solution unless adopted to the exclusion of the other solutions available, reasonable, and appropriate for that problem.[74]

Finnis explains that one ought not be surprised that 'people (or legal systems) who share substantially the same *concept* (e.g. of the human right to life, or to a fair trial) may none the less have different *conceptions* of that right, in that their specifications... differ'.[75]

This account of rights provides a basis for the margin of appreciation in human rights adjudication. It has not been the purpose of this chapter to engage in an analysis of which are the better theories of rights, but rather to highlight the deficiency of proportionality analyses that pay inadequate attention to the margin of appreciation and second-order reasoning, and to show that it is possible for the conception of the margin of appreciation set out in this book to be compatible with at least one theory of rights. The limitation of accounts of proportionality that fail to incorporate the role of second-order reasoning is most clearly seen in relation to Greer's approach to the limitation of rights.

Accounts of proportionality as balancing have also suffered from this limitation, but not universally. In his discussion of the commensurability of rights, Rivers weakens his commitment to commensurability by stating that the 'relative assessments can only be carried out in a crude manner'.[76] This is a sensible move for

---

[71] Letsas (n50) 104: 'This reason-blocking theory can also find some ground in the ECtHR case law, although admittedly less than the interest-based model.'

[72] Finnis (n20) 231–3.

[73] Ibid, 232.

[74] Ibid. This claim is substantiated earlier in Finnis' ch VIII.5, 'The Specification of Rights'.

[75] Ibid, 219 (emphasis in original). See also DL Donoho, 'Autonomy, Self-Governance and the Margin of Appreciation: Developing a Jurisprudence of Diversity within Universal Human Rights' (2001) 15 Emory Intl LRev 391, 429, on the fact that international standards refer to generally indeterminate, abstract norms that require fleshing out.

[76] Rivers (n47) 201. Further, at 193, Rivers argues that 'proportionality is flexible: in certain circumstances it might produce just one legally correct answer, but it need not'. In such circumstances, there is what Rivers calls judicial 'restraint' as a result of the democratic legitimacy of the state.

Rivers to make, leading him to a discussion of what he calls 'variable intensity of review',[77] which dovetails with the approach of this book.

Yutaka Arai-Takahashi similarly refers to the principle of proportionality as 'the other side of the margin of appreciation'.[78] Further, Judge Matscher describes the principle of proportionality as 'corrective and restrictive of the margin of appreciation'.[79] Judge Spielmann identifies the proportionality principle as 'probably the most important—and perhaps even decisive—factor' that impacts the margin of appreciation.[80] These commentators correctly note that proportionality affects the impact of the margin of appreciation in the judicial decision-making process. It is uncommon, though, to find commentary that explains this impact in greater detail, or indeed that considers the matter from the other perspective: namely, the effect that the margin of appreciation has on proportionality. The interconnection between proportionality and the margin of appreciation is explored further in the following sections: first, conceptually; and secondly, with a discussion of examples of that interaction in relevant case law.

a. The conceptual connection between the margin of appreciation and proportionality

It is common to think of proportionality as being a consideration of only the first-order reasons in a case. The balancing metaphor is often described as weighing up the competing reasons in the case, without expressly considering whether or how these first-order reasons are affected by second-order reasons. However, the proportionality assessment need not be so limited: where appropriate, it involves a consideration of both first-order and second-order reasons.

The proportionality assessment, properly understood, is the last stage of the courts' decision-making process. Earlier stages of the process involve the gathering of all relevant facts and information. These include all of the first-order and second-order reasons in the case. The second-order reasons are often, but not always, discussed along with the concept of the margin of appreciation. Some decisions do not require recourse to a proportionality assessment. For example, if the facts reveal a deliberate use of lethal force by the state without legal justification, then there is a clear violation of the right to life. However, many of the most difficult human

---

[77] The difference between this book and the account found at Rivers (n47) 202 is that he uses deference only to refer to 'institutional competence', which is consonant with what this book calls a reason for deference on the basis of expertise. Further, what this book calls 'deference', on the basis of democratic legitimacy, Rivers calls 'restraint'. Rivers does not discuss international consensus, since his account focuses on domestic law.

[78] Y Arai-Takahashi, *The Margin of Appreciation Doctrine and the Principle of Proportionality in the Jurisprudence of the ECHR* (Intersentia, Antwerpen; Oxford 2002).

[79] F Matscher, 'Methods of Interpretation of the Convention' in RSJ Macdonald, F Matscher, and H Petzold (eds) *The European System for the Protection of Human Rights* (Martinus Nijhoff, Dordrecht; London 1993) 79.

[80] D Spielmann, 'Allowing the Right Margin: The European Court of Human Rights and the National Margin of Appreciation Doctrine—Waiver or Subsidiarity of European Review?' (Centre for European Legal Studies Working Paper Series, Cambridge 2012) 22.

rights cases involve the state arguing that its action is justified. In such cases, if it is arguable that the state was justified, the court must undertake a careful assessment of all of the relevant reasons in the case. This can occur only once the relevant factors have been identified, and for this reason the proportionality assessment is the last stage of the courts' decision-making.

What does this last stage of decision-making involve? The tribunal considers the first-order reasons, and applies second-order reasons to them. The second-order reasons may cancel out, strengthen, or reduce the ordinary weighting of first-order reasons. Once the tribunal has considered the composite affect of all of the reasons in the case, it must make a judgment about what the guiding rationale is for its decision. This process can be described as balancing, understood as a heuristic device to illustrate the practical reasoning of the tribunal.

The consideration of first-order and second-order reasons together is somewhat complex. It can be illustrated mathematically, but can by no means be executed mechanically, since the values or weight or strength or importance of the various identified reasons are not fixed by some objective external process, but are determined by human judgment. Nevertheless, using a mathematical formula to illustrate the reasoning process can helpfully show how first-order and second-order reasons interact.

A simple example of the proportionality assessment can be illustrated as follows:

Example 1: $C(A) + B = \text{Decision}$

In Example 1, A is a first-order reason in favour of the respondent state (that is, its reason for reaching the decision on the facts), B is a first-order reason in favour of the applicant, and C is a second-order reason (for example the level of international consensus) relating to A. Depending on the nature of C, there are a number of different ways in which the second-order reason can affect the decision:

(i) C could strengthen A leading to a decision on the basis of A;

(ii) C could weaken A and nevertheless lead to a decision on the basis of A;

(iii) C could weaken A leading to a decision on the basis of B; or

(iv) C could strengthen A and nevertheless lead to a finding of B.

This is the most simplistic illustration. In practice, a realistic illustration would have many iterations. If there were several factors in favour of finding for the state, and several second-order reasons that affected each of these differently, it would become somewhat more complex to set out symbolically. For example:

Example 2: $(D(A + H(B)) + H(C)) + (D(E + F) + G) = \text{Decision}$

Here, in Example 2, the first-order reasons in favour of the state are A, B, and C. The first-order reasons in favour of the respondent are E, F, and G. The second-order reasons are D and H. D affects two of the first-order reasons of both the state (A and B) and the respondent (E and F). H affects only two of the first-order reasons of the state (B and C). D could be the level of international consensus. This could strengthen reasons to agree with the state on A and B, and also reduce the strength of reasons to agree with E and F. H could be the state's expertise relative to that of the tribunal. This might strengthen or weaken the weight that the court attaches to B and C.

There are clearly many variables here. The purpose of this exercise is not to argue that tribunals should set out their reasoning in this quasi-mathematical way: not only would this be inordinately complex, but it would also be unnecessary. For instance, of the many possible iterations of Example 2, it may become clear that C is an irrelevant consideration, or that G does not add anything to the case, or that H will not affect the outcome of the decision. In such situations, it would be unnecessary to mention them in the reasoning.

Instead, the purpose of this exercise has been to illustrate how second-order reasoning and first-order reasoning come together in the decision-making process of the court. This account is a re-articulation of what is commonly called the 'proportionality assessment', or balancing. The process applies equally where the decision under scrutiny affects the ends, means, or side effects of state action.

b. Cases that demonstrate the connection between the margin of appreciation and proportionality

i. *European Court of Human Rights (ECtHR)*

In the ECtHR, there are many cases that employ the language of proportionality and the margin of appreciation, and provide evidence of the conceptual account set out above. In *Odièvre*,[81] France set out its first-order reasons and second-order reasons alongside each other in a paragraph that began as follows: 'With regard to the proportionality of the interference...'[82] Then followed discussion of first-order reasons, such as the importance to women of the ability to decline giving their identity following birth, as well as second-order reasons, such as the international consensus of the state. The ECtHR assessed such first-order reasons and factors for deference together, finding that France sought to 'strike a balance and to ensure sufficient proportion between the competing interests'.[83]

Having identified the relevant factors, both first-order[84] and second-order reasons,[85] the Court analysed their weight, and found the second-order reasons significant in leading to a finding in favour of the state:

Overall the Court considers that France has not overstepped the margin of appreciation which it must be afforded in view of the complex and sensitive nature of the issue of access to

---

[81] *Odièvre v France* No. 42326/98 (2003) (ECtHR (GC)).
[82] Ibid, [37].   [83] Ibid, [49].
[84] Ibid, [44]–[45] (setting out the importance under Article 8 of knowing one's origins and a mother's interest in anonymity, as well as the impact on the wider adoptive family, as well as the aim of preventing illegal abortions and unofficial child abandonment, thus pursuing the right to life), and [48]–[49] (discussing the non-identifying information given to the applicant about her mother, and the new legislation in France).
[85] Ibid, [46]–[47] (mentioning both the legislative aspect of the case and the role of international consensus).

information about one's origins, an issue that concerns the right to know one's personal history, the choices of the natural parents, the existing family ties and the adoptive parents.[86]

Other cases also show the same structure of reasoning, but find instead in favour of the applicant. In *Cumpana and Mazare v Romania*,[87] two journalists wrote an article strongly accusing a judge and a politician of corruption for giving contractual rights to a car parking company on council property. It was claimed that the council had authorized one company to be granted the contract, but that the officials had instead granted the rights to an entirely different company, and that this alternative company had caused damage to cars and yet had received the protection of officials and the police. The domestic court punished the journalists for writing the article by barring them from journalism and with imprisonment. Whilst both of these punishments were not enforced and pardons were granted, the decisions were nevertheless challenged before the ECtHR.

For present purposes, the case is particularly of interest for the way in which the ECtHR found that, when assessing the limitations on the freedom of speech in Article 10 ECHR, the state had a margin of appreciation, and found that the conviction followed an orderly legal process.[88] However, such assessment of the first-order and second-order reasons was not the end of the matter, for it was also necessary for the Court to assess the severity of the punishment. This involved both first-order[89] and second-order reasons.[90] In this case, the second-order reasons strengthened first-order reasons in favour of the state, but nevertheless the first-order reasons in favour of the applicants outweighed these combined considerations, leading to a finding that the state action was 'manifestly disproportionate'.[91]

These two examples from the ECtHR show how second-order reasons, when combined with first-order reasons in a proportionality assessment, do not lead to judicial abdication, but can result in decisions that are in favour of or against the state. Most significantly, though, these examples alone show that it would not be possible to make adequate sense of the proportionality assessment without taking into account the fact that it involves an analysis of both first-order and second-order reasons together.

ii. United Nations Human Rights Committee (UN HRC) and Inter-American Court of Human Rights (IACtHR)

The same ideas can be seen in the UN HRC and IACtHR. In the case of *Herrera-Ulloa v Costa Rica*[92] (in which a journalist claimed breach of freedom of expression for criminal and civil charges brought against him for reporting diplomatic scandals), the IACtHR discussed the first-order[93] and second-order[94] reasoning distinctly in the context of the proportionality analysis. This sort of assessment in the

---

[86] Ibid, [49].   [87] *Cumpana and Mazare v Romania* No. 33348/96 (2004) (ECtHR (GC)).
[88] Ibid, [110].   [89] Ibid, [111]–[114].
[90] Ibid, [115].   [91] Ibid, [120].
[92] *Herrera-Ulloa v Costa Rica* Series C No. 107 (2 July 2004) (IACtHR).
[93] Ibid, [131]–[133].   [94] Ibid, [127].

IACtHR has also been referred to as assessing the 'fair balance' between the conflicting issues.[95]

Before the HRC, the Netherlands has made use of the terminology of balancing in the case of *Zwaan-de Vries v the Netherlands*,[96] in which a woman challenged a requirement to show that she was a breadwinner to access certain unemployment benefits for which men did not have to prove this. The HRC, whilst not using the terminology of balancing or proportionality, followed the structure of proportionality. Moreover, first-order and second-order reasons can be identified in the finding that the state had violated Article 26 of the International Covenant on Civil and Political Rights (ICCPR) (equal treatment and non-discrimination).[97]

5. Conclusion: the structure of decision-making in human rights law

The proportionality assessment is a descriptive label given to the process whereby tribunals make their final analysis of all of the relevant considerations in a case. To understand the proportionality assessment properly, the impact of external factors or second-order reasons must be considered along with the nature of the determination of rights. Too often, commentators focus on the nature of balancing or theories of rights when discussing proportionality without looking at the nature of the reasons that are taken into account in a proportionality assessment. When it is understood that the factors considered are what the philosophy of practical reasoning calls first-order and second-order reasons, the concept of proportionality becomes somewhat less mysterious.

There remains, of course, an element of mystery involved in the judicial decision-making process that this chapter has not intended to eliminate. This mystery is a necessary aspect of all practical reasoning, including the species of practical reasoning involved in tribunals. Nevertheless, the foregoing discussions using formulas as illustrations provide some explanation as to how the second-order reasoning and first-order reasoning interact in reaching a decision before human rights tribunals. This provides a structure and guidance for decision-making in many human rights cases that rely on the margin of appreciation (or deference more generally) and proportionality.

As at other points in this book, this chapter has shown that where reliance on second-order reasoning and the margin of appreciation is relevant, there is room for differences amongst commentators and practitioners about the role of the Tribunals and thus the significance of the margin of appreciation. Where there are differences about the role of the court or the state in the protection of human

---

[95] *Salvador-Chiriboga v Ecuador* Judgment of 6 May 2008, Series C No. 179 (IACtHR), [63].

[96] *Zwaan-de Vries v the Netherlands* CCPR/C/29/D/182/1984 (1987) (HRC), [8.4].

[97] Ibid, [14]. First-order reasons in this case include the impact of the law on married men compared to women. An example of second-order reasoning is of the democratic legitimacy of the state in legislation, implicit in the judgment of the Committee when it finds the impugned legislation 'unreasonable' and says that the state 'seems to have acknowledged' this by changing the law. The reasoning is unfortunately opaque.

rights, this should be set out expressly by the Tribunals. Given that the affect of external factors is inherent in practical reasoning, including that of the Tribunals, consideration of the factors for a margin of appreciation as affecting the balance of first-order reasons should be recognized more clearly. This does not mean that the Tribunals ought to refer to such reasons as 'first-order' and 'second-order' reasons, but it may be helpful for the Tribunals to explain how reasons for a margin of appreciation impact their assessment of the first-order reasons, resulting in greater deference or heightened scrutiny.

One discussion that often comes up in the context of proportionality is whether there is just one proportionality test, or whether there are different tests for different (types of) rights, for example a wider and a narrower or stricter proportionality test. A connected and overlapping issue is whether the 'nature of the right' is a factor that affects the margin of appreciation that the Tribunals leave to states to determine the content of human rights norms. These matters are addressed in the next chapter.

8
Nature of the Right and Type of Case

1. Introduction

It is often said by commentators and judges alike that the nature of the right or the type of case[1] is a factor that affects the width of the margin of appreciation or the amount of deference to be accorded to the state. Similarly, it is often said that there are different proportionality tests for different rights or types of case. There is some truth in these propositions, but they are not entirely accurate. Instead, the 'nature of the right' means that a particular set of first-order reasons relevant to the determination of the dispute are in issue. These are relevant as considerations within the proportionality assessment. Accordingly, as part of the proportionality assessment, the nature of the right has the effect of providing more or less scope for a margin of appreciation. It is only in this sense a factor that *affects* the margin of appreciation; it is not an 'external' or 'institutional' factor intrinsically connected with the margin of appreciation.

Likewise, similar 'types of case' raise the same sorts of first-order considerations as well as similar factors affecting the margin of appreciation. Decisions involving the same type of case provide the Tribunals with guidance about how they might approach similar problems again.

The nature of the right does not in itself provide a reason for (or against) a margin of appreciation: it is not a second-order reason. When, therefore, lawyers, judges, or commentators refer to the nature of the right as a factor *affecting* the margin of appreciation, what they mean is that the nature of the right affects the strength or importance of the first-order reasons that must be overcome by the three factors for a margin of appreciation discussed in Part Two. The final assessment of these factors is undertaken as part of the proportionality assessment (see Chapter 7).

Similarly, the type of case is not strictly so-called a factor *for* a margin of appreciation, but is best understood as a body of knowledge regarding the types of factor that affect the margin of appreciation, including the sorts of cases that will often result in stronger grounds for a margin of appreciation to the state than

---

[1] The 'nature of the right' refers to the first-order attributes of the right in issue, e.g. life, freedom of expression, etc. The 'type of case' refers to groupings of cases that can be within one right or across several rights, e.g. national security (including rights to liberty, fair trial, etc.), cases about state surveillance (a subset of privacy rights), etc., which may share some first-order and second-order considerations.

others. In other words, the type of case 'factor' is shorthand for a reasoning process that has already been accepted in prior case law. When general statements can be found supporting the approach of the Tribunals to the margin of appreciation in particular types of case or when handling particular rights, this lends credence to the idea that the margin of appreciation is in fact a doctrine.[2]

The purpose of this discussion is to clarify how legal arguments in this area work. Cases dealing with particular rights or types of case form a body of decisions that provide guidance to the Tribunals about which first-order and second-order considerations might be relevant in such cases. In this way, accounts of the margin of appreciation or proportionality organized by right or type of case provide helpful categories for lawyers and judges alike.[3] However, such accounts do not accurately explain how the margin of appreciation operates in human rights adjudication. This is best understood by reference to the three factors for a margin of appreciation in Part Two, weighed along with the first-order considerations in the proportionality assessment.

Accounts of the margin of appreciation and proportionality that cite the relevance of the type of right or case are set out in section 2 of this chapter, including more detailed discussion of what the difference is between the 'nature of the right' and the 'type of case'. The remaining two sections of the chapter discuss the main groupings of different rights (section 3) and identify various 'types of case' (section 4). Some cases discussed in this chapter have been selected because they demonstrate how the nature of the right or the type of case as a category can provide useful guidance about the sorts of issues that are commonly relevant to the margin of appreciation and proportionality when faced with similar cases. Other cases have been selected because they demonstrate the opposite—namely, that just because a case falls within a certain 'type' or involves a particular right, there is no guarantee that it will provide clear guidance about the sorts of reasons relevant to the margin of appreciation and proportionality. It is obviously not the purpose of this chapter to provide a comprehensive catalogue of human rights cases involving the margin of appreciation or proportionality, but rather to provide examples that show how previous cases can present useful examples in different types of case and when dealing with different rights in a more systematic way than in other chapters, as well as to show the limitations of this categorization of the case law.

2. How the 'nature of the right' or 'type of case' may affect the margin of appreciation or proportionality

It is commonly said that the nature of the right or the type of case in issue affects the margin of appreciation. In a leading practitioner text on the European Convention

---

[2] See Chapter 1.3.

[3] For example, Y Arai-Takahashi, *The Margin of Appreciation Doctrine and the Principle of Proportionality in the Jurisprudence of the ECHR* (Intersentia, Antwerpen; Oxford 2002) pt II, and HC Yourow, *The Margin of Appreciation Doctrine in the Dynamics of European Human Rights Jurisprudence* (DPhil, University of Michigan 1995; Kluwer Law International, The Hague 1996).

on Human Rights (ECHR), the nature of the Convention right is the first consideration mentioned that affects the margin of appreciation.[4] Other accounts likewise make reference to the nature of the right as a factor that affects deference.[5] The same can be said of the type of case.[6]

It is also commonly said that there are different proportionality tests for different types of case or right, akin to the varying levels of scrutiny in the US Supreme Court (strict scrutiny for First Amendment protection and some other 'suspect classifications' such as race discrimination, heightened review or intermediate scrutiny for claims of sex discrimination, or rational basis review, which is a more general test). The idea of varying proportionality tests can be seen in the dissent of Judge Zupančič in the case of *Burden and Burden v UK*:[7] 'The mildest proportionality (reasonableness) test is applied to social and economic matters such as the one at hand.'

What exactly is meant by the idea of the nature of the right and the type of case being a factor that affects the margin of appreciation or the proportionality assessment? The first thing that can be noticed in accounts that mention the nature of the right or the type of the case as being a factor affecting the margin of appreciation or proportionality is that they rarely provide an explanation as to how these issues are factors at all. Indeed, there is sometimes confusion between terminology of 'nature of the right' and 'type of case'. In one textbook on the ECHR, the authors use 'nature of the right' ostensibly to refer to certain 'types of case' concerning moral issues that reach similar outcomes because they are similarly affected by a margin of appreciation due to the lack of international consensus, where the scope of that issue is 'still in the process of being understood, recognized and accepted'.[8] However, in contrast, the language used confusingly implies that the 'nature of the individual right *determines* the breadth of the margin'.[9]

The meaning attributed in this book to the 'nature of the right' is that each of the rights protected in the Treaties involves a set of first-order reasons relevant to the determination of the dispute. It is not all of the first-order reasons, since many will be case-specific. Rather, the nature of the right refers to the sorts of generally applicable considerations that come into play whenever that right is engaged. For example, the right to life is to be regarded as one of the most important and basic of rights. Its termination involves the termination of access to all other rights. This

---

[4] A Lester, D Pannick, and J Herberg, *Human Rights Law and Practice* (3rd edn, LexisNexis, London 2009) [3.21], 125, although in discussion a page earlier, the body of the text argues that there are two main reasons for discretion in a national context: expertise and democratic legitimacy. For international tribunals, to these two main reasons can be added the common practice of states: see Chapter 5.

[5] M Hunt, 'Sovereignty's Blight: Why Contemporary Public Law Needs the Concept of "Due Deference"' in N Bamforth and P Leyland (eds) *Public Law in a Multi-Layered Constitution* (Hart, Oxford 2003) and T Hickman, *Public Law after the Human Rights Act* (Hart, Oxford 2010).

[6] Lester, Pannick, and Herberg (n4) 126. It is the second criterion mentioned.

[7] *Burden and Burden v UK* No. 13378/05 (2008) (ECtHR (GC)).

[8] R White and C Ovey, *Jacobs, White, and Ovey: The European Convention on Human Rights* (5th edn, OUP, Oxford 2010) 329.

[9] Ibid (emphasis added).

means that when considering the first-order reasons relevant to establishment of the scope of the right, the reasons for limiting this scope will have to be particularly relevant and weighty. This has a clear impact on the exercise of the proportionality assessment.

Similarly, the importance of the right to life is reflected textually in the ECHR. In Article 2, any limitations on the right are required to be 'absolutely necessary', which compares with other Articles, such as the standard limitation clauses applicable to Articles 8–11, which require limitations that are 'necessary in a democratic society', which can again be compared with the interferences to the peaceful enjoyment of property, which need only be 'necessary . . . in accordance with the general interest'.

That the text reflects the differing levels of importance of the first-order considerations of these rights is entirely proper. It is the nature of the right that determines the importance required of reasons for a margin of appreciation rather than the specific wording of the text, important though that is for providing guidance about the nature of the right.

The text does not, however, provide any particular guidance as to the weightiness of first-order reasons for the 'type of the case'. Instead, the type of case is likely to traverse a number of different Articles.[10] The type of case is not strictly a factor affecting the margin of appreciation, but rather an acknowledgement by the Tribunals that certain sorts of cases often result in clearer grounds for a margin of appreciation than others. It is shorthand for a reasoning process that has already been established and accepted in prior case law. The usefulness of prior cases on the margin of appreciation, and discussion of previous decisions in a doctrinal manner are that it can give the Tribunals guidance on the sorts of matters that are prima facie relevant for discerning the applicability and strength of reasons for a margin of appreciation, and importantly, the way in which reasons for a margin of appreciation have affected the balance of first-order reasons in similar cases. This does not mean that the hands of the Tribunals are tied to assign a certain weight to the importance of the reasons for a margin of appreciation, or that a doctrine of precedent has to be followed.[11] On the contrary, all of the reasons of relevance in the case have to be identified and assessed. The argument here is that a doctrine, or prior cases, can assist a court in identifying the reasons and the factors that affect deference.

Positive obligations on the state are often considered to be a factor affecting the exercise of the margin of appreciation.[12] It is commonly said that there are two types of positive obligation:[13] first, where the state is required to implement certain rules to uphold rights, for example where certain categories of person must be admitted in immigration rules, or where birth certificates require adjustment for

---

[10] See, e.g., the discussion of national security at Chapter 6.4.a.
[11] See Chapter 1.3.
[12] Lester, Pannick, and Herberg (n4) 127, fn3, referring to *Abdulaziz, Cabales and Balkandali v UK* No. 9214/80 (1985) (ECtHR), [67]. See also *Christine Goodwin v UK* No. 28957/95 (ECtHR (GC)), [72].
[13] For example, White and Ovey (n8) 338.

transsexuals; and secondly, where the state is required to protect an individual from interferences by other non-state actors. The limits of positive obligations on the state are often regarded as worthy of greater deference than negative obligations since they are likely to involve polycentric considerations.[14] This is particularly the case for the second type of positive obligations since they have the potential to be more amorphous and difficult to delimit.

3. The nature of the right

Each of the rights in the Treaties could be taken in turn and discussed. However, the purpose of this chapter is not to provide a complete analysis of cases involving the margin of appreciation, or to record all of the first-order considerations relevant to the proportionality assessment. Instead, the aim here is more modest—namely, to demonstrate how the nature of different rights impacts the sorts of first-order reasons in a case, and hence impacts the outcome of weighing those first-order reasons and grounds for a margin of appreciation together in the proportionality assessment.

Common categories of rights are: (a) absolute rights; (b) strong rights; (c) qualified rights; and (d) weak rights. For convenience, the subsequent discussion will follow these four categories, giving some more detailed discussion of at least one of the rights discussed within each category.

a. Absolute rights: life and freedom from torture

Rights to life and freedom from torture are frequently described as absolute. Other rights are sometimes regarded as absolute. Some such rights are regarded as absolute because they cannot be subject to derogation in emergencies.[15] Other additional rights that might be regarded as absolute include the right to freedom of thought, which is distinct from the right to freedom of expression.

It is not the purpose here to discuss or assess such a categorization, or the meaning of 'absolute'.[16] Instead, this section sets out a number of cases on the right to life and freedom from torture to show how the nature of these rights results

---

[14] The traditional justification for limiting socio-economic rights, for example, is that they are more difficult to define legally without sufficient expertise in economic matters as a result of polycentricity. See generally L Fuller, 'The Forms and Limits of Adjudication' (1978) 92 Harv LRev 353.

[15] Articles 7 (non-retroactive criminal punishment), 2 (life—except lawful acts of way), 3 (torture), and 4(1) (slavery) ECHR; Articles 6 (life), 7 (torture), 8 (slavery), 11 (imprisonment for contractual breach), 15 (retroactive criminal laws), 16 (juridical personality), and 18 (thought, conscience, and religion) ICCPR; Articles 3 (juridical personality), 4 (life), 5 (humane treatment), 6 (slavery), 9 (retroactive criminal laws), 12 (conscience and religion), 17 (family), 18 (name), 19 (child rights), 20 (nationality), and 23 (right to participate in government) ACHR.

[16] See, e.g., A Gewirth, 'Are There Any Absolute Rights?' (1981) 31 The Philosophical Quarterly 1, M Addo and N Grief, 'Does Article 3 of The European Convention on Human Rights Enshrine Absolute Rights?' (1998) 9 EJIL 510, and J Finnis, *Natural Law and Natural Rights* (Clarendon Press, Oxford 1980) ch VIII.7.

in a stricter application of the proportionality assessment than for some other rights, and how there are often fewer grounds for a margin of appreciation to the state when such rights are in issue.

i. Life

The United Nations Human Rights Committee (UN HRC) has described the right to life as the 'supreme right of the human being'.[17] It is one of the most important rights protected by international treaties. When life is ended, so too are all other human rights. For this reason, the first-order considerations surrounding interferences with this right are particularly weighty. This leads to searching scrutiny of any justification for taking life, and indeed for any failure to protect life. Does this mean that there is no role for deference to the state, as is sometimes claimed?[18] There are, at least, two circumstances in which the Tribunals can appropriately give deference to the state on cases involving the right to life: first, when determining the scope of 'life'; and secondly, when assessing the proportionality of justified use of force that results in the taking of life.

The clearest examples that discuss the scope of the right to life involve cases of the unborn child and whether the right to life entails a right to die. The Tribunals have been cautious in handling the issue of abortion. The European Court of Human Rights (ECtHR) recently decided in *A, B and C v Ireland*[19] that the Convention did not confer a right to an abortion,[20] and that there was a broad margin of appreciation for states as to whether (or not) and how to confer rights to an abortion based on the lack of consensus amongst states on the interplay between privacy rights and the right to life of the unborn.[21] Where the issue of abortion has arisen before the HRC, the Committee likewise did not consider whether the law in that case regulating abortion was itself consistent with human rights laws, nor whether the International Covenant on Civil and Political Rights (ICCPR) included the right to an abortion. Instead, the case was a matter of upholding the rule of law by allowing a young and mentally impaired girl who had been raped to access an abortion to which she was entitled to by law.[22]

In the case of *Vo v France*[23] (no requirement for criminal charge for a doctor who negligently terminated the life of an unborn child by mistakenly conducting a coil removal procedure), despite the fact that the applicant argued that the right to life in Article 2 had a 'universal meaning and definition',[24] the Grand Chamber of the ECtHR, finding that Article 2 had not been violated, came to the following conclusion about reasons for deference to the state:

---

[17] *Suarez de Guerrero v Colombia* CCPR/C/15/D/45/1979 (1982) (HRC), [13.1].

[18] S Greer, *The European Convention on Human Rights: Achievements, Problems and Prospects* (CUP, Cambridge 2006) 243, with respect to Article 2(2).

[19] *A, B and C v Ireland* No. 25579/05 (2010) (ECtHR (GC)).

[20] Ibid, [214].   [21] Ibid, [237].

[22] See *VDA and LMR v Argentina* CCPR/C/101/D/1608/2007 (2011) (HRC).

[23] *Vo v France* No. 53924/00 (2004) (ECtHR (GC)).   [24] Ibid, [47].

[C]onsideration [has been] given to the diversity of views on the point at which life begins, of legal cultures and of national standards of protection, and the State has been left with considerable discretion in the matter, as the opinion of the European Group on Ethics in Science and New Technologies at the European Commission appositely puts it: 'the… Community authorities have to address these ethical questions taking into account the moral and philosophical differences, reflected by the extreme diversity of legal rules applicable to human embryo research… It is not only legally difficult to seek harmonization of national laws at Community level, but because of lack of consensus, it would be inappropriate to impose one exclusive moral code.'[25]

This does not mean that the ECtHR rejected the universality of the right to life, nor the strength of the first-order reasons to protect life. It means rather that the Court accepts that the articulation of the right can legitimately vary under certain circumstances. In *Vo*, the reasons for deference were strong notwithstanding the strength of first-order reasons to protect life, and thus the margin of appreciation became a key part of the decision.[26]

In the case of *Pretty v UK*,[27] the ECtHR was faced again with the scope of Article 2. In this case, there was no recourse to the margin of appreciation. Instead, the reasoning on first-order considerations sufficed to decide that there was no right to die entailed by the right to life.[28] The applicant argued that this finding would place 'those countries which do permit assisted suicide in breach of the Convention'. The Court found this argument unpersuasive. The applicant's argument appeared to be that international consensus did not support the ECtHR's finding. If so, the ECtHR was right to reject it since lack of consensus on whether to allow assisted suicide cannot logically translate into a requirement under Article 2 to allow assisted suicide.

The other area in which a margin of appreciation might feature in right to life cases is assessing the proportionality of the use of force resulting in loss of life. The role of deference in such cases is seen in the case of *McCann v UK*,[29] in which the ECtHR assessed compliance with the ECHR of the shooting dead of suspected Irish Republican Army (IRA) terrorists in Gibraltar. The ECtHR found that the operation had elements of negligence and recklessness.[30] In reaching its conclusion, which differed both from the domestic inquiry and the Commission's findings, the ECtHR placed emphasis on the fact that the jury assessed the action of the police by too low a standard: rather than using proportionality as 'absolute necessity', the inquest instead relied on the concepts of 'reasonable force' and 'reasonable necessity'.[31] This reduced any scope for a margin of appreciation to the original decision-maker, on the basis of superior competence, instead leading to heightened scrutiny by the ECtHR.[32]

---

[25] Ibid, [82].   [26] Ibid, [85].

[27] *Pretty v UK* No. 2346/02 (2002) (ECtHR).   [28] Ibid, [38]–[41].

[29] *McCann v UK* No. 18984/91 (1995) (ECtHR (GC)).   [30] Ibid, [202]–[214].

[31] Ibid, [170]. Note also that, in this paragraph, mention was made of some reasons for deference based on the jury's superior competence to assess the factual matters in the case. Notwithstanding these reasons for deference, the different test reduced the importance of this factor such that the Court decided to place greater emphasis on its own assessment of the facts.

[32] For a similar case in the context of the IACtHR, see *Zambrano-Vélez v Ecuador* Series C No. 166 (2007) (IACtHR), [83]: 'The use of force by law enforcement officials must be defined by exceptionality and must be planned and proportionally limited by the authorities.' In the UN HRC context, see

However, even in assessing the state's actions there could have been scope for a margin of appreciation to the state. Such deference was not observable in the reasoning of the majority, but a strong dissent (nine of nineteen judges) did demonstrate it. The dissenting judges in the decision placed emphasis on the fact-finding of both the Commission as well as the inquiry, deciding that the findings that the use of force had resulted in lawful killings was able to assist the ECtHR in its determinations of whether there had been a violation of Article 2(2), and thus there could still be some deference to these better placed decision-makers.[33] The dissenting judgment continued by taking issue with the approach of the majority on most of the key parts of its judgment on the merits,[34] which included second-order reasons along with the pertinent first-order concerns.[35]

ii. Torture

The right to be free from torture and inhuman or degrading treatment, like the right to life, is a primary fundamental right amongst human rights. There are no limitations in the language of the Treaties for this right: Article 3 ECHR; Article 7 ICCPR; and Article 5(2) of the American Convention on Human Rights (ACHR). This does not mean, though, that there is no role at all for a margin of appreciation to the state in the determination of all cases that raise this issue. International tribunals can appropriately give deference to the state when determining the scope of the meaning of torture or inhuman and degrading treatment.[36]

The ECHR jurisprudence is instructive in giving a margin of appreciation on what treatment amounts to torture or inhuman and degrading treatment. In the case of *Soering v UK*,[37] the respondent state sought to extradite the applicant to the US, where he would face trial in Virginia for murder and potentially face the death penalty. A key part of his claim was that treatment on death row amounted to inhuman or degrading treatment, and that there were substantial grounds to believe

Suarez de Guerrero v Colombia (n17) [13.1]:

> The right enshrined in this article is the supreme right of the human being. It follows that the deprivation of life by the authorities of the State is a matter of the utmost gravity. This follows from the article as a whole and in particular is the reason why paragraph 2 of the article lays down that the death penalty may be imposed only for the most serious crimes. The requirements that the right shall be protected by law and that no one shall be arbitrarily deprived of his life mean that the law must strictly control and limit the circumstances in which a person may be deprived of his life by the authorities of a State.

[33] *McCann v UK* (n29), [7] of the dissent.

[34] Ibid, [8]–[25].

[35] A good example of second-order reasoning is found ibid, [24], where the minority judgment relied on the 'extent of experience in dealing with terrorist activities which the relevant training reflects' to find that the training given was adequate and not deficient; cf the majority judgment at [212].

[36] J Merrills, 'Human Rights and Democratic Values in the Strasbourg System' (2000) 29 Thesaurus Acroasium 37, 85, makes this point as follows: 'Popular sentiment and local culture have a bearing on how a punishment is regarded and hence, as one would expect, may be relevant to its status for Convention purposes.'

[37] *Soering v UK* No. 14038/88 (1989) (ECtHR).

that extradition would entail a real risk of a violation of Article 3.[38] The Court correctly set out the following proposition:

What amounts to 'inhuman or degrading treatment or punishment' depends on all the circumstances of the case .... Furthermore, inherent in the whole of the Convention is a search for a fair balance between the demands of the general interest of the community and the requirements of the protection of the individual's fundamental rights.[39]

These principles show that the scope of 'inhuman or degrading treatment' depends on a variety of factors. In this sense, it is to some extent 'relative',[40] although use of this word is unfortunate, likely to cause confusion, and not to be recommended. It is clear, though, that in some circumstances there may be scope for deference to state views about what is or is not inhuman or degrading treatment. This is because, in order to determine whether a certain action falls foul of Article 3, the purpose and necessity of the action can be relevant to determining whether or not such action is degrading.[41] In *Jalloh v Germany*,[42] the ECtHR applied these principles well. The ECtHR assessed the action of state police who forcibly administered emetics so that the applicant would regurgitate packages of swallowed narcotics. The ECtHR applied the principles as follows:

As regards the extent to which the forcible medical intervention was necessary to obtain the evidence, the Court notes that drug trafficking is a serious offence. It is acutely aware of the problem confronting Contracting States in their efforts to combat the harm caused to their societies through the supply of drugs ... However, in the *present case it was clear before the impugned measure was ordered and implemented that the street dealer on whom it was imposed had been storing the drugs in his mouth and could not, therefore, have been offering drugs for sale on a large scale.* This is reflected in the sentence (a six-month suspended prison sentence and probation), which is at the lower end of the range of possible sentences. The Court accepts that it was vital for the investigators to be able to determine the exact amount and quality of the drugs that were being offered for sale. However, *it is not satisfied that the forcible administration of emetics was indispensable in the instant case to obtain the evidence. The prosecuting authorities could simply have waited for the drugs to pass through his system naturally. It is significant in this connection that many other member States of the Council of Europe use this method to investigate drugs offences.*[43]

In the first emphasized passage in the extract, the Court implies that more intrusive conduct is justifiable for a more serious offence. Such logic makes sense, because it may offer justification for treatment that would otherwise be excessive. Forced use of emetics for a low-time crook would be using a sledgehammer to crack a peanut, whereas if it could lead to evidence that might stop a major drug trafficking league, then the action might be more reasonable. However, this sort of first-order reasoning alone was not determinative. In addition, it was noted that less severe

---

[38] Ibid, [91].   [39] Ibid, [89].
[40] *Enea v Italy* No. 74912/01 (2009) (ECtHR (GC)), [55].
[41] *Soering v UK* (n37) [100].
[42] *Jalloh v Germany* No. 54810/00 (2004) (ECtHR).
[43] Ibid, [77] (emphasis added).

means could be relied upon to access the evidence—namely, that the drugs could pass naturally.

Recourse was also made to second-order reasons to heighten scrutiny of the arguments of the state that such action was necessary. In the second emphasized passage, the practice of the signatory states revealed that other states used less restrictive measures, and thus international practice undermined the approach taken by Germany, providing grounds to increase scrutiny. Since this sort of issue was outside the expertise of the Court and there seemed to be international consensus against Germany, the reasoning of the applicant was strengthened accordingly.

The case of *Jalloh* is an example of where it can be legitimate to assess the proportionality of state action as well as reasons for a margin of appreciation to determine the scope of inhuman or degrading treatment by the state.[44] Whilst *Jalloh* is a good example, the case of *Soering*[45] involves poor use of reasoning with respect to the margin of appreciation and proportionality. In that case, the Court held that the difficulties that states have in prosecuting crime was a factor to be weighed along with the risk of ill-treatment in the receiving state.[46] In applying this principle of proportionality, the Court decided the fact that the UK could have sent the applicant to Germany rather than the US, where he would have been free from risk, was a factor in assessing the proportionality of the extradition decision with Article 3.[47] But this logic cannot be right. It implies that the decision might have been more or less compliant with Article 3 depending on whether the UK had options other than sending the applicant to likely mistreatment. The only relevant factor is whether there were substantial grounds of a real risk of treatment contrary to Article 3. If so, the extradition would be non-compliant with the ECHR. The state would not have any greater expertise than the international court to assess this, nor would there be any grounds for a margin of appreciation on the basis of international consensus or democratic legitimacy. In the case of *Chahal v UK*,[48] in which the ECtHR was asked to determine whether the deportation of an Indian national, a Sikh who had become involved in Punjab resistance and had been ill-treated in India, was contrary to Article 3, the Court corrected the mistake made in *Soering*. In setting out the principles in this area, the Court clarified the law as follows:

It should not be inferred from the Court's remarks concerning the risk of undermining the foundations of extradition, as set out in paragraph 89 of [*Soering*], that there is any room for balancing the risk of ill-treatment against the reasons for expulsion in determining whether a State's responsibility under Article 3 is engaged.[49]

---

[44] See further *Tyrer v UK* No. 5856/72 (1978) (ECtHR), [31], which relied on 'commonly accepted standards in the penal policy of the member States of the Council of Europe in this field'. See too *Ramirez Sanchez v France* No. 59450/00 (2006) (ECtHR (GC)), [119]: 'The Court would add that the measures taken must also be necessary to attain the legitimate aim pursued.' See also the argument of the UK in *N v UK* No. 26565/05 (2008) (ECtHR (GC)), [24], which appears to have been upheld by the Court at [44], although to dissent by Judges Tulkens, Bonello, and Spielmann at [7]–[8].
[45] *Soering v UK* (n37).   [46] Ibid, [89].   [47] Ibid, [110].
[48] *Chahal v UK* No. 22414/93 (1996) (ECtHR).   [49] Ibid, [81].

The UK challenged this ruling in an intervention in *Saadi v Italy*,[50] but the Grand Chamber unanimously upheld the rectitude of the *Chahal* principles.[51]

iii. Summary

This section has argued that even on what are traditionally regarded as absolute rights, it is to be expected that the margin of appreciation and proportionality can, in certain circumstances, be relevant to determining the scope of the international obligations.

b. Strong rights: fair trial, liberty, and derogations

After absolute rights in the hierarchy, there are some rights that can be interfered with only in a very limited number of ways. These might be regarded as 'strong' rights, and include fair trial rights, the right to liberty, and the right of states to derogate from some human rights protections. There are likely to be very few circumstances in which there would be reason to give a margin of appreciation to the state in such circumstances. Thus the nature of these rights do not raise many situations in which second-order reasons are going to be relevant, by virtue of their subject matter; hence their labelling as 'strong'.

This does not mean that there are no occasions on which second-order considerations are relevant to the resolution of a dispute.[52] With respect to rights to liberty, there is not much scope for deference. This is because the meaning of 'liberty' is not particularly contentious. Where there are requirements for setting standards, the context is quintessentially within the purview of the Tribunals. Furthermore, there can be many limits to this right because as long as the deprivation of liberty is lawful, the right itself does not control which laws can justify interferences with liberty. This provides a large degree of differentiation from state to state for which there is no need for a margin of appreciation.[53]

Lastly, the rights to derogate from the Treaties have already been discussed,[54] with respect to how there is a margin of appreciation to the state on the assessment of what is in furtherance of national security requirements, but that such grounds for a margin of appreciation go hand in hand with the scrutiny of all of the first-order reasons in the case, both for and against making a derogation.

---

[50] *Saadi v Italy* No. 37201/06 (2008) (ECtHR (GC)).
[51] Ibid, [138]–[140].
[52] See Chapter 6.5 on fair trial rights.
[53] Of course, such laws depriving citizens of liberty may well be circumspect on other human rights grounds.
[54] See Chapter 6.4.a and discussions there of *Brannigan and McBride v UK* No. 14553/89; 14554/89 (1993) (ECtHR), [43], and *Castillo-Petruzzi v Peru* Series C No. 52 (1999) (IACtHR), [89] and [109].

c. Qualified rights: privacy, and freedoms of religion, association, speech, and non-discrimination

The qualified rights are fertile territory for discussion of the margin of appreciation and proportionality. Decisions in cases that raise these rights are where judicial deference can most often be observed and where reasons for a margin of appreciation have most clearly been developed by the Tribunals. The purpose of this section cannot be to provide a comprehensive treatment of this large corpus of law. Rather the aim here is to show how the nature of each right impacts the Tribunals' assessment of second-order reasons for deference. This will be undertaken by looking at rights to privacy/respect for private life and rights to freedom of speech/expression as examples.[55]

i. Privacy

The nature of rights to privacy is by no means simple. They are often regarded as having dual motivations, first among which is that there is a private sphere of life free from state interference. This motivation can be seen in the European context from an early definition given by the Parliamentary Assembly of the Council of Europe, which has defined 'privacy' as 'the right to live one's own life with a minimum of interference'.[56] This has been reflected in case law. For example, in *Niemitz v Germany*,[57] the ECtHR articulated 'the essential object and purpose of Article 8' as being 'to protect the individual against arbitrary interferences by public authorities'.[58] This case decided that the protections of Article 8 could extend to some business premises.

The second motivation of privacy rights is the creation of an environment conducive to human flourishing, and the discovery and development of one's own personality. This motivation is also widely recognized in European human rights law. Also in *Niemitz*, the ECtHR stated:

The Court does not consider it possible or desirable to attempt an exhaustive definition of the notion of 'private life'. However, it would be too restrictive to limit the notion to an 'inner circle' in which the individual may live his own personal life as he chooses and to exclude therefrom entirely the outside world not encompassed within that circle. Respect for private life must also comprise to a certain degree the right to establish and develop relationships with other human beings.[59]

---

[55] An example in relation to freedom of association can be seen in *Demir and Baykara v Turkey* No. 34503/97 (2008) (ECtHR (GC)), [199]:

> [T]he exceptions set out in Article 11 are to be construed strictly; only convincing and compelling reasons can justify restrictions on such parties' freedom of association. In determining in such cases whether a 'necessity' – and therefore a 'pressing social need' – within the meaning of Article 11(2) exists, States have only a limited margin of appreciation, which goes hand in hand with rigorous European supervision.

[56] Resolution No. 428 of 23 January 1970. See also Resolution No. 1165 of 26 June 1998.
[57] *Niemitz v Germany* No. 13710/88 (1992) (ECtHR).
[58] Ibid, [31].   [59] Ibid, [29].

This second motivation, to create an environment in which individuals can explore their identity, relationships with others, and enjoy personal flourishing, can lead to positive obligations on the state. As mentioned in section 2 of this chapter, where positive obligations are at issue, there may be greater grounds for a margin of appreciation as to whether and how such requirements are implemented and what limits there are.

Both motivations for privacy rights can be seen in the UN HRC context in the case of *Coeriel and Aurik v The Netherlands*,[60] in which the HRC decided that the Netherlands' rejection of two Hindu converts' application for a name change was arbitrary. In reaching this conclusion, the HRC explained that it 'considers that the notion of privacy refers to the sphere of a person's life in which he or she can freely express his or her identity, be it by entering into relationships with others or alone'.[61] In this way, the case engaged the negative 'sphere' of freedom from state interference, as well as revealed the need for states to create an environment within which individuals can explore their identity.

In the European context of Article 8, matters are complicated somewhat by the structure of the right as it appears in the text. It is sometimes argued that the scope of Article 8(1) ECHR should be kept distinct from appropriate limitations of such rights in Article 8(2).[62] Whilst this makes logical sense, the scope of the right is actually determined by an assessment of the rights' limitations. It is accordingly understandable that the ECtHR often merges together these two enquiries, particularly for positive obligations where the same considerations of balancing the competing interest arise. If the ECtHR finds in a particular case that there is a positive obligation on the state to act in a certain way, this will usually involve, on the facts, a finding of a violation of that obligation. In such cases, the finding of a positive obligation will be determinative of the case. An example of this can be seen in *Hatton v UK*,[63] in which the ECtHR argued that same result would be produced, and the margin of appreciation and proportionality reasoning employed, whether the case was dealt with as a positive obligation under Article 8(1) or as an interference under Article 8(2).[64]

Article 8 is very broad. Indeed, the Court has argued that 'the concept of "private life" is a broad term not susceptible to exhaustive definition'.[65] The right has been applied to such diverse matters as the protection of our bodies from physical or

---

[60] *Coeriel and Aurik v The Netherlands* CCPR/C/52/D/453/1991 (1994) (HRC).
[61] Ibid, [10.2].
[62] C Warbrick, 'The Structure of Article 8' (1998) EHRLR 32, 35–6.
[63] *Hatton v UK* No. 36022/97 (2003) (ECtHR (GC)).
[64] Ibid, [98]:

> In both contexts regard must be had to the fair balance that has to be struck between the competing interests of the individual and of the community as a whole; and in both contexts the State enjoys a certain margin of appreciation in determining the steps to be taken to ensure compliance with the Convention.

See also further at [119]. See further *Christine Goodwin v UK* (n12) [74] and [84]–[85], which was handled under Article 8(1), but which clearly employed considerations of proportionality and the margin of appreciation that might ordinarily be considered only under Article 8(2).
[65] *Pretty v UK* (n27) [61].

sexual violation, the police's powers to listen to our telephone conversations, whether we have a right to end our own lives, or whether prisoners should have the right to in vitro fertilization (IVF) treatment. The sheer breadth of this right makes any reliance on the 'nature' of the right as raising common first-order considerations of limited value in providing guidance for the Court when weighing reasons for a margin of appreciation. For this reason, the 'nature of the right' is something of a meaningless concept as a consideration that will provide guidance when undertaking the proportionality assessment and when assessing second-order reasons for a margin of appreciation.

Instead, it might be helpful to recognize that there can be similar types of interest that fall within Article 8, and that the nature of such interests can raise common first-order considerations in similar cases. But even this is doubtful. One example will suffice to demonstrate this. In the case of *Dudgeon v UK*,[66] the ECtHR made the following statement: 'The present case concerns a most intimate aspect of private life. Accordingly, there must exist particularly serious reasons before interferences on the part of the public authorities can be legitimate for the purposes of paragraph 2 of Article 8.'[67] The case involved the criminalization of homosexual conduct. It is difficult to know the boundaries of what was meant by the Court in designating this right a 'most intimate aspect of private life'. Was it the fact that it was related to sexual identity? Or was it the personal nature of the impact?

The case of *Christine Goodwin* confirms the extension of this first-order reasoning in the case of transsexual identity, albeit that this issue of course had to be weighed along with the other considerations in the case.[68] However, in the case of *Hatton v UK*,[69] the applicant attempted to extend this sort of first-order reasoning far beyond sexual identity in the context of protecting the right to sleep undisturbed by night flights. This argument was rightly rejected as extending these ideas too far.[70] Whilst the majority was right to reject this comparison, the example serves to show how there may be some similar principles under Article 8 cases, but also that such principles are not universally applicable in all cases involving Article 8.

ii. Free speech

The right to freedom of speech and expression does not present the same problems of determining the relevant principles as under rights to privacy. Whilst the exact interplay of relevant considerations remains the subject of continuing academic debate, the Tribunals know what the relevant considerations are, and many of the considerations have been identified for some time.[71] These include: the importance

---

[66] *Dudgeon v UK* No. 7525/76 (1981) (ECtHR).   [67] Ibid, [52].
[68] *Christine Goodwin v UK* (n12) [77] and [90].   [69] *Hatton v UK* (n63).
[70] Ibid, [123]: 'the sleep disturbances relied on by the applicants did not intrude into an aspect of private life in a manner comparable to that of the criminal measures considered in *Dudgeon*.'
[71] For example, see the discussion entitled 'The Function of Freedom of Expression in a Democratic Society' in T Emerson, 'Toward a General Theory of the Freedom of Expression' (1962–63) Yale LJ 877, 878.

of free speech to effective political engagement and democratic government; the emergence of truth; the ability of individuals to enjoy moral autonomy; and the prevention of potential harm to other members of society (particularly children or victims of defamation).

The major difficulty with freedom of expression cases is not so much identifying the relevant first-order considerations, but how they are weighed along with the second-order reasons for a margin of appreciation. It is possible to see how the nature of the right here does provide some guidance, and this can be observed most clearly in two main contexts: political speech and obscene expression.[72]

Freedom of speech and expression is regarded as one of the most important rights in a democracy in which different opinions can freely be aired and assessed in the marketplace of ideas.[73] For this reason, when political speech is limited, the Tribunals are likely to place more weight on the protection of political speech as a first-order consideration in a proportionality assessment, and thus require second-order reasons to be stronger before they will have any meaningful impact in the case. Part of the aim of this right is to promote democracy and good governance. This can be seen in the case of *Ceylan v Turkey*,[74] in which a Kurdish trade union leader was charged with the criminal offence of incitement to violence for a publication in which he criticized government 'imperialists'. In the course of its reaching its decision that there was a breach of Article 10 ECHR, the ECtHR articulated that there was less scope for a margin of appreciation where political speech was in issue.[75] A similar sort of protection is also given to journalistic freedom.[76] This is protected on the basis of the importance of a free press to democratic government, but also on the basis of other factors in favour of free speech, such as the emergence of truth and the importance of moral autonomy.

The protections given to political speech and journalistic expression can be contrasted with the level of protection given to what is regarded as obscene expression. This can be seen in the case of *Müller v Switzerland*.[77] In this case, some of an artist's public works were seized and the artist was fined because obscene images of a sexual nature (including bestiality) were on display without any parental warnings. A child was very upset by the paintings, leading to the penal action. The ECtHR gave weight to second-order reasoning in this case in that the national courts' assessment of limiting rights in the protection of public morals was given deference.[78] In this context, in contrast to emphasizing the importance of protecting political

---

[72] For an account that recognizes the difference of approach by the ECtHR between types of speech, see P Mahoney, 'Universality versus Subsidiarity in the Strasbourg Case Law on Free Speech: Explaining Some Recent Judgments' (1997) 4 EHRLR 364.

[73] See the UN HRC case of *Tae-Hoon Park v Korea* CCPR/C/64/D/628/1995 (1998) (HRC), [10.3], which stated: 'The right to freedom of expression is of paramount importance in any democratic society, and any restrictions to the exercise of this right must meet a strict test of justification.'

[74] *Ceylan v Turkey* No. 23556/94 (1999) (ECtHR (GC)).

[75] Ibid, [34].

[76] *Lingens v Austria* No. 9815/82 (1986) (ECtHR).

[77] *Müller v Switzerland* No. 10737/84 (1988) (ECtHR).

[78] Ibid, [35] and [36].

speech or journalistic freedom, the ECtHR placed importance on the fact that exercising expression involves 'duties and responsibilities'.[79]

From these few examples, it can be seen that the nature of the right to freedom of expression furnishes the Court with some similar first-order considerations, some of which are generally weighty. All of the other first-order reasons, such as what exactly the expression was, what its aims were, audience, impact, and consequences, etc., still all need to be considered, and these particularities will affect first-order reasons, such that some political speech may be considered to be less weighty than some artistic expression. Nevertheless, these generalities about the nature of the right can furnish the Tribunals with some assistance when undertaking the proportionality assessment where both first- and second-order reasons are weighed together. Some expression, for example political discourse, may be regarded as providing weighty first-order reasons. Accordingly, this would render some factors for a margin of appreciation of less impact, for example the arguments for a margin of appreciation on the basis that a restriction of such expression was the result of a legitimate, democratically made law.[80] In this way, the nature of the right can furnish some guidance to the courts about how to assess reasons for a margin of appreciation along with first-order reasons, but the first-order reasons regarding the 'nature of the right' must be taken in the context of their facts.

d. Weak rights: property, education, and free elections

Some rights can be limited by a broad range of interests, and thus can be regarded as 'weaker' rights. As a result of this, the first-order considerations are generally less weighty, and leave greater scope for second-order reasons for a margin of appreciation to impact the outcome of the proportionality assessment. This is the case, for example, for rights to property, access to education, and the right to free elections. This section has the modest aim of showing from the jurisprudence of the Tribunals that the nature of such rights means that, on the whole, the first-order considerations are somewhat weak, and that there is greater scope for second-order reasoning, using the right to property as an example. This does not mean the state will always be successful when limiting such rights, but that there will be greater scope for states to govern the exercise of such rights.

In Europe, the text of the right to property itself shows that there is greater scope for state interference with property than other ECHR rights. The drafting of the right itself took a number of different forms before it could be agreed upon, resulting in text that gives the state a large discretion to 'control the use of property in accordance with the general interest'.[81] In the ICCPR context,

---

[79] *Müller v Switzerland*, [34].
[80] This can be seen to some extent in the case of *Tae-Hoon Park v Korea* (n73).
[81] Article 1, Protocol 1, ECHR.

there is no separate right to property, it being only a consideration for which there cannot be discrimination or a denial of equal treatment. The ACHR protects property with similar limitations 'for reasons of public utility or social interest'.[82]

A clear expression by the ECtHR that the nature of Article 1, Protocol 1, ECHR generally leads to weaker first-order considerations can be seen in the case of *Pye (Oxford) Ltd v UK*,[83] in which the Court ruled on whether the rules relating to adverse possession could violate the right to property. In the circumstances, a large amount of valuable farmland was issue. In deciding that the system was Convention-compliant, the ECtHR stated that: 'Such arrangements fall within the State's margin of appreciation, unless they give rise to results which are so anomalous as to render the legislation unacceptable.'[84] This conclusion followed a standard assessment of the nature of an aspect of the rights protected by Article 1, Protocol 1: 'In spheres such as housing, the Court will respect the legislature's judgment as to what is in the general interest unless that judgment is manifestly without reasonable foundation.'[85]

First-order considerations in the case of rights to property are, as has briefly been observed, comparatively weak, and consequently specific circumstances must exist to render the interference with property particularly intrusive before the Tribunals intervene. In this way, the nature of the right can be of assistance in determining the level of influence that second-order reasoning will have in their decision-making. This contrasts with rights such as the right to life and freedom from torture, which prima facie entail much stronger first-order reasons, leaving much less scope for deference to the state.

4. Types of case

Cases of a similar type raise comparable first- and second-order considerations. This does not lead to the strict application of precedent, because each case is decided on its own facts. Instead, all of the relevant reasons in the case have to be identified and assessed. Accounts that discuss similar types of case can provide a useful resource by collating the relevant reasons that have arisen for consideration in future cases. The type of case is not a factor affecting deference, but an acknowledgement that certain sorts of cases often give rise to stronger reasons for deference than others.

No attempt is made here to expound the authorities on different types of case or how reasons for deference are impacted by the type of case. Such accounts exist elsewhere.[86] However, many texts place discussion of the jurisprudence within

---

[82] Article 21 ACHR.
[83] *Pye (Oxford) Ltd v UK* No. 44302/02 (ECtHR (GC)).
[84] Ibid, [83].
[85] Ibid, [75]. For the IACtHR's approach, see *Salvador-Chiriboga v Ecuador* Judgment of 6 May 2008, Series C No. 179 (IACtHR).
[86] Arai-Takahashi (n3), pt II. See also (1998) 19 HRLJ 1.

chapters on different rights.[87] This can lead to repetition when certain types of case commonly raise numerous rights. National security cases, for example, could be discussed under free speech, fair trial, derogation, and private rights. It can be a helpful exercise therefore to study 'types of case' separately, resulting in a catalogue of considerations.

Some 'types of case' have been discussed already in the book in earlier chapters.[88] A non-exhaustive list could include the following categories:

- national security;
- police powers/the surveillance state;
- prisoner rights;
- rights to health care;
- morality;
- socio-economic rights;
- planning;
- sexual identity; and
- immigration cases.

In each of these categories, decisions can be analysed in such a way as to identify the general first-order and second-order considerations in such cases, as well as how such considerations have been particularized in different cases. This can help arguments to be developed that previous cases were wrongly decided, for example by arguing that previous cases erred in placing weight on a particular factor. In this way, such accounts can also help to shape substantive doctrine of the law of particular types of case. Accounts of deference that discuss different types of case can furnish lawyers with greater clarity about how the Tribunals will make their decisions, and how to frame arguments appropriately.

5. Conclusion

This chapter has argued that the nature of the right can provide some assistance in identifying the relevant first-order considerations in a case, and can give indications as to the strength of such reasons. This has implications as to how weighty the second-order considerations need to be before a margin of appreciation will have much impact in any decision made by the Tribunals. The chapter has also argued that the type of right is not a factor that affects the margin of appreciation. Instead, accounts of case law that catalogue and analyse the various factors relied on by

---

[87] For example, DJ Harris, M O'Boyle, C Warbrick, and E Bates, *Harris, O'Boyle & Warbrick: Law of the European Convention on Human Rights* (2nd edn, OUP, Oxford 2009), and White and Ovey (n8).

[88] Chapter 6 included sections on national security, child protection, health-care decisions, educational needs, police and civil servants' organization, economic matters, and legal procedures. Chapter 5 included sections on conflicts of private rights, morality, electoral rights, and cases involving minorities.

the Tribunals can be useful as a record of past decisions and a guide to future arguments.

More work can be done to explain the different ways in which the margin of appreciation impacts accounts based on the nature of the right or type of case. The aim in this chapter has been to show that the account of the margin of appreciation and proportionality defended in this book can lead to a clearer articulation of how reasons for a margin of appreciation impact and interact with the first-order reasoning in human rights cases.

9

Concluding Remarks

This book addresses the question: 'Is the way in which the margin of appreciation in international human rights law affects the reasoning of the Tribunals justified?' The heart of the book's response to this question is found in Chapter 2, which provides an analytical account of how the margin of appreciation in international law operates, drawing on the philosophy of practical reasoning, and in particular the concept of deference as a form of second-order reasoning. Chapter 2 argues that deference is the practice of assigning weight to reasons for a decision on the basis of external factors. The margin of appreciation, a doctrine of judicial deference in international human rights law, is the practice of the Tribunals assigning weight to the respondent states' reasoning in a case on the basis of three such external factors: democratic legitimacy; the common practice of states; and expertise. These concepts provide the foundation for the remainder of the book, which aims to articulate an account of the role, purpose, and function of the margin of appreciation within international human rights law, answering the above question robustly in the affirmative.

The book argues that the margin of appreciation is not analogous to a non-justiciability doctrine, but rather that all relevant reasons must be considered in the Tribunals' deliberations (Chapter 2.5). This deliberation occurs at the stage of the proportionality assessment. Once all of the reasons relevant to resolution of the case have been identified, both first-order and second-order reasons for a margin of appreciation, they are then to be assessed. This assessment, or weighing, of all of the reasons is a somewhat mysterious process, but involves the exercise of judgment by the Tribunals, and is often referred to as the 'proportionality assessment'. The key argument of the book in relation to an understanding of proportionality is that the three external factors for a margin of appreciation affect the first-order balance of reasons in human rights cases. This impact has been illustrated formulaically in Chapter 7, but the process itself is more intangible. The level of impact varies from case to case depending on the nature and strength of the reasons for a margin of appreciation. Sometimes, the weight of those reasons can swing the decision in favour of the state; at other times, notwithstanding consideration of those reasons, the first-order balance of reasons will support the applicant.

In addition to analysing the structure of reasoning involved in the margin of appreciation and proportionality, the book has sought to establish a normative justification of the margin of appreciation. The general approach to the margin of appreciation was explored in Chapter 3, where it was argued that the role of the

Tribunals is compatible with permitting a diversity of standards in human rights and that it is not desirable for the Tribunals to impose uniform human rights standards. This general approach was developed further for each of the three external factors for a margin of appreciation in Part Two. It was argued in Chapter 4 that local norms that are formed through a democratically legitimate process justify a measure of deference to the state, which enables the Tribunals to avoid being accused of judicial supremacy. Chapter 5 argues that the current level of state practice (the 'consensus' factor) is also relevant to the margin of appreciation to be given to the state, on the basis that the legality of treaties is found in the agreement of states and that the Vienna Convention on the Law of Treaties (VCLT) requires the consideration of state practice. Whilst the nature of the Treaties means that the Tribunals are to look beyond state practice to the upholding of human rights standards, where states attempt to implement these standards, their practice provides guidance in cases of ambiguous interpretation. Finally, Chapter 6 argues that where the state has demonstrated expertise, the Tribunals ought to give a margin of appreciation to this ability to assess better the requirements on the ground. This does not reduce the responsibility of the Tribunals to make a determination, but reflects the abilities of the Tribunals to reach a determination accurately.

These arguments provide analytical and normative theories with which to explain and justify the Tribunals' use of the margin of appreciation doctrine. In addition to these theoretical arguments, the book provides a complementary exposition of relevant case law. The theoretical positions defended herein are grounded in and informed by the practice of the Tribunals. Chapters 4–6 in particular categorize the decisions of the Tribunals, providing detailed analysis of how each of the three factors for a margin of appreciation operates in practice.

It is hoped that the account of the margin of appreciation in this book will lead to better understanding and greater control over the arguments involving reasons for a margin of appreciation. It is not hoped that the terminology of 'first-order' and 'second-order' reasons is adopted in legal practice, but rather that the way in which the three factors for a margin of appreciation operate can be better understood. Accordingly, when lawyers rely on the margin of appreciation and when Tribunals consider such arguments, the factors in favour of a margin of appreciation will be carefully assessed and then expressly deployed either to strengthen deference to or heighten scrutiny of the views of the state.

Discussion of just one case in the European Court of Human Rights (ECtHR) suffices to demonstrate the approach to the margin of appreciation taken throughout this book. Many other cases from the Tribunals could have been chosen.[1] In *A, B and C v Ireland*,[2] the Grand Chamber was required to assess Ireland's approach to abortion, and for the first time in its history to consider whether the Convention confers a right to an abortion. In Ireland, abortion is illegal (and a serious criminal offence contrary to the Offences Against the Person Act 1861) when undertaken

---

[1] For other examples, see Chapter 2.5.
[2] *A, B and C v Ireland* No. 25579/05 (2010) (ECtHR (GC)).

for any reason other than one exception provided by the Irish Supreme Court in *Attorney General v X and others*[3]—namely, where there is a substantial risk to the life of the mother. The applicants claimed violations of the Convention on the basis that the Irish law prohibiting abortion on health and well-being grounds violated their rights under Articles 2 (C only), 3, 8, 13, and 14 of the European Convention on Human Rights (ECHR). The Court rejected the claims on the basis of Article 2 and 3 as manifestly ill-founded. The judgment focuses on arguments about Article 8. It is obvious that the issues dealt with in this book were central to the case:

> The Court considers that the breadth of the margin of appreciation to be accorded to the State is crucial to its conclusion as to whether the impugned provision struck [a] fair balance [between, on the one hand, the right to respect for the applicants' private lives under Article 8 and, on the other, profound moral values of the Irish people as to the nature of life and consequently as to the need to protect the life of the unborn].[4]

The Court went on to consider factors for a margin of appreciation and also other factors in the case. The Court stated that 'Where a particularly important facet of an individual's existence or identity is at stake, the margin allowed to the State will normally be restricted'.[5] This makes reference to the strength of the first-order considerations in such Article 8 cases, recalling the discussion of the 'type of case' in Chapter 8. Accordingly, grounds for a margin of appreciation in this situation needed to be strong in order to result in deference to the state.

The Court then referred[6] to the fact that where there is no consensus within the member states of the Council of Europe, the margin will be wider (as discussed in Chapter 5), and also to the fact that the state authorities are better suited to assess the 'exact content of the requirements of morals' in their country, which recalls the discussion on democratic legitimacy in Chapter 4. The Court noted that the 'acute sensitivity' of the moral and ethical issues raised could not be doubted, and determined that the margin of appreciation on this issue was wide.[7] The Court also noted the 'lengthy, complex and sensitive debate in Ireland...as regards the content of its abortion laws' from which 'a choice has emerged'. This recalls the importance of the level of public debate in according a wide margin of appreciation to the state on the basis of democratic legitimacy discussed at Chapter 4.6.c.

The issue of consensus (discussed in Chapter 5) was more complicated.[8] The Court found that there was a consensus amongst contracting states allowing abortion on broader grounds than the Irish state, but argued that this consensus was not decisive on the basis that there was no consensus as to when the right to life begins, and accordingly no consensus as to how the right to life should be balanced against Article 8. Although it was not mentioned by the Court, it may have been influenced by the argument made by counsel for Ireland that there *was* a consensus amongst contracting states that these matters should lie within the margin of

---

[3] *Attorney General v X and others* [1992] 1 IR 1.
[4] Ibid, [231].   [5] Ibid, [232].   [6] Ibid.
[7] Ibid, [233]. See the discussion at Chapter 4.5.b.
[8] Ibid, [234]–[237].

appreciation, evidenced by the signing of a legally binding Decision of the heads of state or government of the twenty-seven member states of the European Union (EU) that the Lisbon Treaty would in no way affect the right of Ireland to regulate its prohibition of abortion, as it had done in the Constitution of Ireland.[9]

The Court identified a number of first-order considerations, such as the requirement that the women would have to travel abroad to receive a legal abortion, and the fact that this was psychologically, physically, and financially arduous.[10] As already noted, such considerations would require more of arguments for a margin of appreciation in light of the importance of this case on the individual's existence or identity. The Court explained that the arguments for a margin of appreciation applied *to* such considerations.[11] This recalls the interaction between the arguments for a margin of appreciation and other factors discussed in Chapter 7.4.a in relation to assessing the proportionality of the measure in question. The crux of the decision in *A, B and C* in relation to the first two applicants was made once each of the first-order factors and factors for a margin of appreciation had been considered, as follows:

Accordingly, having regard to the right to lawfully travel abroad for an abortion with access to appropriate information and medical care in Ireland, the Court does not consider that the prohibition in Ireland of abortion for health and safety and well-being reasons, based as it is on the profound moral views of the Irish people as to the nature of life... and as to the consequent protection to be accorded to the right to life of the unborn, exceeds the margin of appreciation accorded in that respect to the Irish State. In such circumstances, the Court finds that the impugned prohibition in Ireland struck a fair balance between the right of the first and second applicants to respect for their private lives and the rights invoked on behalf of the unborn.[12]

This excerpt helpfully demonstrates the method of adjudication undertaken by the ECtHR, and in particular it shows factors for the margin of appreciation affecting the weight of first-order factors in the case as part of the proportionality assessment. There are certainly ways in which to criticize the decision, whether as to its substance or its structure. For example, it might be said that the majority erred in placing importance on the lack of consensus in relation to Article 2 on the rights to life of the unborn, having already found that there was a relevant consensus by contracting states in favour of more liberal abortion rights, which has necessary implications for rights to life of the unborn. The majority would probably have done better in this case to refocus its consensus argument by noting that, notwithstanding an emerging trend amongst contracting states to provide more liberal rights of abortion, there was also a clear consensus that the matter remained within Ireland's margin of appreciation, by reference to the twenty-seven EU member states' Decision to allow Ireland to maintain its constitutional approach to the prohibition of abortion. Consequently, any consensus was not a weighty factor in favour of an authoritative interpretation of the Convention that would lead to a

---

[9] See ibid, [102], for the text of this Decision.
[10] Ibid, [239].   [11] Ibid, [240].   [12] Ibid, [241].

right to abortion on grounds of health and well-being. The Court would also have done well to place more clear reliance on the importance of the broad democratic support in Ireland for its abortion laws. It is noteworthy that the dissenting judgment placed reliance on the same structure of adjudication, although the argument placed a different emphasis on factors for the margin of appreciation, arguing that it should have been narrower on the basis of the consensus in favour of broader rights to abortion.

The decision in *A, B and C v Ireland* supports the approach to the margin of appreciation articulated in this book. It is important to note that the Court's reliance on arguments about the margin of appreciation did not drive its decision; nor did it result in the Court finding matters to be non-justiciable. Rather, it showed that the Court considered relevant considerations for deference to the state, and considered them along with the first-order considerations in the case. The same approach could have led to a different outcome if the Court had placed different weight on the factors that it considered, as demonstrated by the approach of the dissenting judgment. Furthermore, the same approach, albeit considering different factors, led to the finding of a violation in respect of the third applicant on the more specific basis that accessing an abortion in life-threatening circumstances was unacceptably uncertain. It cannot be said that the structure of adjudication, with reliance on factors for a margin of appreciation, considered along with other factors as part of the proportionality assessment, was determinative of the applicants' cases. Rather the structure provides the opportunity for the Tribunals to present the relevant factors clearly, and to explain, as far as it is possible to do so, how those factors influenced their decision.

The account of the margin of appreciation defended in this book shares one important characteristic in common with the approach to human rights adjudication taken by critics of the margin of appreciation: both the 'standard-unifying' and 'diversity-permitting' approaches to the role of the Tribunals result in decisions that set the international minimum standards protected by the Treaties. This commonality between the two approaches might lead some to say that both approaches can be reduced to the same thing, or that the dispute is somehow sterile: one approach, the 'diversity-permitting' approach, uses the language of the margin of appreciation; the other, the 'standard-unifying' approach, does not.

Of course, this comment is correct on one level. Both approaches do result in an international norm that sets a 'minimum standard'. However, the comment is mistaken for two important reasons. First, the method of assessing the norm is fundamentally at odds between these two different approaches to the role of the Tribunal. The 'diversity-permitting' approach places value on the role of the state in the interpretation of the international standard, both in terms of assessing the democratic quality and expertise of local interpretations of the right, as well as paying attention to the practice of states for the purposes of interpreting the Treaties. The 'standard-unifying' approach does not regard such matters as significant. Secondly, the nature of the international standard formed by the two accounts has one drastic difference: under the 'diversity-permitting' approach, the international standard formed is variable from state to state. Whilst there are situations in which there is a unified minimum standard of international human rights application, there will be other international minimum standards that have variable implementation requirements, and which may look different from state to state. In states 'X' and 'Y' there may be an international minimum requirement 'A' for freedom of speech, and in state Z that requirement may not apply. In each of these states, there is an international minimum standard, but its application is different between them (in state Z, consideration A may be entirely irrelevant). This sort of international norm would not be acceptable under the 'standard-unifying' account. Either there is or there is not an international standard.

One criticism of the margin of appreciation still requires a response. This is the problem of the doctrine's name or label. Rabinder Singh has criticized the 'conceptual inadequacy of the margin of appreciation' on the grounds that it is a 'conclusory label that only serves to obscure the true basis on which a reviewing court decides whether or not intervention in a particular case is justifiable'.[13] It is true that sometimes the margin of appreciation has been used as a conclusory label, without articulation of the process that has led to its application. This book has sought to counter such abuses of the doctrine by promoting greater understanding of the role and function of deference. It is simply not true to say that a phrase ('the margin of appreciation') 'prevents' the articulation of the courts' reasons. Singh claims that 'the better question is not "what is the scope of the margin of appreciation?" but "what is the appropriate intensity of review?"'.[14] The same result can be reached by saying that the latter question is another way of articulating the first question. This book is neutral as to which label is employed to convey the meaning. Whether deference, 'due deference', 'variable intensity of review', or the 'margin of appreciation' is used, what is important is the substance of the judicial exercise, not its label. Hunt has criticized the labelling of the margin of appreciation for its 'spatial metaphor'.[15] Hunt claims that this metaphor implies non-justiciability. This book has sought to counter the view that deference or the margin of appreciation leads to non-justiciability. Hunt is mistaken to say that the margin of appreciation 'contemplates there being a zone or area of decision-making in which a decision-maker is immune from any interference by the court'. There is no inexorable logic that requires this. Instead, the zone is the context within which there is legitimate differentiation, thus leading to deference by the court, which is dependent upon the issues being justiciable.

In the context of the ECtHR, it is unlikely that the margin of appreciation terminology will be discarded given its prominence. In other contexts, if it were considered that another phrase would better capture the essence of the doctrine, the arguments of this book would apply in the same way. However, it is likely that

---

[13] R Singh, 'Is There a Role for the "Margin of Appreciation" in National Law after the Human Rights Act' (1999) 1 EHRLR 15, 20–1.

[14] Ibid, 21.

[15] M Hunt, 'Sovereignty's Blight: Why Contemporary Public Law Needs the Concept of "Due Deference"' in N Bamforth and P Leyland (eds) *Public Law in a Multi-Layered Constitution* (Hart, Oxford 2003), 344–9.

many 'labels' will furnish criticism.[16] The best way in which to counter such criticism is to have a clear account of the practice so that such criticisms can be avoided.[17]

One of the core aims of the Tribunals is to interpret the Treaties and to set standards. But this standard-setting rightly involves an affirmation of the importance of states in protecting and implementing human rights. The margin of appreciation helpfully reflects this principle of subsidiarity in international human rights law. Whilst international human rights institutions have an important standard-setting and accountability role, it is states that are both the primary implementers and protectors of human rights. As the human rights movement continues, it is the enforcement of human rights internationally that is an increasingly important priority,[18] and it is the state parties to the Treaties that must be empowered and held responsible to this end. This emerging priority offers an added practical imperative for adopting the approach to the margin of appreciation taken in this book, since it affirms the responsibility of states for the protection and implementation of international human rights norms, undergirded by the international accountability offered by the Tribunals. The margin of appreciation doctrine can have the desirable effect of encouraging an increasing number of states to submit to international judicial review, as those states observe the Tribunals giving appropriate deference to states' interpretations of their international human rights obligations.

---

[16] Lord Hoffmann's reference to the 'overtones of servility' of the word 'deference' in *R(ProLife Alliance) v BBC* [2004] AC 185 (HL), [75].

[17] For example, Hoffmann's concern that the doctrine might lead to judicial bowing to other agencies can be overcome where it is made clear that deference is not a matter of authority, but of valuing the role of the agency, and consequently is conditional on that value and various other factors, none of which deny jurisdiction.

[18] See G Haugen and V Boutros, 'And Justice for All: Enforcing Human Rights for the World's Poor' (2010) 89 Foreign Affairs 51.

Bibliography

BA Ackerman, *We the People* (Harv UP, Cambridge, Mass 1991)

M Addo and N Grief, 'Does Article 3 of the European Convention on Human Rights Enshrine Absolute Rights?' (1998) 9 EJIL 510

R Alexy, *A Theory of Constitutional Rights* (OUP, Oxford 2002)

TRS Allan, 'Human Rights and Judicial Review: A Critique of "Due Deference"' (2006) 65 (3) CLJ 671

P Alston, 'The Unborn Child and Abortion under the Draft Convention on the Rights of the Child' (1990) 12 HRQ 156

American Law Institute, *Restatement of the Law, the Third, the Foreign Relations Law of the United States* (American Law Institute Publishers, St Paul, Minn 1987)

M Andenæs and E Bjorge, '*Preventive Detention No. 2 BvR 2365/09*' (2011) 105 (4) AJIL 768

Y Arai-Takahashi, *The Margin of Appreciation Doctrine and the Principle of Proportionality in the Jurisprudence of the ECHR* (Intersentia, Antwerpen; Oxford 2002)

D Beetham, 'Human Rights as a Model for Cosmopolitan Democracy' in D Archibugi, D Held, and M Köhler (eds) *Re-imagining Political Community: Studies in Cosmopolitan Democracy* (Polity Press, Cambridge 1998)

J Bell, 'Mechanisms for Cross-Fertilisation of Administrative Law in Europe' in J Beatson and T Tridimas (eds) *New Directions in European Public Law* (Hart, Oxford 1998)

E Benvenisti, 'Margin of Appreciation, Consensus, and Universal Standards' (1999) 31 International Law and Politics 843

S Besson, 'Sovereignty in Conflict' in C Warbrick and S Tierney (eds) *Towards an 'International Legal Community'? The Sovereignty of States and the Sovereignty of International Law* (BIICL, London 2006)

C Binder, 'The Prohibition of Amnesties by the Inter-American Court of Human Rights' (2004) 12 German Law Journal 1203

I Brownlie, *The Rule of Law in International Affairs: International Law at the Fiftieth Anniversary of the United Nations* (Martinus Nijhoff, The Hague; London 1998)

——, *Principles of Public International Law* (6th edn, OUP, Oxford 2003)

PG Carozza, 'Subsidiarity as a Structural Principle of International Human Rights Law' (2003) 97 (1) AJIL 38

A Cassese, *International Law* (2nd edn, OUP, Oxford 2005)

M Delmas-Marty, 'The Richness of Underlying Legal Reasoning' in M Delmas-Marty and C Chodkiewicz (eds) *The European Convention for the Protection of Human Rights: International Protection versus National Restrictions* (Martinus Nijhoff, Dordrecht; London 1992)

M-B Dembour, *Who Believes in Human Rights? Reflections on the European Convention* (CUP, Cambridge 2006)

P van Dijk and GJH van Hoof, *Theory and Practice of the European Convention on Human Rights* (3rd edn, Kluwer Law International, The Hague; London 1998)

DL Donoho, 'Autonomy, Self-Governance and the Margin of Appreciation: Developing a Jurisprudence of Diversity within Universal Human Rights' (2001) 15 Emory Intl LRev 391

R Dworkin, *Taking Rights Seriously* (Duckworth, London 1978)

——, *Freedom's Law: The Moral Reading of the American Constitution* (Harv UP, Cambridge, Mass 1996)

——, *Law's Empire* (Hart, Oxford 1998)

DM Dwyer, *The Judicial Assessment of Expert Evidence* (CUP, Cambridge 2008)

D Dyzenhaus, 'Law as Justification: Etienne Mureinik's Conception of Legal Culture' (1998) 14 SAJHR 11

R Ekins, *Legislative Intent and Group Action* (MPhil, Oxford University 2005)

JH Ely, *Democracy and Distrust: A Theory of Judicial Review* (Harv UP, Cambridge, Mass 1980)

T Emerson, 'Toward a General Theory of the Freedom of Expression' (1962–63) 72 Yale LJ 877

T Endicott, *Vagueness in Law* (OUP, Oxford 2000)

——, ' "International Meaning": Comity in Fundamental Rights Adjudication' (2001) 13 (3) IJRL 280

——, *Administrative Law* (OUP, Oxford 2009)

T Farer, 'The Rise of the Inter-American Human Rights Regime: No Longer a Unicorn, Not Yet an Ox' in DJ Harris and S Livingstone (eds) *The Inter-American System of Human Rights* (Clarendon Press, Oxford 1998)

B Fassbender, *The United Nations Charter as the Constitution of the International Community* (Martinus Nijhoff, Leiden 2009)

C Feingold, 'The Doctrine of Margin of Appreciation and the European Convention on Human Rights' (1977–78) 53 Notre Dame LRev 90

D Feldman, 'Freedom of Expression' in D Harris and S Joseph (eds) *The International Covenant on Civil and Political Rights and United Kingdom Law* (Clarendon Press, Oxford 1995)

J Finnis, *Natural Law and Natural Rights* (Clarendon Press, Oxford 1980)

——, 'On Reason and Authority in *Law's Empire*' (1987) 6 Law and Philosophy 357

——, 'Commensuration and Public Reason' in R Chang (ed) *Incommensurability, Incomparability and Practical Reason* (Harv UP, Cambridge, Mass 1997)

M Fordham and T de la Mare, 'Identifying the Principles of Proportionality' in J Jowell and J Cooper (eds) *Understanding Human Rights Principles* (Hart, Oxford 2001)

TM Franck, *Fairness in International Law and Institutions* (Clarendon Press, Oxford 1995)

L Fuller, 'The Forms and Limits of Adjudication' (1978) 92 Harv LRev 353

P Gallagher, 'The European Convention on Human Rights and the Margin of Appreciation' (UCD Working Papers in Law, Criminology and Socio-Legal Studies Research Paper No. 52/2011, 2012), <http://papers.ssrn.com/sol3/papers.cfm?abstract_id= 1982661?>

J García Roca, *El Marge de Apreciación Nacional en la Interpretación del Convenio Europeo de Derechos Humanos: Soberanía e Integración* (Civitas, Madrid 2010)

RK Gardiner, *Treaty Interpretation* (OUP, Oxford 2008)

J Gerards, 'Pluralism, Deference and the Margin of Appreciation Doctrine' (2011) 17 ELJ 80

A Gewirth, 'Are There Any Absolute Rights?' (1981) 31 The Philosophical Quarterly 1

F Gibbs, 'Human Rights: Is it Time to Sever Ties with the European Court?' (2011) *The Times* 23 February, 55

MA Glendon, *A World Made New: Eleanor Roosevelt and the Universal Declaration of Human Rights* (Random House, New York 2001)

GS Goodwin-Gill, *Free and Fair Elections* (Inter-Parliamentary Union, Geneva 2006)

B Goold, L Lazarus, and G Swiney, *Public Protection, Proportionality and the Search for Balance* (Ministry of Justice Research Series 10/07, HMSO, London 2007)

C Greenwood, 'The Unity and Diversity of International Law', 33rd Annual FA Mann Lecture (Lincoln's Inn, London 4 November 2009)

S Greer, *The Margin of Appreciation: Interpretation and Discretion under the European Convention on Human Rights* (Council of Europe, Brussels 2000)

——, *The European Convention on Human Rights: Achievements, Problems and Prospects* (CUP, Cambridge 2006)

J Habermas, *Between Facts and Norms: Contributions to a Discourse Theory of Law and Democracy* (MIT Press, Cambridge, Mass 1998)

D Harris, 'The International Covenant on Civil and Political Rights: An Introduction' in D Harris and S Joseph (eds) *The International Covenant on Civil and Political Rights and United Kingdom Law* (Clarendon Press, Oxford 1995)

——, 'Regional Protection of Human Rights: the Inter-American Achievement' in DJ Harris and S Livingstone (eds) *The Inter-American System of Human Rights* (Clarendon Press, Oxford 1998)

DJ Harris, M O'Boyle, C Warbrick, and E Bates, *Harris, O'Boyle & Warbrick: Law of the European Convention on Human Rights* (2nd edn, OUP, Oxford 2009)

HLA Hart, *The Concept of Law* (2nd edn, Clarendon Press, Oxford 1972)

G Haugen and V Boutros, 'And Justice for All: Enforcing Human Rights for the World's Poor' (2010) 89 Foreign Affairs 51

L Helfer, 'Consensus, Coherence and the European Convention on Human Rights' (1993) 26 Cornell Intl LJ 133

T Hickman, *Public Law after the Human Rights Act* (Hart, Oxford 2010)

R Higgins, *Problems and Process: International Law and How We Use It* (Clarendon Press, Oxford 1994)

D Hovell, 'The Deliberative Deficit: Transparency, Access to Information and UN Sanctions' in JM Farrall and K Rubenstein (eds) *Sanctions, Accountability and Governance in a Globalised World* (CUP, Cambridge 2009)

M Hunt, 'Sovereignty's Blight: Why Contemporary Public Law Needs the Concept of "Due Deference"' in N Bamforth and P Leyland (eds) *Public Law in a Multi-Layered Constitution* (Hart, Oxford 2003)

M Janis, R Kay, and A Bradley, *European Human Rights Law: Text and Materials* (3rd edn, OUP, Oxford 2008)

T Jones, 'The Devaluation of Human Rights under the European Convention' (1995) Public Law 430

S Joseph, J Schultz, and M Castan, *The International Covenant on Civil and Political Rights: Cases, Materials and Commentary* (OUP, Oxford 2000)

——, *The International Covenant on Civil and Political Rights: Cases, Materials, and Commentary* (2nd edn, OUP, Oxford 2004)

A Kavanagh, 'Participation and Judicial Review: A Reply to Jeremy Waldron' (2003) 22 (5) Law and Philosophy 451

——, 'Deference or Defiance: The Limits of the Judicial Role in Constitutional Adjudication' in G Huscroft (ed) *Expounding the Constitution: Essays in Constitutional Theory* (CUP, Cambridge 2008)

D Kennedy, *International Legal Structures* (Nomos, Baden-Baden 1987)

M Koskenniemi, *From Apology to Utopia: The Structure of International Legal Argument* (CUP, Cambridge 2005)

W Kymlicka, *Liberalism, Community and Culture* (Clarendon Press, Oxford 1989)

P Leach, *Taking a Case to the European Court of Human Rights* (2nd edn, OUP, Oxford 2005)

A Legg, *Towards a Principled Doctrine of the Margin of Appreciation in International Human Rights Law* (MPhil, University of Oxford 2007)

P Legrand, 'How to Compare Now' (1996) 16 Legal Studies 232

A Lester, 'Universality versus Subsidiarity: A Reply ' (1998) 1 EHRLR 73

A Lester, D Pannick, and J Herberg, *Human Rights Law and Practice* (3rd edn, LexisNexis, London 2009)

G Letsas, 'Two Concepts of the Margin of Appreciation' (2006) 26 (4) OJLS 705

——, *A Theory of Interpretation of the European Convention on Human Rights* (OUP, Oxford 2007)

AV Lowe, 'Book Review of *From Apology to Utopia: The Structure of International Legal Argument*' (1990) 17 Journal of Law and Society 384

——, *International Law* (Clarendon Press, Oxford 2007)

M Luteran, *Some Issues Relating to Proportionality in Law and Ethics, with Special Reference to European Human Rights Law* (DPhil, Oxford University 2009)

N MacCormick, *Questioning Sovereignty: Law, State, and Nation in the European Commonwealth* (OUP, Oxford 1999)

RSJ Macdonald, 'The Margin of Appreciation' in RSJ Macdonald, F Matscher, and H Petzold (eds) *The European System for the Protection of Human Rights* (Martinus Nijhoff, Dordrecht; London 1993)

P Mahoney, 'Universality versus Subsidiarity in the Strasbourg Case Law on Free Speech: Explaining Some Recent Judgments' (1997) 4 EHRLR 364

——, 'Marvellous Richness of Diversity or Invidious Cultural Relativism?' (1998) 19 HRLJ 4

S Marks, 'Civil Liberties at the Margin: The UK Derogation and the European Court of Human Rights' (1995) 15 OJLS 69

——, *The Riddle of All Constitutions: International Law, Democracy and the Critique of Ideology* (OUP, Oxford 2000)

S Marks and A Clapham, *International Human Rights Lexicon* (OUP, Oxford 2005)

F Matscher, 'Methods of Interpretation of the Convention' in RSJ Macdonald, F Matscher, and H Petzold (eds) *The European System for the Protection of Human Rights* (Martinus Nijhoff, Dordrecht; London 1993)

C McCrudden, 'A Common Law of Human Rights? Transnational Judicial Conversations on Constitutional Rights' (2000) 20 (4) OJLS 499

——, 'Legal Research and the Social Sciences' (2006) 122 LQR 632

D McGoldrick, *The Human Rights Committee: Its Role in the Development of the International Covenant on Civil and Political Rights* (Clarendon Press, Oxford 1991)

A McHarg, 'Reconciling Human Rights and the Public Interest: Conceptual Problems and Doctrinal Uncertainty in the Jurisprudence of the European Court of Human Rights' (1999) 62 MLR 671

JG Merrills, *The Development of International Law by the European Court of Human Rights* (2nd edn, Manchester UP, Manchester 1993)

——, 'Human Rights and Democratic Values in the Strasbourg System' (2000) 29 Thesaurus Acroasium 37

AR Mowbray, *Cases and Materials on the European Convention on Human Rights* (2nd edn, OUP, Oxford 2007)

A Orakhelashvili, 'Restrictive Interpretations of Human Rights Treaties in the Recent Jurisprudence of the European Court of Human Rights' (2003) 14 EJIL 529

JM Pasqualucci, *The Practice and Procedure of the Inter-American Court of Human Rights* (CUP, Cambridge 2003)

S Perry, 'Judicial Obligation, Precedent and the Common Law' (1987) 7 OJLS 215

——, 'Second-Order Reasons, Uncertainty and Legal Theory' (1988–89) 62 SCalLRev 913

J Raz, *The Authority of Law: Essays on Law and Morality* (Clarendon Press, Oxford 1979)

——, *The Morality of Freedom* (OUP, Oxford 1986)

——, 'On the Authority and Interpretation of Constitutions: Some Preliminaries' in L Alexander (ed) *Constitutionalism: Philosophical Foundations* (CUP, Cambridge 1998)

——, *Practical Reason and Norms* (OUP, Oxford 1999)

——, *Value, Respect and Attachment* (CUP, Cambridge 2001)

J Rivers, 'Proportionality and Variable Intensity of Review' (2006) 65 (1) CLJ 174

D Sarooshi, *International Organizations and their Exercise of Sovereign Powers* (OUP, Oxford 2005)

M Schmidt, 'The Complementarity of the Covenant and the European Convention on Human Rights: Recent Developments' in D Harris and S Joseph (eds) *The International Covenant on Civil and Political Rights and United Kingdom Law* (Clarendon Press, Oxford 1995)

R Singh, 'Is There a Role for the "Margin of Appreciation" in National Law after the Human Rights Act?' (1999) 1 EHRLR 15

P Soper, *The Ethics of Deference: Learning from Law's Morals* (CUP, Cambridge 2002)

D Spielmann, 'Allowing the Right Margin: The European Court of Human Rights and the National Margin of Appreciation Doctrine—Waiver or Subsidiarity of European Review?' (Centre for European Legal Studies Working Paper Series, Cambridge 2012)

JA Sweeney, 'Margins of Appreciation: Cultural Relativity and the European Court of Human Rights in the Post-Cold War Era' (2005) 54 ICLQ 459

E Tiller and F Cross, 'What is Legal Doctrine?' (2006) 100 Northwestern ULRev 517

L Tribe, 'The Puzzling Persistence of Process-Based Theories' (1980) 89 Yale LJ 1063

S Tsakyrakis, 'Proportionality: An Assault on Human Rights?' (2009) 7 (3) IJCL 468

J Tsen-Ta Lee, 'Interpreting Bills of Rights: The Value of a Comparative Approach' (2007) 5 International Journal of Constitutional Law 122

H Waldock, 'The Effectiveness of the System Set Up by the European Convention on Human Rights' (1980) 1 HRLJ 1

J Waldron, *Law and Disagreement* (Clarendon Press, Oxford 1999)

N Walker, 'Human Rights in a Postnational Order: Reconciling Political and Constitutional Pluralism' in T Campbell, KD Ewing, and A Tomkins (eds) *Sceptical Essays on Human Rights* (OUP, Oxford 2001)

M Walzer, *Thick and Thin: Moral Argument at Home and Abroad* (University of Notre Dame Press, Notre Dame, Ind 1994)

C Warbrick, 'The Structure of Article 8' (1998) EHRLR 32

A Watson, 'Comparative Law and Legal Change' (1978) 37 CLJ 313

GCN Webber, *The Negotiable Constitution: On the Limitation of Rights* (CUP, Cambridge 2009)

J Weiler, *The Constitution of Europe: 'Do the New Clothes Have an Emperor?' and Other Essays on European Integration* (CUP, Cambridge 1999)

R White and C Ovey, *Jacobs, White, and Ovey: The European Convention on Human Rights* (5th edn, OUP, Oxford 2010)

HC Yourow, *The Margin of Appreciation Doctrine in the Dynamics of European Human Rights Jurisprudence* (DPhil, University of Michigan 1995; Kluwer Law International, The Hague 1996)

Index